A COMPARATIVE STUDY OF THE PRĀTIMOKṢA

BUDDHIST TRADITION SERIES

VOLUME 31

Edited by
ALEX WAYMAN

A Comparative Study of the Prātimokṣa

On the Basis of its Chinese, Tibetan, Sanskrit and Pāli Versions

W. PACHOW

MOTILAL BANARSIDASS PUBLISHERS
PRIVATE LIMITED • DELHI

First Edition: Santiniketan, 1955
Revised and Enlarged Edition: Delhi, 2000

ISBN: 81-208-1572-6

Also available at:

MOTILAL BANARSIDASS

236, 9th Main III Block, Jayanagar, Bangalore 560 011
41 U.A. Bungalow Road, Jawahar Nagar, Delhi 110 007
8 Mahalaxmi Chamber, Warden Road, Mumbai 400 026
120 Royapettah High Road, Mylapore, Chennai 600 004
Sanas Plaza, 1302 Baji Rao Road, Pune 411 002
8 Camac Street, Calcutta 700 017
Ashok Rajpath, Patna 800 004
Chowk, Varanasi 221 001

Printed in India

BY JAINENDRA PRAKASH JAIN AT SHRI JAINENDRA PRESS,
A-45 NARAINA, PHASE-I, NEW DELHI 110 028
AND PUBLISHED BY NARENDRA PRAKASH JAIN FOR
MOTILAL BANARSIDASS PUBLISHERS PRIVATE LIMITED,
BUNGALOW ROAD, DELHI 110 007

DEDICATED TO

PROF. TAN YUN-SHAN

FOR

His Selfless Service and Devotion to Promoting Sino-Indian Studies and Renewing the Cultural Interchange Between India and China.

Foreword

This excellent coverage by W. Pachow of the Prātimokṣa code of Buddhist Vinaya originally appeared in parts in *Sino-Indian Studies* (Santiniketan) in its Vol. IV (1951) and in its Vol. V (1955). Pachow is correct in stressing the importance of this code as going back to earliest Buddhism, besides implicating early Buddhist Councils. The meaning of 'comparative' in his title is that Pachow does not restrict himself to Pāli, but usually presents in addition many other traditions, such as the Sarvāstivādin. After much useful introduction, Pachow gives his translation of the text, with both Pāli and Sanskrit equivalents, and alternate renderings for the terms, including references to the Tibetan version (as it had been translated into English).

Of course, the reprinting of the entire text required some re-editing; and this has probably improved the text for the reader of the final version, which is an invaluable scholarly account of the early Buddhist Vinaya.

ALEX WAYMAN

New York City, April, 1999

Preface

Being unable to solve the mystery manifested in the universe, ancient Indian seers turned to the inner consciousness searching for the infinite and the eternal, so that they may attain to enlightenment and emancipation. By treading the Aryan path of spiritual realization, Gautama Buddha achieved his ultimate objective and created a religion on the foundation of righteousness and morality. The doctrines and practices taught by him are rational, practical and easy to understand. As a sequel the growth of Buddhism was rapid and people of all walks of life flocked to him for refuge and became his disciples. This group of mendicants (bhikṣus) has been known as the Buddhist Saṅgha. As each of these bhikṣus came from a particular social or religious background the new communal life under the supervision of the Buddha may cause discordance without a set of regulations to be observed by all. It was under these circumstances there arose the necessity of a code of conduct for them. The disciplinary rules established by the Buddha on numerous occasions were later on classified into eight sections amounting to about two hundred fifty precepts entitled, *Bhikṣu Prātimokṣa Sūtra.* If anyone should violate a particular precept, certain penalty or punishment would be imposed on the guilty individual. Depending on the nature of the offence the punishment may be light or severe. Being a religion of compassion, expulsion is the worst sentence an offender would ever receive. In comparison to a normal secular chastisement, the Buddhist way is very mild and humane.

The present work discusses the religious background and other factors which influenced the formation of the Buddhist code of conduct, the fortnightly recitation of the *Prātimokṣa Sūtra*, the rationale or cause for establishing a particular rule, the function and authority of the *Prātimokṣa* in relation to the Saṅgha, the development of the text among the Buddhist sects, the importance of the *Prātimokṣa* in Buddhist history and other associated topics. By obeying the admonition of the Buddha and observing the code of conduct, members of the Saṅgha will lead a life in purity, harmony and emancipation.

In the early nineteen forties when I was studying at the Visva-Bharati University, Santiniketan, India (This Institute was founded by poet Rabindranath Tagore, winner of the Nobel Prize in literature), this work was prepared for a Ph.D. degree in the University of Bombay, India. In the preparatory stage I was profoundly indebted to Prof. V.V. Gokhale of the University of Poona, my teacher and supervisor for his learned advice on various matters concerning my thesis, to the late Prof. P.C. Bagchi, Research Professor of the Visva-Bharati Cheena-Bhavana for consultation on ancient Indian religious traditions and to the late Prof. Tan Yun-shan, Director of the Visva-Bharati Cheena-Bhavana and founder of the Sino-Indian Cultural Society for his advice and guidance on academic and other matters. I am extremely grateful to them for their magnanimous blessings. With the assistance of these scholars it was published by the Sino-Indian Cultural Society, Santiniketan, in 1955. Being a scholarly dissertation the number of printed copies was severely limited. It was out of print within a few years of its appearance. Now, it is heartening to learn that the management of Motilal Banarsidass Pvt. Ltd., a leading Indological publisher in Delhi, India has proposed to publish it in the 'Buddhist Tradition' series. I appreciate greatly this welcome opportunity and hope that its availability may facilitate, in a small measure, the advancement of Buddhist studies, and it may generate some interest among scholars in the area of Asian religions and literature.

W. PACHOW

Iowa City, Iowa
U.S.A.
March, 1999

Contents

SECTION III—APPENDICES

Abbreviations

A.	Aṅguttara-Nikāya: PTS, London 1885
ab.	absent (or missing)
Adhik.	Adhikaraṇaśamatha Dharmas
Ani.	Aniyata Dharmas
Apa.	Āpastamba (SBE, vol. II)
Asod.	Aśokāvadāna: Nanjio no. 1343
Aśoka	Aśoka, the Buddhist Emperor of India: By Vincent A. Smith, London 1909
BBPS	Bruchstücke des Bhikṣuṇī-Prātimokṣa der Sarvāstivādins: By Ernst Waldschmidt, Leipzig 1926.
BI	Buddhist India: By Rhys Davids, London 1903
Bu-ston	History of Buddhism in India and Tibet: By Bu-ston, Heidelberg 1932
Childers	A Dictionary of the Pāli Language: By R.C. Childers, London 1875
Cv. or CV	Cullavagga (Vinaya-Piṭaka, II): Edited by H. Oldenburg, London 1880
CR	Le concile de Rājagṛha: By Przyluski, Paris 1926
D.	Dīgha-Nikāya: PTS, London 1890
Dg.	Dīrghāgama-Sūtra, Nanjio no. 545
Dh. or Dharmg.	Dharmagupta: Nanjio no. 1155
Dhmp.	Dhammapada (SBE, vol. X)
Dhv.	Dharmagupta Vinaya: Nanjio no. 1117
Dip.	Dipavaṃsa: Edited and Translated by H. Oldenburg, London 1879
D.P.	Different Phraseology
EBJ	Early Buddhist Jurisprudence: By Durga Bhagavat, Poona 1939
EBM	Early Buddhist Monachism: By S. Dutt, London 1924

Eko.	Ekottarāgama-Sūtra: Nanjio no. 543
EMB	Early Monastic Buddhism (vol. I): By N. Dutt, Calcutta 1941
Fa-hien	The travels of Fa-hien: Trans: By H.A. Giles, Cambridge 1923
Gau.	Gautama (SBE, vol. II)
Gil.	Gilgit Manuscripts: Ed. By N. Dutt, Srinagar-Kashmir 1939
Grh.	Gṛhyasūtra: By Śāṅkhāyana (SBE, vol. XXIX)
Hil.	History of Indian literature: By M. Winternitz, Calcutta 1933
HPL	History of Pāli literature: By B.C. Law, London 1933
IA	Indian Antiquary (Bombay)
IB	Indian Buddhism: By Rhys Davids, London 1881
IHQ	Indian Historical Quarterly (Calcutta)
JA	Journal Asiatique (Paris)
JASB	Journal of the Asiatic Society of Bengal (Calcutta)
JDL	Journal of the Department of Letters, Calcutta University, Calcutta
JPTS	Journal of the Pāli Text Society (London)
JRAS	Journal of the Royal Asiatic Society (London)
Kath.	Kathā-vatthu: PTS, London 1915
Kern.	Manual of Indian Buddhism: By H. Kern Strassburg 1896
Ksy. or Kāśy	Kāśyapiyaḥ: Nanjio no. 1108
Nei-Hsio.	Journal of the Nanking Cheena Buddhist Institute, Nanking
LHSB	Literary History of the Sanskrit Buddhism: By G.K. Nariman, Bombay 1923
M.	Majjhima-Nikāya: PTS, London 1888
Mahā.	Mahāvaṃsa (PTS): Ed. and Translated by W. Geiger, London 1908
Mg. or Madhy.	Madhyamāgama-Sūtra: Nanjio no. 542
Mhs. or Mahīś.	Mahīśāsaka: Nanjio no. 1157
Mhsv.	Mahīśāsaka Vinaya: Nanjio no. 1122
Milin.	Milinda-pañho: Ed. By H. Kern, London 1880
MPS	Mahā-Parinirvāṇa-Sūtra or Mahā-Parinibbāna-Sutta
MPT or Mpt.	Mahāvyutpatti: Tokyo, 4th year of Taisho, Kyoto, 5th year of Taisho

MRBL	Manuscript Remains of Buddhist Literature Found in Eastern Turkestan: By A.F. Rudolf Hoernle, London 1916
Msg. or Mahāsg.	Mahāsaṅghika: Nanjio no. 1159
Msgv.	Mahāsaṅghika Vinaya: Nanjio no. 1119
Msv.	Mūlasarvāstivādin: Nanjio no. 1110
Msvv.	Mūlasarvāstivādin Vinaya: Nanjio no. 1118
MV. or Mv.	Mahāvagga (Vinaya-Piṭaka I): Ed. By H. Oldenburg, London 1879
Nanjio	A Catalogue of the Chinese Translations of the Buddhist Tripiṭaka: By B. Nanjio, London 1883
n.c.	not corresponding
NIA.	New Indian Antiquary (Poona)
Np.	Niḥsargika Pātayantika Dharmas
Oldb. Life	Buddha, His Life, His Doctrine, His Order: By H. Oldenburg, Berlin 1920, English Translation, Calcutta 1927
Oldb. Vin.	Oldenburg's Introduction to the Vinaya Piṭaka: Edited by Him, London 1879-83
Pā.	Pātayantika Dharmas
Pāli	Pāli Text of the Prātimokṣa: By St. Petersburg 1869, Poona 1939
Pd.	Pratideśanīya Dharmas
PE Dict.	Pāli-English Dictionary: Ed. by Rhys Davids and W. Stede, Chipstead, Surrey 1921
Pj.	Pārājika Dharmas
PLL	Pāli Literature and Language: By W. Geiger, Calcutta 1943
Pmk.	Prātimokṣa or Pātimokkha
P.T.S. or PTS	Pāli Text Society
PPN Dict.	Dictionary of Pāli Proper Names: By G.P. Malalasekara, London 1937
Roc.	The Life of the Buddha: By W. Woodville Rockhill, London 1884
S.	Saṃyutta-Nikāya: PTS, London 1884
Saṃ.	Saṃghāvaśeṣa Dharmas
Samp.	Samanta-pāsādika or Vibhāṣā-Vinaya: Nanjio no. 1125, Pāli: Samp, London 1924
SBE	Sacred Books of the East: Ed. By F. Max Mulier
SBBS	Early History of the Spread of Buddhism and Buddhist Schools: By N. Dutt, London 1925
s.d.	sliggtly different

SE Dict.	Sanskrit-English Dictionary: By M. Monier Williams, London 1899
Sg.	Saṃyuktāgama-Sūtra: Nanjio no. 544
Sk.	Śaikṣa Dharmas
Skt.	Sanskrit Text of the Sv. Prātimokṣa (JA 1913)
STEV.	Sanskrit-Tibetan-English Vocabulary: Ed. By Csoma de Körös, Calcutta 1910
SUV. or Suv.	Sutta-Vibhaṅga (Vinaya Piṭaka III, IV): Ed. by H. Oldenburg, London 1881-82
Sv. or Sarv.	Sarvāstivādin: Nanjio no. 1160
Svbh.	Sarvāstivāda-vinaya-vibhāṣā: Nanjio no. 1135
Svs.	Sarvāstivāda-vinaya-Saṅgraha: Nanjio no. 1127
Svv.	Sarvāstivādin-vinaya: Nanjio no. 1115
T.	Taisho Edition of the Chinese Buddhist Tripiṭaka, Tokyo
Tar.	Taranatha's Geschte des Buddhismus in Indien, aus dem Tibetischen übersetze, von A. Schiefner: St. Petersburg 1869
Tib.	Tibetan Text of Prātimokṣa of the Mūlasarvāstivādin (JASB, 1915)
Upp.	Upāli-paripṛcchā-Sūtra: Nanjio no. 1109
V.	Vasumitra's Buddhist Schools: Nanjio no. 1286
VDPS	Vinaya-dvāviṃśati-prasannārtha (?)-śāstra: Nanjio no. 1139
Vim. Vis.	Vimuttimagga and Visuddhimagga—A Comparative Study: By B.V. Bapat, Poona 1937
Visd.	Visuddhimagga: Ed. by Kosambi, Bombay 1940
VNS	Vinayanidāna-sūtra: Nanjio no. 1130
YC	On Yuan Chwang's travels in India: By Thomas Watters, London 1904

Note 1. We have taken the Prātimokṣa text of the Sarvāstivādin School as the standard text for comparison.

2. In quoting the Skt. text, all brackets introduced by the editors, have been omitted by us.

I

INTRODUCTION

Introduction

After a thorough investigation into the relevant documents concerning the history of ancient India, one gets an impression, that the records supposed to possess a good deal of historical importance are unhappily mixed up with legends and interpolations which often cause a profusion of confusion in the minds of scholars and consequently lead to sharp controversies. The reason is that our information, in the first place is not always derived from very authentic and reliable sources and are mostly based on hearsay. Secondly, the ancient writers belonging to different religious sects do not hesitate to invent fantastic tales, so that their religion or sect may be benefited in some way. They appear to possess little sense of what is called 'history' in the modern sense of the term. We presume, that it was the habit of the sages in ancient India to attach hardly any importance to chronology of events as we do today. Hence, we find that India did not make much progress in the development of a historical sense as China did in her old days. Being deprived of the facilities of authentic history, the workers in this field have to labour extremely hard; they have to sift the distorted facts from a heap of legends, study the archaeological data, and investigate the original literature preserved in Chinese, Tibetan and other languages and also to get confirmation from early foreign travellers who came to India mainly from China and Greece, with the hope that a flood of light may be thrown on unsolved problems and fairly reliable conclusions drawn from them. This method has been applied, accepted and now well-established by the modern savants of both the West and the East. In our present investigation, we shall also endeavour to observe the same principles of historical criticism and deliver an independent judgement based on whatever clear evidence we can gather.

The various reasons and testimonies, discussed and presented in the following treatment of the subject show that the Prātimokṣa (Pāli: Pāṭimokkha) is one of the oldest texts in the Buddhist Canon and the oldest text also in the Vinaya-Piṭaka. Its significance and importance to the students of ancient Indian history and culture is manifold, though primarily it is a collection of liturgical formularies governing the conduct of the Bhikṣus and Bhikṣuṇīs. The text and its commentaries furnish us with such minute details, that we are confronted with a distinct picture of the social, political, economic and religious conditions that must have prevailed in the time of the Buddha, that is, about the fifth century B.C. The significant characteristic of the Pmk. is that it deals with the daily affairs (individual or communal) of the Buddhist Order. It used to be and still[1] is recited every half-month in the assembly of Bhikṣus, so that they may confess their sins, and purify themselves if they had committed a transgression of the rules mentioned. It shows quite a realistic outlook and is unlike such texts e.g. *Mahā-Sudassana-Suttanta* of the *Dīgha-Nikāya,* which gives fantastically coloured and figurative descriptions. As it evidently possesses a considerable amount of historicity as well as antiquity, it will be undoubtedly worth our while to arrive at some definite results, which will throw more light on this particular problem in Indian history.

I. THE MEANING OF PRĀTIMOKṢA

Regarding the meaning of the word Prātimokṣa[2] (Pāli: Pāṭimokkha), we find that there are different interpretations of it in the Pāli and the Northern translations. We shall first see how it has been defined in the Pāli Canon and then pass on to other records. The references quoted below are from the Pāli sources:

1. 'Pāṭimokkhan ti ādim etaṃ mukhaṃ etaṃ pāmukhaṃ etaṃ kusalānan dhammānam teṇa vuccati pāṭimokkhan[3] ti'—'Pāṭimokkhaṃ', it is the beginning, it is the face (*mukhaṃ*), it is the principal (*Pāmukhaṃ*) of good qualities; therefore, it is called 'Pāṭimokkhaṃ'.
2. 'Yo taṃ pāṭirakkhati taṃ mokkheti moceti apāyikādidukkhehi tasmā pāṭimokkhan ti vuccati—whosoever observes (the rules of Pāṭimokkha), him it releases, delivers from sufferings such as of the inferior states, and so it is called Pāṭmokkha'—from an old Ṭīkā, quoted by Subhuti.[4]

1. We find the Bhikṣus in Tibet and in Ceylon still observe this custom. See JASB 1915, nos. 3 and 4, p. 30.
2. This is said to be a wrong adaptation in Skt. Its correct form should be 'Prātimokṣya' PE Dict.
3. Mv., II.3.4.
4. See Childers, p. 363; Visd., ch. I, p. 43.

3. 'Pāṭimokkhan ti atimokkhaṃ paṭippāmokkhaṃ atiseṭṭhaṃ ati-uttamaṃ—The Pāṭimokkha is that which is the highest, the extraordinary high, the very best and very highest.'

In the Chinese[5] and Tibetan[6] translations, this is interpreted as: 'Deliverance, liberation or emancipation for each and every one' and at all occasions, that is, 'prāti' stands for 'each', every and 'mokṣa' for 'Deliverance'. The *Prātimokṣa Vinaya*[7] (or Sūtra), a text of the Kāśyapīya School, translated into Chinese by Gautama Prajñāruci in A.D. 543 is called 'Chieh-t'o-chieh-pan-ching', which means: The Vinaya text for deliverance. The Tibetan *So-sor-thar-pa*, literally signifies: 'Disburdenment of each individual's sins.[8] Etymologically, it seems that Pāli 1, and 3, have derived it from 'Mukha' and the Skt. from the root 'Muc'. For Prāti-muc (muñcati) Monier Williams[9] has given the following meaning: 'To set at liberty, release, let go, send away, along with other senses.' Rhys Davids and H. Oldenberg[10] have expressed their doubts as to how a word having the meaning of 'Over against, standing close, in front' could become the title of a book of the liturgy of confession such as the Pāṭimokkha.

Other Vinaya works in the Chinese translations have interpreted this word as 'Deliverance' in almost all the cases, excepting the Mahīśāsaka[11] which gives an interpretation corresponding with the 'mukha' explanation. It runs as follows:

> 'Prātimokṣa means that by (observing) the Śīla (chieh) one will protect one's sense organs and hence one's meritorious qualities (*saddharma*) will be increased. It is the first entrance (ch'u-men) to all the good Dharmas. Therefore, it is called Prātimokṣa.'

The 'muc' explanation is found in the following works:

The *Pi-ni-mu-lun* or *Vinaya-mātṛkā-Śāstrā*[12] (ch. 2) says: 'Prātimokṣa means that one remains in the practice of Śīla and Vinaya. It is therefore,

---

5. T'ing fu-po's: The great Buddhist Dict., p. 1541; Mūlasarvāstivādin Vinaya, ch. I, Introduction verses.
6. So-sor-thar-pa: JASB 1915, vols. xi, nos. 3 and 4 (n.s.).
7. Nanjio no. 1108.
8. See note 6.
9. SE Dict. under Prātimuc.
10. SBE, vol. XIII, p. xxvii.
11. Msv., ch. 18, on Uposatha.
12. Nanjio no. 1138.

called Prātimokṣa.'

The (Pi-na-ya) *Chieh-yin-yüan-ching* or *Vinayanidāna-Sūtra*[13] (ch. 1) in reply to the question about the best of Śīlas, says: 'A Bhikṣu who observes the Śīla, adorns himself with the ornament of Pmk., the Śīla-deliverance (chieh chieh t'o). A habit thereby will be formed by him that he will be afraid of committing even the most insignificant offence and whatever he does will be in perfect concord with Śīla or Vinaya.'

The *Mūlasarvāstivāda-nikāya-vinaya-saṅgraha*[14] (ch. 1) composed by Jinamitra of Nālandā has given another clear confirmation to the derivation of 'Prātimokṣa' from 'muc'. It states that: 'The Prātimokṣa' means that he who practises according to the *Prātimokṣa-Sūtra,* will gradually cut off the minutest doubts of the nine divisions...and attain deliverance from all evil dispositions (*kleśa*)—it is called Prātimokṣa.'

It is not impossible that the different Vinaya works mentioned above, in connection with the etymology of 'muc', have drawn on very old tradition that was probably prevalent during the lifetime of the Buddha or after his death. Inasmuch as we find similar expression in the *Madhyamāgama* (ch. 10, Sūtra[15] 42-43) which, as we shall see later, contains a comparatively older tradition:

> By observing the 'Śīla, one will be freed from repentance, thence one will acquire the benefit of joy, the equanimity of mind, preceiving things in their reality, detached from desires, and *attain deliverance* from longing, anger and ignorance (*Rāga, Doṣa* and *Moha*)...'

Here, the Sūtra does not attempt to state clearly the definition of Pmk. but nevertheless the renowned fourfold formula of Śīla, Samādhi, Prajñā and Vimukti turns up, as though by its own accord. *Mukti* or deliverance is the final goal of all the religious mendicants in ancient India, as well as of the Buddhists. To observe the rules laid down in the Pmk. is the proper means through which the Buddhists would achieve their ends. So even theoretically we are strongly supported by the Buddhist general doctrine that 'muc' fits in better than 'mukha' in the present case.

13. Nanjio no. 1130.
14. *Ibid.*, 1127; Jinamitra lived about 600 A.D. See On Yuan Chwang II.169.
15. *Ibid.*, 542 (cf. A. X.1), *Kimatthiya;* Taisho I, p. 485.

The prefix 'prāti' has the sense[16] of 'towards, near to, against, in the direction of, about, with regard to, every, severally and on every...' Accordingly, we find both the senses of 'each, every, individually' common in the Vinaya works and also 'towards, on way to or following' in *tsung chieh t'o* 'following Deliverance', a translated term for Pmk. e.g., in the *Madhyamāgama* (ch. 5, Sūtras[17] 21-22) regarding a Bhikṣu observing the disciplinary rules, protecting the Pmk., behaving properly and with great awe when he sees the slightest offence, the 'prāti' is rendered as 'towards'. That is one of the earliest renderings in Chinese translations, because Gautama Saṅghadeva translated this work into Chinese in 397-398 A.D.

Taking all the aforesaid data into consideration, we are inclined to believe that there used to be two different interpretations of the word 'prātimokṣa'. It has been interpreted as 'Deliverance' on the one hand, the 'Chief' or the 'Principal' on the other. These two seem to have taken the word 'mukha' and the root 'muc' respectively for the purpose of derivation current at the same time.

The suggestion made by H. Kern[18] that Pmk. was taken in the sense of Cuirass, or something serving as a (spiritual) Cuirass does not appear to us to be convincing, because so many texts of the Northern tradition as we have seen above, clearly and undoubtedly, base their explanations on the root 'muc'[19] in spite of the fact that Dr. S. Dutt[20] seeks to defend that explanation. He quotes *Amarakoṣa* to strengthen his assertion, but immediately confesses that he has not been able to discover any instance of the use of the word precisely in that sense in Sanskrit.[21]

II. NUMBER, DATE AND AUTHORSHIP OF THE PRĀTIMOKṢA RULES

The number of the Pmk. rules shown in the texts belonging to different schools is of the greatest significance to the students of Buddhist history. It indicates unmistakably the comparative antiquity

16. SE Dict. under Prātimuc.
17. Cf. A., II.4.5-6: 'Idhāvuso bhikkhu sīlava hoti pāṭimokkha-saṃvara-sambhuto viharati ācāra-gocara-sampanno anumattesu vajjesu bhayadassāvi samādāya sikkhati sikkhāpadesu', vol. I, pp. 63-67; Av., 166; Nirodha; Sv., 187; EBM, pp. 88-90; PPN Dict., vol. II, p. 183.
18. Kern, p. 74, n. 5.
19. SE Dict. under Prātimuc.
20. EBM, pp. 89-90.
21. Other references regarding the interpretation of the Pmk., see Winternitz's HIL, vol. II, p. 22, n. 2; Samp. (PTS), vol. IV, p. 787; Vim. Vis., p. 11.

of the texts as well as the line of development followed by each school. Before dealing with the exact figures taken from the various works, it would be appropriate to make inquiries with regard to the numerary references found in the Canonical literature other than the Vinaya-Piṭaka.

According to the tradition of the Saṃmitīya[22] School, it is said that the Tathāgata had established 420 (actually 419) precepts, namely: 200 in the P'o-shou-tou (Posadha) Vinaya; 120 in the U-po-ti-sha (Upadeśa) and 99 in the *Bhikṣuṇī Vinaya*. The first of these three is probably meant to refer to the Pmk. rules in the earliest times.

Other records found in the Pāli Nikāya cited in the *Milindapañha*,[23] on the one hand, and the Chinese Āgamas on the other, help us to determine the correct number. The Pāli gives 150 rules, whereas the *Saṃyuktāgama-Sūtras*[24] 819 (cf. A. III.87 Sādhika), 821 (cf. A. III.85-86 Sekha) and 829 (cf. A. III.83 Vajjiputta) give 250. Both these numbers have been given in connection with the half-monthly recital of the Pmk. Sūtra. We find a striking similarity between the passages found in Chinese Sam. no. 829 and Pāli A. III.83 as shown below, and as other evidences aslo testify to their correctness, we may logically conclude, that both the Pāli and Skt. have their grounds to state the foregoing figures. For clarification we quote the following relevant passages of both the Sūtras:

> Pāli A. III.83. .....Atha kho aññataro Vajjiputtaka Bhikkhu yena Bhagava ten'upasankami....ekamantam nisinno kho so Vajjiputtako bhikkhu Bhagavantaṃ etad avoca: "Sādhikam idam bhante *diyaḍḍhasikkhāpadasatam* anvaddhamāsam uddesaṃ āgacchati nāham bhante ettha sakkomi sikkhitum ti."
>
> "Sakkhasi pana tvam bhikkhu tisu sikkhāsu sikkhituṃ—adhiśīlasikkhāya adhicittasikkhāya adhipaññasikkhāya[25] ti."

Chinese Sam., ch. 29, Sūtra 829: "Thus have I heard, once the Blessed One was staying in the village of the Vajjians and the venerable Vajjiputta was attending upon him. Now, the venerable Vajjiputta went

---

22. See VDPS: Nanjio no. 1139, ch. 1, composed by Buddhatrāta and translated by Paramārtha in 568 A.D.
23. Miln.: 'Diyaḍḍhesu sikkhāpadasatesu samādāya', pp. 143, 232; A. III.83.85.86.87 (vol. 1, p. 232). In passing, is it possible to maintain, that the word 'diyaḍḍha' was also interpreted in the sense 2½ instead 1½?
24. T., vol. II, pp. 210, 212.
25. Cf. A., III.88, n. 1.

to the place where the Lord Buddha was. Having saluted him with his head touching the feet, he stood on one side and said: "O Blessed One, the Lord Buddha has laid down (literally:) 'more than 250 rules' (Vinaya chieh) and asked the sons of the community to recite the *Prātimokṣa-Sūtra* every half month as well as let them learn (them) according to wish. Lord, I am now not able to learn according to the Rules."

The Buddha said to Vajjiputta: "Will you be able to learn the Three Śikṣā-padas? . . . you should always learn the Śikṣās of Adhiśīla, Adhicitta and Adhiprajñā."

The word 'sādhikam' in the Pāli version is very significant here, because it indicates that Pmk. is something 'more than 150'. We know that the actual number in the text is 227. That is to say this 'something more' means actually 77 rules! We are tempted to believe, that this is attributable to the role of the Śaikṣa dharmas, because their sum total is 75 in the Pāli version. Moreover, in all the Pmk. texts and Vinaya works, including the accounts given in most cases, with reference to the Rājagṛha Council, the number of rules in all other sections of the Pmk., excepting the Śaikṣa dharmas, has been distinctly stated. We know, the numerary significance apportioned to that section is 'Bahu Śaikṣa Dharmas' or 'many rules that should be learnt'. As this 'many' is indefinite, it is not unlikely that the editors of the Nikāyas thought it convenient to quote the conventional figure by saying '150 etc.'. We can hardly subscribe to the opinion[26] expressed by Dr. B.C. Law that the 7 Adhikaraṇaśamatha and the 75 Śk. dharmas had no place in the first Buddhist Council and were later additions.[27] His argument is that the later *Suttavibhaṅga* scheme makes room for the 75 Śk. rules, therefore the Pmk. code with its total of 152 rules may be shown to have been earlier. But as there is evidence to show the existence of both the Śk. and the 7 Adhik. dharmas in such works (e.g. Sg., ch. 9, discussed below) that are definitely much older than the *Suttavibhaṅga*, we cannot but infer that the omission of the 75 Śk. rules in the A. III.83 may be intentional, and that the 7 Adhik. dharmas were obviously included in the '150 and more' Rules, as B.C. Law himself later on admits.[28] The Saṃ., ch. 9, Sūtra 253 (cf. S., 35, 133, Verahaccāni) described an incident as to how the Brāhmanī (Pi-nin-ka-chien-yen) Verakātyāyana(?) of the Kāmaṇḍāya (Chu-pan-tu) village was refused three times instruction

---

26. History of Pāli Lit. (HPL), vol. I, pp. 20-21.
27. For the 7 Adhik. dharmas, see Mg., ch. 52, no. 196; Taisho, vol. I, p. 754 (cf. M. 104, Samāgama Sutta).
28. HPL, vol. I, p. 21; EBM, pp. 92-93.

by the Venerable (Mahā) Udāyi[29] (Yu-dha-yi) on account of her: 1. Wearing best shoes made of leather; 2. Covering her head with cloth; 3. Preparing a higher seat for herself; 4. Wearing an appearance of looking down upon the Bhikṣus; and 5. Sitting with impudence. All these are obviously direct references to the Śk. dharmas:

1. Refers[30] to Sarv. Śk. 104—not to preach to a person who puts on leather shoes.
2. Refers to Sarv. Śk. 95—not to preach to a person who covers his head.
3. Refers to Sarv. Śk. 92—not to preach to a person who is in a high position whereas the Bhikṣu is in a low position.

The Śk. dharmas or rules of decorum were not merely observed and practised by the members of the Buddhist Saṅgha. They had such a wide and universal appeal that even the Kings and Rulers at that time had to acquaint themselves with some of these etequettes. It was then a social code for the highly cultured circles. Several Sūtras[31] in the Saṃ., and *Ekottara* state that King Bimbisāra and King Prasenajit had on many an occasion paid visits to the Buddha. Before their approach to him, they had to withdraw the five insignia of a King, namely, (i) the crown, (ii) the canopy, (iii) the fan or the duster, (iv) the sword, and (v) the shoes. Among these, (i), (ii), (iv) and (v) correspond to 96, 106, 107 and 104 of the Sarv. Śk. dharmas[32] respectively.

It is evident then that the Śk. rules had, in reality, occupied a prominent and a more or less customary position in the society during the time of the Buddha.[33] Regarding their omission in the Pāli account, we can hardly offer any satisfactory explanation, in the face of all this solid testimony. On the other hand, the number given in the Saṃ, ch. 29, Sūtra 829 amounting to over 250 Rules leads us to believe that the editors of the *Āgamas* had actually got them. For conveying a clear idea of the actual numbers existing in the different versions and their commentaries, we give an illustrative Table spread on pages 11-13.

The reference we obtain from the VDPS of the Saṃmitīya School to the number of different sections is the same as that of the Sarv. except

29. PPN, Dict. vol. II, p. 376; S., iv.121-4.
30. For the corresponding number in the various Pmk. texts, see Appendix, IV.vii.
31. Saṃ., ch. 38, Sūtra 1074 (cf. Mv., I.22.); ch. 40, Sūtra 1115 (cf. S., XI.1.9; 5, Isayo); ch. 13, Sūtra 1.
32. See Appendix, IV.vii.
33. For the comparative estimate of the Bhikṣunī-Prātimokṣa, see Ernst Waldschmidt's Bruchistücke des Bhikṣunī-Prātimokṣa der Sarvāstivādins, p. 2.

	Pārājika	*Saṃghāvaśeṣa*	*Aniyata*	*Niḥsargika-Pātayantika*	*Pātayantika*	*Pratideśanīya*	*Śaikṣa*	*Adhikaraṇa Śamatha*	*Total*
Sarvāstivādin[34]	4	13	2	30	90	4	113	7	263
Sanskrit[35]	4	13	2	30	90	4	113	7	263
Vinayanidāna Sūtra[36]	4	13	2	30	90	4	113	7	263
Sarvāstivāda-Vinaya[37]	4	13	2	30	90	4	108	7	257
Sarvāstivāda-Vinaya-vibhāṣā[38]	4	13	2	30	90	4	91	7	241
Mūlasarvāstivādin and Comm.[39]	4	13	2	30	90	4	98	7	248
Tibetan[40]	4	13	2	30	90	4	108	7	258
Mahāvyutpatti[41]	4	13	2	30	90	4	105[48]	7	255
Dharmagupta and Comm.[42]	4	13	2	30	90	4	100	7	250
Mahīśāsaka and Comm.[43]	4	13	2	30	91	4	100	7	251
Kāśyapīya[44]	4	13	2	30	90	4	96	7	246

	Pārājika	*Saṃghāvaśeṣa*	*Aniyata*	*Niḥsargika-Pātayantika*	*Pātayantika*	*Pratideśanīya*	*Śaikṣa*	*Adhikaraṇa Śamatha*	*Total*
Upālipariprcchā Sūtra[45]	4	13	...[49]	30	92	4	72	...[49]	224 215
Pāli[46]	4	13	2	30	92	4	75	7	227
Mahāsaṅghika and Comm.[47]	4	13	2	30	92	4	66[50]	7	218

34. Shih-sung-lü-pi-ch'iu-chieh-pen or Prātimokṣa of the Sarvāstivāda-vinaya: Nanjio no. 1160, trans. by Kumārajīva, about 404 A.D. A reference and discussion concerning an older lost version of the Sv. will be found below.
35. Le Prātimokṣa-sūtra des Sarvāstivādins, texte Sanskrit, par M. Louis Finot avec la version Chinoise de Kumārajīva, traduite en Francais par M. Edouard Huber, JA, 1913.
36. Chieh-yin-yüan-ching or Pi-nai-ya=Vinaya: Nanjio no. 1130, translated by Chu Fo-nien, 378 A.D.
37. Shih-sung-lü or Vinaya of Ten Recitations: Nanjio no. 1115, trans. by Puṇyatāra, together with Kumārajīva, 404 A.D., 65 fasciculi, 10 adhyāyas or divisions, 29 sections.
38. Sa-p'o-to-p'i-ni-pi-p'o-sha: Nanjio nos. 1135, 1136, the translator of the work is unknown.
39. (A) Text. Ken-pen-shou-yi-chieh-yu—shih-ching: Nanjio no. 1110, trans. by I-Tsing 710 A.D.
(B) Comm. Mūlasarvāstivāda-nikāya-vinaya: Nanjio no. 1118, trans. by I-Tsing, 703 A.D., 50 fasciculi.
40. So-sor-thar-pa, or a Code of Buddhist Monastic Laws, being the Tibetan version of Prātimokṣa of the Mūlasarvāstivāda School: Ed and trans. by Satis Chandra Vidyabhusana, JASB, 1915, nos. 3-4.
41. Mahāvyutpatti, Minayeff: Sec. 257-264; Sakaki: cclvii-cclxiii; Csoma de Körös: clii (243)-clviii (249); Wogihara: 257-264.
42. (A) Text. Szu-fen-chieh-pen or Prātimokṣa of the Dharmaguptanikāya: Nanjio no. 1155, trans. by Buddhayaśas, A.D. 403-413. An English translation of the same, see Beal's Catena of Buddhist Scriptures from the Chinese, pp. 206-239.

(B) Comm. Szu-fen-lü-tsang or Dharmagupta Vinaya: Nanjio no. 1117, trans. by Buddhayaśas, together with Chu Fo-nien, A.D. 405, 60 fasciculi.

43. (A) Text. Wu-fen-chieh-pen or Prātimokṣa of the Mahīśāsaka-nikāya: Nanjio no. 1157, trans. by Buddhajīva, A.D. 423-424.
(B) Comm. Mi-sha-sai-pu-wu-fen-lü or Mahīśasāka-vinaya: Trans. by Buddhajīva, together with Chu Fo-nien, A.D. 423-424, 30 fasciculi, 5 Vargas or divisions.

44. Chieh-t'o-chieh-pen-ching or Prātimokṣa-Sūtra of the Kāśyapīya-nikāya: Nanjio no. 1108, trans. by Gautama Prajñāruci, A.D. 538-543.

45. Yu-po-li-wen-ching: Nanjio no. 1109, trans. by Guṇavarman, A.D. 431, 1 fascicule.

46. Pāṭimokkha: Edited by Minayeff with a Russian translation, St. Petersburg 1869; the same, edited by R.D. Vadekar in Devanāgarī Characters, Bhandarkar Oriental Series, no. 1, Poona 1939; English translation, SBE, vol xiii.

47. (A) Text. Po-lo-ti-mu-cha-san-c'hi-chieh-pen or text of the Prātimokṣa Saṅghika-vinaya: Nanjio no. 1159, trans. by Buddhabhadra about A.D. 416.
(B) Comm. Mo-ho-san-c'hi-lü or Mahāsaṅghika Vinaya, trans. by Buddhabhadra, together with Fa-hien, A.D. 416, 46 fasciculi, 18 sections.

48. We find in Csoma de Körös's STEV, p. 232 only 102 rules.

49. These two sections are left out uncommented.

50. This refutes H. Kern's statement: 'The Pāli version is unquestionably the oldest and, accordingly, the shortest'; *Manual*, p. 74.

that the section of the Śk. dharmas has been left unmentioned. *The Sarv. Vinaya-Śāstra* of Jinamitra, a word for word commentary on the Pmk. of the M-sarv. school has only expounded 62 rules of the Śk. and the division relating to 'preaching' therein is absolutely untouched. The number of other sections corresponds to the Msv. text.

Thus we see that 263 rules in the Sarv. is the highest and 218 in the Mahāsaṅghika the lowest. There is no variance in I, II, III, IV, VI, and VIII, of all the texts. The most divergent section is the VII (Śk. dharmas) which runs from 66 to 113 rules. Regarding its growth and development, we shall have occasion to discuss it later in a separate section allotted for the purpose.

It has been admitted[51] by all eminent scholars that Pmk. is one of the oldest texts in the Buddhist Canon. But none[52] is quite certain with regard to the rules which were comparatively older and were laid down by the Buddha himself. The precise date of the promulgation of such rules, of course, is beyond our knowledge,[53] but there are abundant scattered data in the Buddhist literature that give us the clue to the approximate time of their fixation.

The events given in the *Suttavibhaṅga* and attached to each particular rule, which although generally considered as imaginary and unreliable, cannot be totally discarded as untrue. As a rule, the truth of ancient Indian history has to be sifted from the conventional legends. The references found in the Sūtra-Piṭaka may indicate that at least some of the rules had been laid down by the Buddha, naturally they are the older ones in the Pmk. We shall now endeavour to search for such references from the Āgamas and Nikāyas to confirm our statement.

(A) **The 3rd Pārājika-Sarv.**

There is a large number of references to this incident:

1. The Bhikṣus who lived in the Sa-lo-li (Sarali) forest[54] on the bank of Valgumudā river in Vajragrāma were disgusted with their lives due to the practice of Aśubhāsmṛti visualization. They commited suicide in various ways and some of them requested Mṛgavana Brahmin to kill them with a knife. Consequently sixty

51. Oldb. Vin., pp. xvi, xx; Kern, p. 2; LHSL, p. 173; PLL, p. 15.
52. SBE, vol. xiii, pp. xii and xiv.
53. The Nidāna of the Msg. text has given a definite date of the 4 Pārājikas and they are said to have been established by the Buddha himself.
54. Saṃ., ch. 29, no. 809 (cf. S., 54.9, Vesali); T., vol. II, p. 207 (cf. Suv. Pārājika, 3).

Bhikṣus died in this way.

2. Pūrṇa said to the Buddha:[55] "If the Sonāparāntakas of the West were to kill me, I would think that the disciples of the Lord had been weary of their lives. In order to put an end to it, they committed suicide with a sword, or taken poison, or hanged themselves with a piece of rope or thrown themselves from a precipice . . ."
3. Thera Vakkali[56] (Po-chia-li) of Rājagṛha was suffering from a serious disease. He could not endure it any longer and committed suicide with a sword.
4. Thera Channa[57] of the Naḍa (Na-lo) village who was suffering destroyed his life in the same manner as that of Vakkali.[58]

(B) **The 1st Pārājika and 8th Saṃghāvaśeṣa-Sarv.**

The story of Mettiyabhummajoka[59] requesting his Bhikṣuṇī-sister to accuse Dabba Mallaputta falsely that the latter had committed a Pārājika offence by violating her chastity, throws a flood of light on the existence of those two rules in the lifetime of the Buddha, and shows that there was such a code as *Prātimokṣa*. In reply, the Bhikṣuṇī said: 'How can I charge a Bhikṣu, who observes the Brahmacaryā with a Pārājika offence?' That involves and links up both the rules mentioned above.

(C) **The 10th and 11th Saṃghāvaśeṣa-Sarv.**

The endeavour of Devadatta to cause a schism in the Saṅgha[60] and destroy the life of the Buddha is too notorious. His conspiracy with King Ajātaśatru has been recorded in the Sūtra and Vinaya literature as well as by the Chinese travellers.

(D) **The 13th Saṃghāvaśeṣa-Sarv.**

A Bhikṣu who lived in a forest in Kosala country used to play

55. Saṃ., ch. 13, no. 311 (cf. S., 35, 88, Punna and M. 145, Punnavada); T., vol. II, p. 89.
56. Ekottara, ch. 19; T., vol. II, p. 642; Saṃ., ch. 47, no. 1264 (cf. S., 22, 47, Vakkali); T., vol. II, p. 347.
57. Saṃ., ch. 47, no. 1266; T., vol. II, p. 348 (cf. S., 35, 87).
58. Other cases of attempting to commit suicide, see Saṃ., ch. 50, no. 1344 (cf. S., 9, 8, Ogāḷho); T., vol. II, p. 370; Eko., ch. 35; T. vol. II, p. 742.
59. Saṃ., ch. 39, no. 1075 (cf. Cv., IV.4.4-11).
60. Cv. VIII.3.3-9; *Ibid.* VIII.4.3; Dhv., ch. 46; Fa-hien, 34, 35, 37; YC., vol. I, p. 390; Rock., p. 94; Eko., ch. 47; T., vol. II, p. 803; Eko., ch. 9; T., vol. II, p. 590; Mahāsaṅgh., ch. 27; T., vol. I, p. 601.

(games) with the ladies of the locality. Great ill-fame later on assailed him and he finally attempted to commit suicide.[61]

(E) The 18th, 19th, and 20th Niḥsargika-pātayantika-Sarv.

The village chief of Maṇicūlaka[62] questioned the Buddha whether it was lawful for the disciples of the Buddhist Order to keep gold, silver and other precious articles. He, of course, replied in the negative and enjoined the Bhikṣus that thenceforth they might beg wood, grass, cart and labourers if needed, but should never accept gold, silver and other precious metals. This prohibition which has been set forth in the 10th Np. enjoins that a Bhikṣu should not personally accept the robe-fund, but let an agent act on his behalf. It is also very significant here that the Saṃ. does not mention the section of offence such as Np. to which this unlawful practice belongs. It is quite likely that the injunction was decreed by the Buddha much earlier than the time of its inclusion in the present classification.

(F) The 21st and 22nd Pātayantika-Sarv.

The Buddha told the Bhikṣus that he could no longer preach[63] to the Bhikṣuṇīs as he was too old for that. He therefore instructed the disciples to preach to the Bhikṣuṇīs by turn. When Nanda's turn came, he was disinclined to peform that duty. This is relevant here, because this practice of exalting the Bhikṣuṇīs was initiated by the Buddha whereas the Pmk. mentions only the deputation sent by the Saṅgha. That shows obviously a traditional practice being continued by the Buddhist Order.

(G) The 37th Pātayantika-Sarv.

1. The Blessed One told the Bhikṣus to eat once[64] in the day, because that enhanced strength and kept one in the best of health. Bhikṣu Bhaddāli informed the Lord that he was unable to do so on the ground of his poor health.

2. The same Sūtra[65] relates further that Udāyin who was of a very dark complexion, once had gone to beg alms in a dark and stormy night. On seeing him, the lady of the house who was pregnant, took him for a

61. Saṃ., ch. 50, no. 1344 (cf. S., 9, 8, Ogāḷho); T., vol. II, p. 370 (cf. Gil., vol. III, pt. 3, p. 15 foll.).
62. Saṃ., ch. 32 (cf. S., 42, 10, Maṇicūla); T., vol. II, p. 228; Eko., ch. 25; T., vol. II, p. 685.
63. Saṃ., ch. 11, no. 276 (cf. M., 146, Nandakovāda); T., vol. II, pp. 73-74.
64. Eko., ch. 47 (cf. M., 65, Bhaddāli and M. 66, Latukikopana); T., vol. II, p. 800.
65. *Ibid.*

ghost, was frightened and screamed. As a result thereof her foetus was destroyed then and there. When the public took notice of it, they disapproved such practices of the Bhikṣus.

3. '...He who praises[66] those who eat once a day, then he is praising me, because I often praise such practices; but he who disapproves and scolds the same, then, he is insulting me...' said the Buddha.

(H) **The 55th, 56th and 57th Pātayantika-Sarv.**

1. A Bhikṣu named Ariṭṭha[67] (and Gaddhabādhi Pubba) asserted that there is no harm in indulging oneself in the practice of the lustful act even after being admonished by the Bhikṣus for three times, and even maintained the same statement while facing the Buddha. He was later on accused of being guilty and condemned as a big fool.

2. Bhikṣu Moliyaphagguna[68] (mou-lo-p'o-chün) made himself very closely associated with the Bhikṣuṇīs even living together with them. The laity passed undesirable remarks on him. As a reply to the public censure, he said: 'I understand the teaching of the Buddha that the offence of violating the vow of chastity is insignificant.' He too was admonished by the Bhikṣus and scolded by the Blessed One.

There are other references with regard to Saṃ;[69] the 2nd, 13th, 48th, 49th, 76th[70], 79th[71] and 82nd[72] Pātayantika-Sarv., the 7 Adhik.[73] dharmas and so forth in both the Nikāyas and Āgamas. Thus far, we have gathered over 30 rules belonging to the I, II, IV, V, VII,[74] and VIII sections of the Pmk. It is beyond any shadow of doubt that they are among the oldest Rules collected and directly promulgated by the Buddha. We have reason to believe that he had a hand in shaping them. For instance, we are told[75] by Saṅgāramalla that many of his disciples attained their insight when he decreed only a few rules, but few reached such state when many more rules were added later on. As an echo of this, the *Cullavagga*[76] goes further to relate how the Buddha proclaimed and exalted the learning of the Vinaya. One thing to be borne in mind

66. Eko., ch. 5; T., vol. II, p. 570.
67. MG, ch. 54, no. 220 (cf. M. 22, Alagaddūpama); T., vol. I, p. 763.
68. Eko., ch. 48 (cf. M. 21, Kakacūpama); T., vol. II, 812-13.
69. Mahā., ch. 29, no. 116 (cf. A. viii.51, Gotamī); Cv. X.I; T., vol. I, p. 606.
70. Eko., ch. 16 (cf. M. 48, Kosambiya, M. 128, Upakkilesaya); T., vol. II, p. 626.
71. Saṃ., ch. 33, no. 936 (cf. S., 55, 24, Sarakāni); T., vol. II, p. 239.
72. Eko., ch. 42 (cf. A. 45, Pavesana); T., vol. II, p. 777.
73. Madhy., ch. 52, no. 196 (cf. 104, Sāmagāma Sutta); T., vol. I, p. 754.
74. About the Śk. dharmas, we have mentioned elsewhere.
75. Madhy., ch. 35, no. 143 (cf. A., III.60, Saṅgārava); T., vol. I, p. 650.
76. Cv., VI.13.i; SBE, vol. xiii, p. xiii.

is that this does not mean that he created the whole of the Pmk., but merely a minor portion of it. In other words, it should be said that the authorship of the present Pmk. text was shared by many unknown hands.[77] Its earliest part should reach far back to the neighbourhood of 500 B.C. and the final shape of the Pāli and the Mahāsaṅghika texts may at the most take 100 years to undergo their fullest development, including the Śaikṣa dharmas. Its growth may thus have been completed in about 400 B.C. Ryhs Davids was also of the opinion[78] that the great bulk of it must be older than the year 450 B.C. and its final touches about a century later. This looks probable, if we make a comparative survey of the development of all the versions of the schools. In any case, the latest date of its recension cannot possibly be placed[79] after 272 B.C. or just before Aśoka's coronation in 269 B.C. The reason is very obvious; in the Bhabra[80] Edict, Aśoka recommends seven texts of the Buddhist Canon to the Saṅgha. Amongst these, the first one is 'Vinaya-samukase'[81] which might have had some connection with the Pmk. as Oldenberg and Rhys Davids have suggested.

These texts mentioned by Aśoka must have been very popular and much in vogue before his ascent to the throne. To gain such a popularity, it is necessary to take a considerable length of time. Making allowance for all possibilities, we would like to side with the view that the oldest Rules of the Pmk. dated back to 500 B.C. and the latest could not possibly be later than 250 B.C.

III. PRĀTIMOKṢA AND THE COUNCILS

According to tradition, the number of Buddhist Councils amounts to eight.[82] They had been held from time to time by different groups of

77. The Sarv., ch. 5, Np. III gives us a testimony to this effect that even during the lifetime of the Buddha, the Bhikṣus proclaimed a Pātayantika rule prohibiting the members to see the Blessed One except at the time of sending him food and performing the Uposatha. This was probably a temporary measure.
78. IB, p. 43.
79. Oldb. Vin., p. xxxviii, '265 B.C.'; PLL, p. 13; Aśoka, p. 63.
80. Aśoka, p. 142. Out of the remaining six, five have been identified with the works in the Sutta Piṭaka, namely: 2. Aliya Vasāni (cf. D., Saṅgāti Sutta); 3. Anāgata Bhayāni (cf. A., iii.105-108); 4. Muni Gāthā (cf. A., Sutta-Nipāta, 206-220); 5. Moneya Sūte (cf. Itivuttaka no. 67, A., i.272); 7. Lāghulovāde Musāvādam Adhigichya (cf. M., i.414-420). Regarding the D., Saṅgāti Sutta, see PLL, p. 11, n. i; HIL, vol. II, p. 16 ff.
81. SBE, vol. XIII, p. xxvi.
82. EMB, p. 324.

Bhikṣus, at various places. As we are chiefly concerned with the *Prātimokṣa,* it is better to confine ourselves to what has relevancy to the subject-matter. We shall deal with only the councils of Rājagṛha, Vaiśāli and Pāṭaliputra held during the reign of King Aśoka.

The Council of Rājagṛha

This Council has been a subject of heated discussion among the Orientalists. Oldenberg was one of the first persons[83] to express his doubt that it is not history, but pure invention, on the ground that 'the author of the *Mahāparinibbāna Sutta* (MPS) did not know anything of the first council'.[84] But many earlier and later scholars have collected materials on the subject from various sources[85] and made more through investigation. Amongst these, we may mention Louis de la Vallée Poussin's *Conciles de Bouddhisme,*[86] Przyluski's *Le concile de Rājagṛha* and Otto Franke's *The Buddhist Council at Rājagaha and Vesāli.*[87] All these have contributed much to the furtherance of Buddhistic studies and their efforts are worthy of attention, though we may not agree with some of their verdicts. As to whether there is any mention of the first council at Rājagṛha in the MPS, we may state that there is at least one version of the MPS which gives us the answer in the positive. It is in the 2nd chapter of the *Buddha-Parinirvāṇa-Sūtra,*[88] translated by Po Fa-tsu, in A.D. 290-306. We find there immediately after the account of cremation of the remains of the Buddha, the statement that the Bhikṣus who gathered at Kusinārā formed the desire to collect the teachings of the Master. Ānanda was selected as the suitable person for reciting the Sūtra section, but it was feared that the might keep a closed fist to himself. So the Saṅgha forced him by tactics. They first censured him for the seven errors committed by him during the Buddha's lifetime, and immediately relieved him of the anxiety of being a moral criminal by asking him to recite the Sūtras of the Canonical literature.[89] He did as directed and it is said that the four Āgamas were collected through him. We find support of this tradition, in the Mahāsaṅghika V. ch. 32, the

83. For the opinions of Minayeff, see Recherches sur le Boudhisme, trans. from the Russian by R.H. Assier de Pompignan, 1894.
84. Oldb. Vin., vol. I, pp. xxvii-viii.
85. By Wassilief, Schiefner and Rockhill from Tibetan, by Suzuki and Beal from Chinese, by Trunour, Rhys Davids, Gieger and others from Pāli.
86. Le Museon, vi, pp. 213-323, trans. into English in the IA, 1908.
87. JPTS, 1908, pp. 1-80.
88. Nanjio no. 552; T., vol. I, p. 175.
89. Cf. CR, pp. 79-85.

Mūlasarvāstivāda-vinaya-saṃyuktavastu[90] and Bu-ston's *History*[91] *of Buddhism in India and Tibet.* It is not improbable that Louis Finot[92] and Obermiller[93] have hit the nail on the head by suggesting that MPS and the CV XI-XII (which deal with the two Councils) were originally united in one work, possibly of much older tradition, but were later on arbitrarily divided and awkwardly thrown into the Piṭakas without an endeavour being made to fit them in their new setting. This being the case, Oldenberg's principal argument falls to the ground. We are therefore, compelled to form our judgment differently. Nor can the opinion of Otto Franke[94] who drew his evidence chiefly from the Pāli sources, be justified.

For various reasons it has been generally admitted by scholars that the first council was a historical event.[95] Firstly, it contains an ancient nucleus of authentic tradition of holding discussions on points of Vinaya or Discipline, and secondly, it assumes the symbolical aspect of a regular council which put together the essential elements of Buddhist literature, though its date may not be placed just after the death of the Master. The whole Canon in the present shape was incomplete at that time.

The story of its genesis[96] and its chief tenets have been told in different ways by the various schools. However the most important ones may be briefly summed up here:

1. When Mahākaśyapa[97] heard the frivolous utterances of an old Bhikṣu, he was distressed and made up his mind to hold a general assembly so that they might gather the sayings of the Buddha.
2. The Buddha had already permitted that certain minor[98] rules, as told by himself might be abandoned, should the Saṅgha so wished.

---

90. Nanjio no. 1121, ch. 39.
91. Bu-ston, pt. II, p. 72.
92. IHQ, vol. VIII, 1932, p. 244.
93. *Ibid.*, p. 784.
94. JPTS, 1908, p. 68.
95. IA, 1908, p. 18, cited Minayeff: Kern thinks it to be a party function of the Sthavira School, Manual, p. 103; Przyluski considers that it was an annual function of the Bhikṣus after the Vassa. But the one which was held for the first time after the death of the Buddha had occupied a greater significance in the eyes of later generations; CR, p. 373.
96. Mahāvaṃsa, Intro. p. liii.
97. Poussin, IA, 1908, p. 2 and n. 3.
98. Cv., XI.i.9.10; MPS., VI.3.

3. Ānanda became an Arhat and he was censured[99] by the Saṅgha for his shortcomings, the number of which rises from six to eight.
4. The Brahmadaṇḍa[100] should be imposed on Bhikṣu Channa.
5. The passing away of Gavaṃpati[101] and Purāṇa's insistence on holding his own views.
6. Upāli recited the section of Vinaya and Ānanda recited that of the Sūtra.

It is not our intention to investigate the differences regarding these events any further, inasmuch as we do not think it essential to our present purpose.

Leaving this point aside, therefore, we shall now see, to what extent the number and sections of the Pmk. have been mentioned in the Vinaya of the various schools and other records, so as to find out if possible, some traces of the discussions re: the Pmk. rules, which must have taken place in the first council of Rājagṛha and of which mention is made in all the schools.[102]

Sarv. v., ch. 60, Sect. I.1 at Vaiśāli for Sudinna Kalanda-putra.

Sarv. v., ch. 60, Sect. I.2 at Rājagṛha for Dhanika Kumbhakāra-putra.

Sarv. v., ch. 60, Sect. I.3 and 4 at Vaiśāli for the Bhikṣus who lived on the bank of the Valgumudā river.

Sarv. v., ch. 60, Sect. II.1 at Śrāvasti for Kālodayi.

Sarv. v., ch. 60, Sect. II.2-4 at Śrāvasti for Kālodayi.

Sarv. v., ch. 60, Sect. II.5 at Śrāvasti for Kālo Bhikṣu, son of Milikkha. (And in this manner the Vinaya Piṭaka was recited.)

Regarding the question, as to what minor and insignificant rules might be given up, the complete sections mentioned are: III (2 rules); IV (30 rules); V (90 rules); VI (4 rules); and VII (7 rules).

Dharm. v., ch. 54, Sect. I.1.2.3 and 4 are the same as those of the Sarv. above.

Sect. II.1 is the same as Sarv. II.1.

Sect. III.1 at Śrāvasti for Bhikṣu Kālodayi.

Sect. IV (The exact number is not mentioned) at Śrāvasti for a

---

99. A detailed comparison of these errors, see IA, 1908, pp. 4-5; Bu-ston, II, p. 79.
100. MPS, VI.4.
101. IA, 1908, p. 5; Bu-ston, II, p. 73 ff.
102. It should be noted that the Kāś. has no commentary and the Mūlasarv. v., Nanjio no. 1110, does not mention the events of the councils.

group of six Bhikṣus.

Sect. V.1 at Sa-ki-she (Sāṅkāśya?) for Hastibala.

Sect. VI.1 at Śrāvasti for Utpalavarṇā Bhikṣuṇī. (...the 2nd, the 3rd and the 4th are also being questioned and answered in the same manner.)

The total number in each section here is Sect. I=4; II=13; III=2; IV=30; and V=90 rules.

Mahīś. v., Sect. I.1.2.3 and 4 are the same as those of the Sarv. mentioned above.

The other sections being referred to are IV, V and VI, but the definite number is not given.

Msgv. v., ch. 32. There is no mention of places at which the rules had been established as well as the persons with whom they were concerned. The number of sections being given here is III=2; IV=30; V=92; VI=4 and VIII=7 rules.

Samantap.[103], ch. I, Sect. I.1 is the same as Sarv. I.1 (....even so up to the 4th Pārājika).

The following sections are mentioned II (number of rules not mentioned); III=2; IV=30; V=92; VI=4; VII=75 and VIII=7 rules.[104]

Cv. Sect. I.1.2.3 and 4 are the same as those of Sarv. stated above.

And in like manner, both[105] the Vinaya of the Bhikṣus and of the Bhikṣuṇīs were being questioned. Other sections referred to are: II=13; III=2; IV=30; V=92 and VI=4 rules.

Aśokāvadāna[106] (A-yu-wang-ching), Sect. I.1 is the same as the Sarv. I.1.

The rest are questioned in like manner.

From the above comparisons, one observes that although the texts differ in details of the rules under question, yet one thing is certain, viz. that some of the rules at least, had existed before the first council of Rājagṛha took place. This, without question, is an evidence of the antiquity of the *Prātimokṣa.*

The Council of Vaiśāli

About this council, it is said[107] that 100 or 110 years after the death of the Blessed One, the Vajjian Bhikṣus of Vaiśāli indulged themselves

103. Samp., ch. 1 (cf. Pāli Samp. PTS).
104. The Bhikkhunī-Pāṭimokkha was also being questioned. This shows clearly that the Burmese manuscripts read 'Ubhato vibhaṅga in lieu of Ubhato Vinaya' which is a mistake (cf. HPL, p. 10).
105. Cv., XI.1.8, n. 1.
106. Aśoka, ch. 4; Nanjio no. 1343.
107. Cv., XII.1.1.

in the practice of ten tenets which were considered as going against some of the rules of the Pmk. They were therefore, subject to censure. The Sthavira Yaśas, son of Kākandaka who as a true apostle of the Buddha announced publicly their misbehaviour and evil conduct. As a consequence, an assembly of 700 Sthaviras coming from different regions was held. There they discussed those propositions and delivered their final judgment.

For a detailed information about the whole episode, we have to consult the *Cullavagga* which has devoted an entire chapter, namely, the 12th Khandhaka, to it. In Kern's *Manual* (pp. 103-9) and Poussin's[108] *Conciles de Bouddhisme,* one also sees a good summary of the same. As we don't wish to reiterate the story here, the readers are requested to refer to the aforesaid works. We shall however examine, how far this Council owes its origin to and is related with the Pmk. rules, and to what degree the statement, that another Council, held by the heretical Bhikṣus in all ten thousand, who where denounced by the Sthaviras who had held the Second Council, founded the School which bears the name of Mahāsaṅghika,[109] is true.

The interpretations of the ten points differ quite a good deal in the Southern and Northern traditions. It is probably due to the fact that some of them are of local importance. It is clearly illustrated in the case that a learned Sthavira like Sabbakāmi (Sarvakāmi) did not apprehend what exactly those ten propositions meant, except the last two, for he questioned all the first eight.[110]

In order to show the differences, we give below side by side the interpretations found in the existing records:

(i) ***Singilona***

Pāli. Carrying salt in a horn.
Sarv. Keeping aside salt.[111]
Dharm. v. Same as Sarv.[112] (7th)
Roc. Keeping salt as long as one lived.[113] (4th)
Mahīś. v. Keeping aside salt and ginger.[114]

108. IA, 1908, pp. 81-7; Roc., p. 171.
109. Maha., V.3-4.
110. Cv., XIII.2.8.
111. Sarv., ch. 61.
112. Dh. v., ch. 54.
113. Mhsv., ch. 30.
114. Roc., p. 171.

(ii) ***Dvangula***

Pāli. Taking meals when the sun's shadow showed two finger breadth after noon.

Sarv. Having finished eating, picking up food with two fingers that was not left-over food.

Dharm. v., Mahiś. v., Roc. The same as Sarv. This is the 1st in Dhv., and 6th in Roc.

(iii) ***Gāmāntara***

Pāli. Going to a village intending to eat again.

Sarv. Obtaining food by going to a village but without observing the ceremony of food-being-left-over.

Dharm. v. -Do-.

Mahīś. v. -Do-. (4th)

Roc. Eating food during journeys when they are a yojana or a half yojana away from their Vihāra. (5th)

(iv) ***Āvāsa***

Pāli. Holding Uposatha separately within the same boundary.

Sarv. -Do-. (5th)

Dharm. v. Holding a Karma or proclamation separately inside the temple. (3rd)

Mahīś. v. Not corresponding.

Roc. Not corresponding.

(v) ***Anumati***

Pāli. Doing an act and obtaining sanction for it afterwards.

Sarv. Performing a wrong act at first and then asking recognition of the Saṅgha. (6th)

Dharm. v. -Do-. (4th)

Mahīś. v. Holding a separate Karma first and then seeking others' permission. (9th)

Roc. Not corresponding.

(vi) ***Acinna***

Pāli. To do anything adopted as a practice by his Upajjhāya.

Sarv. (Certain offences mentioned in the Prātimokṣa, such as depriving of life etc. are considered impure whether one does them or not—8th); not corresponding.

Dharm. v. Doing an act that is in accordance with the usual way. (5th)

Mahīś. v. To perform the same acts that he used to do when he was a layman.

Roc. Not corresponding.

(vii) ***Amathita***

Pāli. To eat curd after the midday-meal.

Sarv. Taking a mixture of unboiled milk, curd and butter. (4th)

Dharm. v. Taking a mixture of ghee, honey, curd, honey (from caves) and butter after the meal is over. (6th)

Mahīś. v. -Do-., taking at the wrong time. (5th)

Roc. Drinking a mixture of half-milk and half-curd.

(viii) ***Jalogi***

Pāli. Drinking unfermented toddy.

Sarv. Drinking liquor, because the living condition is poor. (7th)

Dharm. v. Drinking Ja-lou-lo (jalogi) wine. (8th)

Mahīś. v. Drinking unfermented wine called Jaloga. (6th)

Roc. To suck fermented drinks as would a leech. (7th)

(ix) ***Adasaka (Adasalaṃ Nisīdanaṃ)***

Pāli. The use of a borderless rug or mat to sit on.

Sarv. Making a seat-rug without taking a piece of one span's length from the old rug to add to the border of the new one. (9th)

Dharm. v. Making a seat without patch-works. (9th)

Mahīś. v. No limitation of the size of making a rug or a mat to sit upon. (7th)

Roc. Using a mat without patching it around the edge (the width of) a Sugata's span. (9th)

(x) ***Jātarūparajata***

Pāli. To receive gold and silver.

Sarv. Receiving gold, silver and other valuable articles.

Dharm. v. Accepting gold and silver.

Mahīś. v. Keeping gold, silver and money.

Roc. Obtaining gold, silver and other treasures (p. 73).

The contents differing most from those of the Pāli text are found in the Tibetan translation, presented by Rockhill, from which we have:

1. The practice of the exclamation *Alala.*[115]

---

115. This might have been influenced by the exclamation in Mahādeva's 5 points. See Watters· YC, I, p. 268.

2. Indulging in enjoyment.
3. Digging the earth with his own hand or have it dug.

Besides this, there is one more dissimilar point in the Mahīś. v. namely:

'To sit and eat'. (4th)

As it does not give us any explanation as to what it exactly means, we are unable to grasp the proper shade of meaning.

The propositions however agree to a considerable extent with some of the rules in the Pmk. The following Table will show distinctly to what degree they are related to the Pmk.

Point	(i)	Pāli	Sect.	V.38	Sarv.[116]	Sect.	V.38
Point	(ii)	Pāli	Sect.	V.37	Sarv.	Sect.	V.37
Point	(iii)	Pāli	Sect.	V.35	Sarv.	Sect.	V.34
Point	(iv)[117]	Pāli	...	...	Sarv.	...	...
Point	(v)[118]	Pāli	...	...	Sarv.	...	...
Point	(vi)	Pāli	...	...	Sarv.	...	...
Point	(vii)	Pāli	Sect.	V.37	Sarv.	Sect.	V.37
Point	(viii)	Pāli	Sect.	V.51	Sarv.	Sect.	V.79
Point	(ix)	Pāli	Sect.	V.89	Sarv.	Sect.	V.89
Point	(x)	Pāli	Sect.	IV.18	Sarv.	Sect.	V.18
The 3rd point given in Roc. "Digging the earth" corresponds with the		Pāli	Sect.	V.18 and	Sarv.	Sect.	V.73

Out of the above ten (points), eight are found in the Pmk. and two, (4 and 5) are referred to in the Vinaya MV. If the date of the Second Council can be trusted, i.e. 100 or 100+10=110 years[119] after the death of the Master[120] (369 or 379 B.C.), then, it is obvious that the Vinaya literature, by that time, had made a rather rapid progress. It does not

116. From this, the equivalent rules of other texts can be found.
117. MV, II.8.3.
118. MV, IX.3.5.
119. Bu-ston, II, p. 96.
120. Oldenberg takes it to be somewhere around 383 B.C.: Vin. xxxix, PTS.; Rhys Davids was of the opinion that it may be placed within thirty years of 350 B.C.; SBE, vol. XIII, p. xxiii.

merely indicate that the Pmk. was in its fully developed stage, but the minute regulations regarding the daily activities of the Saṅgha as found in the *Sutta-Vibhaṅga* and the bulk of the Khandakas[121] had also emerged into existence. As a result, we are led to believe that the incident which caused Yaśas to break away from the Vṛjian Bhikṣus on point of 'receiving gold and silver is unlawful', and the transgression of other nine points aforesaid were two separate events which did not occur at the same time but were brought together as one. The literary evidence, found in the Mahāsaṅghika tradition, which will be treated below, goes to show, that the process would be something like this: A considerable time had elapsed after the demise of the Master. Some members of the Saṅgha, probably due to regional,[122] traditional and linguistic reasons observed the Vinaya rules in a different manner. The drinking of a mixture of curd and butter, or taking meals when the shadow of the sun showed two finger breadths after noon is, in fact, to them as well as to us not of great importance. It therefore went on unnoticed, until Yaśas took notice of one of these illegal practices and made it a subject of public censure. However, this point, as the evidence shows has nothing to do with other nine, but they were somehow welded together with it by later compilers, perhaps because of its dramatic effect. They might have happened much earlier than the 'gold and silver' incident. The endeavour of Yaśas and its consequence, has obviously a historical basis, if the legendary[123] elements such as his rising up into the sky, the presence of the 140-year old Sthavira Sarvakāmin and other great disciples of the Buddha are taken out from the scene. We should bear in mind that when Yaśas requested the laity to give him support, it was the 11th of Niḥsargika Pātayantika at issue. So, we find how he first quoted the Four Stains,[124] amongst which, to accept gold and silver is one. And then, he quoted the Blessed One's reply to Maṇicūḷaka's query that gold and silver were not allowed.[125] Further, he said that the Buddha had distinctly laid down a percept by which gold and silver were forbidden.[126] He never mentioned anything before this in connexion with the other nine points.

121. SBE, vol. XIII, p. xxii.
122. Relaxation was given to the Bhikṣus who lived in the paccantima janapadas in order to suit the physical conditions there. SBBS, pp. 183, 212, 214; Csoma de Körös—The different Systems of Buddhism.
123. Cv., XII.i.8; Kern, p. 105 and n. 3.
124. *Ibid.*, XII.1.3.
125. *Ibid.*, i.4; Saṃ., ch. 32; T., vol. II, p. 685. (cf. S., 42, 10, Maṇicūḷā).
126. *Ibid.*, XII.i.5; Pmk. Sect. IV.18.

We first see the appearance of the ten points on the occasion when[127] he went to Sambhūta Śānavāsi, and later on when he questioned Revata on them. It is obvious at this juncture that the compilers combined the two into one. *A very singnificant evidence that we possess is that the Mahāsaṅghika V. knows nothing*[128] *of the other nine points* although it relates that the Vṛjian Bhikṣus were begging money from the laity and that Yaśas went to Sthavira Dasapāla at Mathura for righting the wrong. *At its conclusion, the council assembled by Yaśas, summed up that one may beg for bowls, robes and medicines if in need, but it was in no way permissible that one should ask for gold, silver or money.*

This is almost a certain indication that the ten theses are a combination of incidents happening at different junctures and all referring back to the Pmk. That gives further testimony to the possibility of the text being completed around 400 B.C., though the date of the Vaiśāli Council has not been quite fixed.[129] Secondly, the account of another council held by the losing party that was called the Great Council (Mahāsaṅgīti), belonging to the Mahāsaṅgha[130] (Mahāsaṅghika) found in the Sinhalese documents is rather doubtful even according to their own statement.[131] The story of the two councils had probably a historical basis in a different sense. The reasons are: 1. The Vinaya of the Mahāsaṅghika school mentions only one council, namely the council summoned by Yaśas to discuss the evil practice of Pmk. Sect. IV.18. 2. This text knows nothing of the other points. Therefore, its compilation is in a way older than the Vinaya texts of other schools in which, the ten points have been mentioned. 3. If there was really a different redaction of the canonical scriptures carried out by the Mahāsaṅghikas[132] in a different council at that time may we ask then, how is it that the point in question (receiving gold and silver) is still retained not merely in the Pmk. of that school but also in its commentary? Why should they not say something in defence of their practice of accepting money, instead of comdemning it? One thing is quite sure that the Pāli chronicles have made us doubt their truthfulness, and that the existence of the Mahāsaṅghika school does not

---

127. Cv., XII.i. 8; *Ibid.*, i.10.
128. Mahās. v., ch. 33.
129. Kern, p. 109.
130. 'The heretical Bhikṣus, subdued by the Theras who held the Second Council, in all ten thousand, founded the school which bears the name Mahāsaṅghika.' Mahā. V.3-4.
131. Dip., IV.52; Vasumitra 20, 25; Mahā., p. lvi; Kern, p. 105.
132. Mahā., p. lvi.

seem to have appeared for the first time in connexion[133] with the Second Council as pictured by the Pāli tradition.

The Council of Pāṭaliputra

This was simply a party meeting of the Theravādins or Vibhajyavādins and the date is quite uncertain,[134] though the Pāli chronicles state that it was held in the reign of King Dharmāśoka when 236 years had passed after the Buddha's Nirvāṇa. As this council had hardly any connection with the Pmk., except that its origin was connected with non-observance of the Posatha ceremony[135] by the Bhikṣus, we may drop the matter here.

IV. TEXT AND THE SCHOOLS

The existing documents regarding the Buddhist schism and the development of the schools as a result thereof, have caused such a great confusion that it is not very easy to grasp the real situation. The cause of this split in the Saṅgha, is said to be the ten propositions[136] in relation to the Council at Vaiśāli, on the one hand, and the five tenets of Mahādeva[137] on the other, about one hundred and odd years after the death of the Buddha. As we have discussed in the previous chapter that the Mahāsaṅghika school had positively very little to do with the other nine propositions, the Pāli statement cannot induce us to believe in its authenticity with regard to the alleged schism at Vaiśāli. Moreover, it is clear that indications given in the literature of the schools prove that the cause of the schism was more on the side of doctrine than on that of disciplinary rules. Thus we find such statements maintained by different authors on the division of the eighteen schools:

(a) Vasumitra[138] takes it to be the five tenets, namely: 1. The Arhats are tempted by others; 2. They have ignorance about their attainment of Arhatship; 3. They have doubt regarding the truth; 4. They realise Arhatship by the help of others; 5. The realization of the Path is ascertained by utterances. It was due to these differences of opinion that the first schism took place

133. Kern, p. 107; Watters: YC, II, p. 161; JDL, 1920, p. 5.
134. Kern, p. 110.
135. Mahā., V.229.
136. Kath., p. 3; Māhā., pp. lix and lxii; YC, I, p. 268; JDL, 1920, p. 5.
137. Bu-ston, p. 96 mentions a person named Bhadra instead.
138. JDL, 1920, pp. 5-11; Nanjio no. 1286 (cf. Tar. IHQ, vol. VII, p. 150, n. 3); SBBS, p. 229.

between the Sthavira and the Mahāsaṅghikas and again the Sthavira school subdivided itself into various sects, on the same account.

(b) Bu-ston[139] maintains that the origin of the dissension was due to linguistic differences in reciting the scriptures.

(c) Commenting on this, Bhavya[140] simply says that it occurred on account of some controversial questions. Since there is a separate account about the ten propositions of the Vaiśāli Council in the Tibetan[141] sources, we take it for granted that these 'controversial questions' should mean invariably some dogmatical differences.

Besides, in the names of the schools, we find very clear reflections on their theoretical adherences e.g. Lokottaravāda[142] means that the Tathāgata is not subject to worldly laws but one who is beyond the world; Sarvāstivāda[143]—that all things exist in all times; and Mahīśāsaka—that their teaching rests on the properties of all the great mass of the earth (*mahī*) and of human beings who will have no other existence and so forth. Therefore, we presume that the split of the schools was caused by differences of doctrine rather than by those of discipline.

Regarding the date of the first schism that is the time when the Sthaviras and the Mahāsaṅghikas established separate schools for themselves, it is rather difficult to come to a definite conclusion at the present moment from the confused mass of statements. It is given as: a hundred and odd years[144] A.B. by Vasumitra; the hundredth[145] year A.B. by Yuan Chwang; one hundred and sixty years A.B. when King Dharmāśoka[146] was reigning in Kusumapura by Bhavya; one hundred and thirty-seven years A.B. when the Kings Nanda and Mahāpadma were reigning, and 160 years A.B. in the reign of King Aśoka given by Bu-ston.[147] We find that out of the five dogmas of Mahādeva, four have been recorded in the *Kathāvatthu.*[148] The commentary of the said text[149] has stated that they

139. Bu-ston, pp. 96-98.
140. Roc., p. 183.
141. *Ibid.*, p. 171.
142. *Ibid.*, p. 183.
143. *Ibid.*, pp. 184-5.
144. JDL, 1920, p. 5.
145. YC, I, p. 267.
146. Roc. p. 132.
147. Bu-ston, p. 96.
148. Kath., ii.2, ii.3, ii.4, ii.6.
149. Kath., ii.i.

were the current views held by the Pubbaseliyās and Aparaseliyās, the two branches of the Mahāsaṅghika schools at that time. The *Kathāvatthuppakaraṇa,*[150] which is said to have been composed by Tissa Moggaliputta in the Third Council at Pāṭaliputra under the patronage of King Aśoka also refers to the five tenets of Mahādeva. It thus seems probable: 1. That there was a dispute over the five tenets of Mahādeva[151] and finally it led to the dissension in the Saṅgha, before the Council of Pāṭaliputra, as described in the Pāli tradition, had taken place. 2. That the date of this schism might fall somewhere between 100 and 150 years after the Nirvāṇa of the Buddha. It would not be a surprise to us if there were two 'Second Councils with a historical basis' one being held from the viewpoint of Vinaya and the other from that of the doctrine (see ante). If this hypothesis can be accepted, it would solve the riddle of so many date (100, 110, 137, 160 A.B.) being attributed to only one council, whether disciplinary or doctrinal. Equally intricate is the question of the date of King Aśoka in relation to the councils. However, in the light of scientific researches conducted by various scholars, it is accepted that he appeared on the scene as a King around[152] 270 B.C. That being settled, the rest would be comparatively easier.

As our chief concern here is the relationship[153] between the Pmk. and the schools, we shall therefore, not indulge ourselves much in the growth of the schools but shall take particular care to see if: 1. The Pmk. text of one school, especially, of the Mahāsaṅghika and the Sthavira schools has any similarity when compared with others; 2. There is any evidence of those schools being branched off from the main trunk as stated in the Northern and Southern traditions; and 3. We may point out which is the oldest amongst them.

The number of the Buddhist schools, both according to the N. and S. traditions, is counted from 18 to 20. The former represents the real group, the latter being the result of local additions. In theory, we suppose each of them had in its possession a copy of the Pmk. of its own, but unfortunately, there is no evidence to prove it. The schools which

150. Mahā., V.278.

151. Poussin: The five points of Mahādeva and the Kathāvatthu; JRAS, 1910, p. 413 foll.

152. His coronation in 269 B.C.: Aśoka, p. 63, 265 B.C.; Oldenberg Vin., p. xxxviii; Rhys Davids, 270 B.C.; BI, p. 272; W. Geiger, 269-264 B.C.; according to the Southern Tradition: Mahā., p. xlvi.

153. Roc., p. 182 foll; JDL, 1920, pp. 6-7. Tar., pp. 270-274; Bu-ston, p. 99; Mahā. V. Dip., 5, 39 foll.; Mahā., Appendix B: The Buddhist Sects.

possess still a rich Vinaya-Piṭaka are but a few, namely:

1. Mahāsaṅghika
2. Sthavira
3. Sarvāstivāda
4. Mūlasarvāstivāda
5. Mahīśāsaka
6. Dharmaguptaka
7. Kāśyapīya (without Comm.)
8. Saṃmitīya

The Vinaya literature, including the Pmk. texts of the first seven schools mentioned above, has been variously preserved viz. in Tibetan and Chinese translations, in the Pāli original and in Sanskrit manuscripts[154] (chiefly in fragments except in the case of the Ms. found by the Pelliot[155] Mission in the ruins of Douldouraquor, at Kucha). Of the last two (7 and 8), the former has only a Pmk. text without commentary and the latter has none. There are instead traces[156] of the existence of a Pmk. text of this last school, which seems to have agreed with that of the Dharmaguptaka school in all sectional numbers, excepting that of the Śaikṣa-dharmas which in general, are not numbered by any of the schools.

Besides the literature of the foregoing schools, there is a text, *Upāli-paripṛcchā-Sūtra*[157] by name, which has the mixed character of both a text of the Pmk. and a brief commentary dealing with persons who had transgressed any of the prescribed precepts. It has 92 rules in § V and 72 rules in § VII. A comparison of the latter section with the 75 rules in the Pāli and the 66 rules in the Mahāsaṅghika in § VII reveals definite signs of its great antiquity, though we are not quite certain as to which school it belongs. It may belong to the early Sarvāstivādins, and may be even older than the Pāli text. Yet we do not consider this to be the original one nor that of the Mahāsg. or the Pāli text. We are firmly convinced that there was a fountain-head, from which, the cardinal schools like Mahāsaṅghika and Sthavira drew their inspiration and source. When the dissensions in the unified Saṅgha took place and later on each school possessed a copy of the Pmk. of its own, the original

154. Gilg., vols. I-II; Fragments du Vinaya des Sarvāstivādin, par Jean Filliozat et Hōryū Kuno; JA, 1938.
155. Hoernle's MRBL.: JA, 1913.
156. VDPS, p. 42, Nanjio no. 1139; Nei-Hsüeh, vol. III, pp. 54-56.
157. Nanjio no. 1109.

Pmk. must have developed to such a formidable extent, that the number of almost all the sections except § VII, had come to be already fixed up. We find therefore, in our comparative table (see ante) that the § VII is the most varied one. Starting from 66 in the Mahāsg. it goes up to 113 rules in the Sarv. That enables us to trace the development of those schools and find a clue to their relative antiquity.

The original text before reaching its highest development, must have undergone several changes in the process of editing and redacting, as such traces have been retained in the existing texts. The cardinal precepts, as a rule, are not laid down once for all, but as occasion arises, they are added and gradually give rise to the present form. Take for instance, the 1st of Pārājika—to perform the act of intercourse with the opposite sex—Maithunaṃ dharmam. We may divide it into four stages:

(i) Such an act with a female is prohibited.
(ii) It may be permitted if one has declared one's weakness and withdrawn from the Order.
(iii) To perform it with any one, other than a female.
(iv) To peform it with an animal.

The commentaries of the schools assert, without any exception, that the rules came into existence as there was actual occurrences during the lifetime of the Buddha. It seems quite natural that when a Bhikṣu committed an offence which is against the principle or the spirit of a rule such as the 1st Pārājika, it had to be included or amended in that very precept, i.e. to say that his object is not a woman but an animal, or that he did it without declaring his weakness or abandoning the life of a Brahmacārin beforehand. Thus it grew stage by stage, first the principal precepts and later on, rules of secondary importance, supplementing the cardinal ones of a similar nature. To prove this, there is evidence and proof in the *Sutta-Vibhaṅga.* The Buddhists, like the Āraṇyakas of ancient India attached a great significance to the observance of celibacy or Brahmacaryā. It is stated[158] in the *Mahāparinibbāna-s.* that in the later days of the Buddha, when Ānanda put the question as to what the attitude of the Bhikṣu towards women should be, the Buddha warned them not to have any association with them and not even to talk to them. So, in conformity with that idea, there exist more than 25 rules classified in different sections bearing on the principle of the 1st Pārājika:

158. MPS, V.23; SBE, vol. XI.

Five Rules in Section II (Sarv.)

1. Emission of semen.
2. Bodily contact with woman.
3. Addressing women with wicked words.
4. Praising women for offering bodily service.
5. Acting as a go-between.

Two Rules in Section III (Sarv.)

1. Sitting in a concealed place fit for lustful purposes.
2. Sitting in the open, fit for a lustful act.

Three Rules in Section IV (Sarv.)

4. Receiving a robe from an unrelated Bhikṣuṇī.
5. Having a robe washed by an unrelated Bhikṣuṇī.
17. Having wool washed by an unrelated Bhikṣuṇī.

Thirteen Rules in Section V (Sarv.)

5. Speaking to a woman beyond five or six words.
21. Exhorting the Bhikṣuṇīs without deputation.
22. Exhorting the Bhikṣuṇīs after sunset.
24. Travelling with a Bhikṣuṇī by appointment.
25. On Board a boat with a Bhikṣuṇī by appointment.
26. Giving a robe to an unrelated Bhikṣuṇī.
27. Making a robe for an unrelated Bhikṣuṇī.
28. Sitting with a Bhikṣuṇī in secret.
29. Sitting alone with a woman.
30. Food procured by the intervention of a Bhikṣuṇī.
43. Sitting secretly with a woman in a family that is taking food.
65. Sleeping in the same place with a woman.
70. Travelling together with a woman by appointment.

Two Rules in Section VI (Sarv.)

1. Accepting food from an unrelated Bhikṣuṇī in the house of a lay disciple.
2. Accepting food at a Bhikṣuṇī's direction in the house of a lay-man.

Among the rules seen above, such as V.30 and VI.1 and VI.2 have hardly anything to do with the grave offence of the 1st Pārājika, but because the person with whom the Bhikṣus came into contact was a Bhikṣuṇī, that was likely to bring public censure on them. It is therefore considered better for them to keep aloof from her.

The same principle can be applied to other[159] cardinal offences such as killing, stealing and uttering false words. Around each of these, there emerged minor precepts which are of a supplementary nature and are scattered among the various sections in the Pmk. It would not be unreasonable to say that the code of discipline of the Saṅgha is but, an enlarged edition of the 'Pañcaśīla' which have been adopted by the Buddhists and the Jains[160] from the Brāhmaṇical ascetics. And under various circumstances, they have developed subsidiary rules in order to meet various requirements on various occasions. This appears to us to be the line of development through which the growth of these rules could be explained.

Our next inquiry would be with regard to the classification of the original Pmk. It appears that at the beginning when the rules were in the making, there had not been any readymade sections as we see them now. The offences, heavy or light, came into existence under circumstances necessitating their formulation. To assume that the first sections like Pārājika and Saṃghāvaśeṣa had the privilege of being proclaimed at an earlier date than those of the later sections such as the Śaikṣa dharmas would be a great blunder. We believe that some of the Śaikṣa dharmas, on the contrary, are amongst the oldest rules of the Pmk. The classification here is determined more by the nature of the offence than by the chronological[161] order. When the bulk of the proclaimed regulations had grown in size, it became impossible for anyone to learn it by heart in this disorderly manner. The compilers thought it necessary to classify them into different groups and sections, according to their nature, the gravest ones on the top and the lightest at the end:

I. That for which one should be excommunicated—Pārājika.
II. That for which one should undergo a period of confinement—Saṃghāvaśeṣa.
III. The offence to be determined according to circumstances—Aniyata
IV. That for which one should repent and for which one's articles should be forfeited—Niḥsargika P.
V. That which should be repented for and confessed to the Assembly of the Saṅgha—Pātayantika.
VI. That which is blameworthy—Pratideśanīya.

159. See Appendix I.
160. Jain Sūtras: SBE, vol. XIV, p. 275.
161. In Suttavbh., ch. 9, it is said, that the Śaikṣa dharmas were first collected. They were placed in the last section, because the nature of offence is therein much lighter than elsewhere.

VII. Good manners which should be learnt—Śaikṣa.
VIII. Ways for settling disputes—Adhikaraṇaśamatha.

This division of offences cannot be said to be satisfactory, because the Section VII is not actually concerned with any legal dealing. One is not likely to receive any punishment even if one has violated the rules prescribed therein. Likewise are the Sections III and VIII. The former is a necessary procedure leading to the decision of being charged under any of the three sections viz., Pārājika,[162] Saṃghāvaśeṣa and Pātayantika. That shows the pre-existence of the aforesaid sections. We are puzzled as to how it could be placed in the 3rd position as it has no significance either from the viewpoint of offence or antecedence in proclamation. The latter (Sect. VIII) is, speaking strictly, a formula as to how to settle a dispute according to the circumstances. It may be said to be an appendix to the code of discipline but cannot be admitted as the essential *element of Buddhist Law. Moreover*, this Section, according to the *Sarvāstivāda-nikāya-vinaya-mātṛkā*[163] (ch. 3) is placed after the Section VI and before the Śaikṣa dharmas. This indicates that there is a different arrangement of its positions, but all the same, it is not of great consequence.

The sections of gross offences being arranged, we are confronted with minor groups in each of the lengthy ones like the IV, V and the VII. For the first two, the Pāli text has made ten rules in a group and named them as:

1. Cīvara-section
2. Eḷakaloma-section
3. Patta-section

Totalling 30 rules in Section IV of the Pmk.:

1. Musāvāda-section
2. Bhūtagāma-section
3. Bhikkhunovāda-section
4. Bhojana-section
5. Acelaka-section
6. Surāpāna-section
7. Sappaṇaka-section

162. Cf. Sect. I.I; II.2-3, V.29 in relation to the sitting alone with a woman.
163. Nanjio no. 1132.

8. Sahadhammika-section[164]
9. Ratana-section

Totalling 92 rules in Section V of the Pmk. For Section VII it simply divides it into 8 groups,[165] of 10 rules each, without giving any particular name to each of them.

The compilers of the Mūlasarv. school being more particular about the accuracy of the number of rules, endeavoured to compose index-verses (*uddāna*) and adding them to each of the eight main sections; and separate clue verses at the end of the Sections IV and V. On this point, both the Chinese and Tibetan translations of the Mūlasarv. agree. But we don't find such similarities in other schools. This would invariably mean that these divergences have been developed after the 'original text of the Pmk.' had come to the end of its growth. If this assumption be correct, then we shall be enabled to explain how the order of the rules and their interpretations have been so differently represented in the schools.

Looking at the concordance[166] tables of the texts (ante), one will be surprised to notice that there is very little agreement between the numbers in the Sections V and VII. This shows: (i) That when the schools used to be located at different places[167]—the Sarvāstivādins at Kashmir, the Mahāsaṅghikas at Pāṭaliputra, the Sthaviras at Rājagṛha and so forth, it seemed inevitable for them to follow the order of rules rather loosely, because they had probably lacked the necessary writing material and had solely to depend on a powerful memory. (ii) That as there is no specific number of the Śaikṣa dharmas, the schools were at liberty to add[168] to them according to their wish. This brought about the discrepancy between the texts of various schools. (iii) That schools claiming a very old origin show great discrepancy in regard to the number of rules. For instance, the Mahāsg. school in general, agrees with the Pāli text so far as the order of the rules is concerned. But it suddenly jumps in a striking manner[169] from 51 to 61, 5 to 63, 8 to 80! Nobody would be inclined to believe that it is older than others because of such peculiarities. However, although the Mahāsg. has also the same

164. This Section amounts to 12 rules, from 71 to 82.
165. The last Section contains 5 rules only.
166. See the Appendices.
167. See N. Dutt: Buddhist Sects, B.C. Law Volume, pt. I, p. 282.
168. The Mūlasarv. school is said to be of a later origin, but its number of Śk.-dharmas is much less than the Sarv. It is likely that they have reduced some of the rules. Roc., p. 183., n. 1.
169. See Appendix, IV.v.4.9 and 61.

peculiarity as the above, in the arrangement of the Śaikṣa dharmas, we have to treat it in a different manner. This will be clear from the Table given below, showing the dissimilar arrangements of the numbers:[170]

Sarv. VII	*Mahāsg. VII*
17. Entering well-covered	3
18. Sitting well-covered	14
21. To enter without casting glances	4
22. To sit without casting glances	15
27. Entering with a little sound	5
28. Sitting with a little sound	16
31. To enter without covering the head	7
32. To sit without covering the head	18
35. To enter without being akimbo	10
36. To sit without being akimbo	22
41. To enter without tucking up the robe	8
42. To sit without tucking up the robe	19

From this Table, one will see the traces of an original text being adopted by different schools with arrangements according to their conveniences. We have good reason to believe that the Mahāsg. has preserved older forms of the 'Original Pmk.' better than any other school wihout excepting the Sthaviravāda. It seems that the Mahāsg. school, tries to group the rules separately according to the actions of 'sitting' and 'entering', while the Sarv. takes successive pairs of these two actions. It is psychologically easier to repeat the same thing with a slight change (changing from 'entering' to 'sitting') at the same time than to perform it all afresh. That is to say the Sarv. school has rearranged the order and changed the original (Mahāsg. VII) number:

3, 14 to 17, 18
4, 15 to 21, 22
5, 16 to 27, 28

And if we look at the above three sets of rules of the Mahāsg. vertically, it gives us a serial number of

3, 4, 5 14, 15, 16

Of course, the new arrangement is definitely better for the purpose of memorising, but because of that, one cannot help suspecting that the Mahāsg. text is closer to the original text of the the Pmk.

170. For a detailed comparison of other schools, see Appendix, IV.vii.

Based on such observation and study of the texts as noted above, we may roughly divide the existing texts into four classes in accordance with their comparative extents:

1. The Mahāsg. the Upāli-paripṛcchā and the Pāli.
2. The Kāśy., the Mahiś. and the Dharmag.
3. The Mūlasarv. (including Mahāvyutpatti, the Chinese and Tibetan translations).
4. The Sarv. (including Skt. and the Chinese translations).

1. In this group, the three texts agree more or less in number, viz., each has 92 rules in Sections V whereas all other texts contain 91 or 90 only. And their number in Section VII is 66, 72 and 75 respectively. People may question as to how the older texts show 92 rules while the later ones show only 90? Our answer to this would be that some of the schools did not adopt[171] the Pāli (Sthavira) V.23 and 82[172], probably on the ground that the Pāli V.21.22 and 81 are similar[173] to them in nature, it was therefore, thought advisable to leave[174] them out. And probably a round number like 90 would be easier to remember and better to calculate!

The Pāli and the Upāliparipṛcchā texts share an old common origin. The former has most likely been influenced[175] by the latter, because it is one of the old Sthavira Pmk. texts. The Mahāsg. appears to have preserved more faithfully the older tradition than the other two, particularly as we have been able to discover in it an older way of arranging the Śaikṣa dharmas.

2. The Dharmag. follows very closely the Pāli text in most cases, not merely in numbering the series but also in contents, except the VII Section in which, it adds 26 prohibitory rules regarding the Stūpa. And that is unique among all the available texts. According to Vasumitra, the Dharmaguptaka school issued from the Mahīśāsakas. But so far as our comparisons go, we do not find any remarkable evidence concerning this fact in the texts of the Pmk. though the number of rules in both of them

171. The texts that dropped them are: Dharmag., Sarv., Skt., Mūlasarv., Tib. and Mahāvyutpatti.
172. The contents of the former are concerned with going to the Bhikṣuṇīs' residence on the proper occasion and exhorting them; and of the latter with diverting to the use of any individual, the property dedicated to the Saṅgha.
173. See Sarv., V.21.22 and 9.
174. For a detailed account see Appendix II.
175. See Nei-Hsüeh, vol. III, p. 52.

is the same. Their dissimilarity in arrangement may be seen below:

Mahiś Section IV	*Dharmag. Section IV*
21 to 27	11 to 17
11 to 13	23 to 25

The numbering of the Kāśyapīya is at times in agreement with the Pāli and at other times with the Dharmag. and Mahiś. In the VII Section it has only 96 rules, which is 4 less than the other two schools.

3. The number of the Śaikṣa dharmas of the Mūlasarv. appears differently in the translations. It is 99 in Chinese, 108 in Tibetan and 105 in the Mahāvyutapatti. These evidently are based on three different recensions of the same text. We may note here, that the distinction sought to be made by some scholars on the basis of the title 'Ārya',[176] prefixed to the names of the schools, e.g. Sarvāstivāda[177] etc. does not deserve much attention. The Mūlasarv. school claims to have preserved more of the original (Mūla) traditions of the Sarv. than the Sarv. itself, as its name implies. But its emergence must be attributed to a later period than that of the Sarv. and in fact, it must have branched off from the Ārya-sarvāstivāda[178] school. Our explanation about the minor rules in the VII Section of this school shows that in most cases, it has omitted the rule 'to sit' after 'to enter' for example:

Sarv. VII	*Mūlasarv. VII*
17. Entering well-covered...	12. The same
18. Sitting well-covered...	Nil
19. Entering well-controlled...	11. The same
20. Sitting well-controlled...	Nil
27. To enter with a little sound...	13. The same
28. To sit with a little sound...	Nil
29. To enter without kneeling down...	24. The same
30. To sit without kneeling down...	Nil
31. To enter without covering the head...	15. The same
32. To sit without covering the head...	Nil
35. To enter without the arms being akimbo...	25. The same
36. To sit without the arms being akimbo...	Nil
41. To enter without tucking up the robe on one side...	16. The same

176. HIL, vol. II, p. 231, n. 2; SBBS, p. 271.

177. The name of this school has been mentioned in the inscription of the Mathura Lion-capital (Circa 100 A.D.)—Epigraphia Indica vol. IX, n. 17, p. 139.

178. Roc., p. 183, n. 1.

Sarv. VII	*Mūlasarv. VII*
42. To sit without tucking up the robe on one side...	Nil
43. To enter without tucking up the robe on the left and right side...	17. The same
44. To sit without tucking up the robe on the left and right side...	Nil
47. To enter without swinging the arms...	26. The same
48. To sit without swinging the arms...	Nil

There are other traces[179] that could be easily found from our concordance Table.

4. We place the Sarv. in the last group, not because it is of a later origin, but because it is the most advanced and developed one. We have taken this as the standard text for our comparison. An older recension of this text has been commented upon in the *Sarv. v. vibhāṣā*. It contains 91 Śaikṣa dharmas. It belongs to the Sarv. school and is older than that of the Skt. and its Chinese translation of Kumārajīva. But we are no more in possession[180] of it now.

According to the data presented above, and supported by the traditional history of the origin of the schools, the development of the Pmk. texts may be illustrated in the following Table:

RELATION OF THE PRĀTIMOKṢA TEXT AND THE SCHOOLS

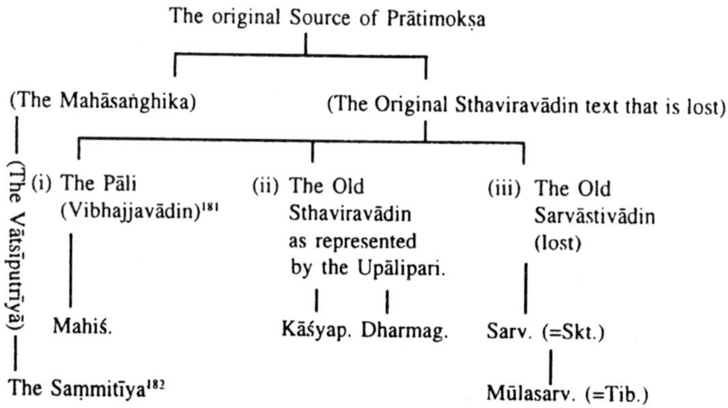

179. Appendix IV.vii.
180. In 372 A.D. T'a-mo-chi'h translated one Pmk. text of the Old Sarv. but it has been lost. Nei-Hsüeh, vol. III, p. 51.
181. Roc., p. 186.
182. Vasumitra, JDL, 1920, p. 7.

For the differences and an account of the schools which seceded from the chief sects, and for their relations with one another, reference may be made to the works which have dealt with them in the minutest details.[183]

V. DIFFERENCES OF INTERPRETATION

An enquiry into the minor differences that occur in the various texts, leads us to believe that they were due to: 1. the ambiguity of the original meaning; 2. the different traditional explanations handed down by the schools; and 3. occasional additions of a local nature, besides the linguistic differences in which the Pmk. texts were written. We are told by Vinitadeva[184] that the Sarvāstivādins, the Mahāsaṅghikas, the Saṃmitīyas and the Sthaviravādins used the following four languages viz., Sanskrit, Prakrit, Apabhraṃśa and Paiśācī respectively in recording their literature. Of course, at this stage of our knowledge, to say anything about translating or copying done by one school from another or mutual influences, would be premature. So much however, is certain that when an original text is translated into four different languages, it is bound to be divergent, howsoever much the translators might have endeavoured to be faithful to the original.

To make the matter clear, we shall illuminate the points by taking examples from our comparison:

1. In Sarv. V.42 and 43, the subject-matter is 'Sabhojane kule' which means, according to the Mahāsg. and the Pāli, a family is taking food. But the Tib. (Mūlasarv.) V.42 has given it quite a different interpretation. It runs thus:

> 'Whosoever Bhikṣu knowing that a man and a woman are sleeping together in a house, goes there and sits on a couch...'[185]

It is quite obvious that the phrase 'Sabhojane kule' has been

183. JDL, 1920, p. 7; Nanjio no. 1286; Roc., pp. 182-6: Beal: The eighteen schools of Buddhism; IA, ix, p. 299; Rhys Davids: The sects of the Buddhists; JRAS, 1891, p. 409 foll.; Minayeff: Recherches sur le Boudhissme; Mahā., 5; Dip., 5, 39 foll.; Kathāvatthuppakaraṇa-aṭṭhakathā, pp. 2-3, 5 and *passim* JPTS, 1899; Mrs. Rhys Davids: Prefatory notes to the Kat., pp. xxix-liv; W. Geiger, Mahā. Appendix B; The Buddhist Sects; Bu-ston, pp. 97-101; Tar., pp. 270-274.

184. HIL, II, p. 226; Csoma de Körös: Tibetan Studies, pp. 74-5, Calcutta, 1912.

185. SBE, vol. XIII, p. 41, n. 3.

misunderstood here, or perhaps, commentary had given such an interpretation.

In the same way (V.42) regarding the place where one sits in such a family, we have the following:

Sarv. V.42. In the sleeping place.
Skt. 42. Āsanam kalpayet.
Pāli 43. Anupakhajja nisajjaṃ kappeyya.
Dharmag. 43. To sit in a place by force where valuable articles are kept in the house.
Kāśyap. 42. To sit in a house by force.
Mahāsg. 54. In a covered place.
Mūlasarv. 42. To arrange his seat by force.
Mahāvy. 42. Sabhojana-kula-nisadya.

The word 'to-sit-by-force' appearing in Dharmag. Kāśyap. Mūlasarv. is closely connected with the Pāli word 'Anupakhajja'.

2. The confusion becomes amazing when the texts face the word 'Ratna' in Sarv. V.82. The gist of that rule is that—'If a Bhikṣu very early in the morning, before the rise of the dawn, when jewels have not yet been collected, is seen going away from the threshold or by the side of the threshold of a King...' as stated by the Sarv. We just see below what differences have been shown by all others texts:

Skt. 82. Aniṣkrānte rājñi anigṛhīteṣu ratneṣu.
Pāli 84. Anikkhantarājake aniggataratanake—when the King has not gone forth, and the Queen(!) has not with drawn (SBE, vol. XIII, p. 52).
Dharmag. 81. If he passes the threshold before the King has not yet come out.
Mahiś. 65. Similar to Dharmag. 81.
Kāśyap. 82. Enters the gate of the palace when the King is not out yet.
Mahāsg. 82. Passing the threshold of the gate when the Queen has not kept aside the jewels.
Mūlasarv. 82 and *Tib.* 82 are more or less the same as those of the Sarv. but add 'jewel like articles'.

This confusion may be divided into 3 classes:

(a) Ratana—goes to mean: Queen, and then the Queen collecting jewels as well.
(b) The word 'entering' the palace by a Bhikṣu, leads to the meaning that the Bhikṣu himself is seen 'going away' from

there.

(c) The interpretation of the word 'Rājñī' or 'Rājake' as obtained in Skt. and Pāli, which, probably, must be carried back to an original reading containing the word 'rajanī'=night, which underlies the Sarv.='before the day breaks'.

On the whole, we think that the Sarv. has preserved the correct tradition here and the Pāli and Skt. texts give a wrong meaning.[186] Moreover, in the Pāli V.83 to 85, all three rules are dealing with 'Jewels'. In fact, that section is called 'Ratana-section'.[187] It would be against the natural order of things, to speak something about a woman (Queen) in the first rule and 'Jewels' in the next two in such a section of Ratana. The Dharmag. Mahiś. and Kāśy. are closely related to the Pāli.

3. As the schools follow their own traditional interpretations, we find at times that a word has two or more meanings. That can be well-illustrated from the example of the word 'Antargṛha' or 'Antaraghara':

Sarv. VI.1. In the house.
Pāli VI.1. Entered within the houses[188] (village).
Dharmag. and *Kāśy.* VI.1. A Bhikṣu enters a village.
Mahiś VI.1. On the street or in the lane.
Mahāsg. VI.2. Lives in the house.
Tib. and *Mūlasarv.* VI.1. On a highway during her visit to a village.

In the present case, it seems the interpretation of 'in the village or on the street', is more predominant than others. And it is later on supported by the *Milindapañho*: 'Antaragharaṃ[189] piṇḍāya paviṭṭha 'amhāti'—we entered the village or street for begging alms.' P.V. Bapat[190] has tried to show that the word: 'Antaraghare' means 'in the village' by quoting Buddhaghosa's and other works from the Pāli canon. But the use of 'in the house' in the Skt. and Pāli Vinaya literature, is in no way less popular. The following instances will bear witness to the statement:

(i) 'Adhivāsayatu me ārya upasenaścantargṛhe bhaktena sārdhaṃ bhikṣusaṅgheneti—May the noble Upasena consent to take a

186. SBE, vol. XIII, p. 52, n. 2.
187. *Ibid.*, p. 55.
188. *Ibid.*, p. 56. n. 1.
189. Milin., p. 11.
190. NIA, vol. I, pt. 1, P.V. Bapat's 'Antaragṛham'.

meal in my house along with the Bhikṣusaṅgha' and 'Citreṇa gṛhapatinā bhikṣusaṅgh'-antargṛhe bhaktenopanimantritaḥ—'The Bhikṣusaṅgha was invited to have their meals in the house by Citra, the householder'.[191]

(ii) 'Na sāmisam udakam antargṛhihe chorayiṣyāmaḥ santaṃ gṛhiṇam anavalokya.' Mahāvyut. VII.71. The commentary to this last passage (Mūlasarv. VII.67) says, that the Chabbaggiya Bhikṣus were taking a meal upstairs in the house of Bodhi, the householder. They threw away their bowl-washing water on the well-decorated floor.

(iii) In *Mahāniddesa,*[192] p. 230, we have 'Antaragharaṃ paviṭṭho itthiṃ vā kumāriṃ vā evamāha—itthaṃ-name itthaṃ-gotte, kiṃ atthi?....Entering the inner part of the house, addresses thus a woman or a maiden, 'so and so, what have you got?....'

Thus, the expression: 'Antaragṛhe' would lose its proper sense, if we interpret it as 'in the village' in the foregoing cases.

The same considerations may be applied to some of the Śaikṣa dharmas. In the Sarv. VII.17 to 61, we have such pairs of rules as e.g. 'to enter the antargṛha' and 'to sit in the antargṛha'. If we adopt the interpretation of antargṛha (lane, street) mentioned above, it is possible to conceive a Bhikṣu entering in between the houses (street or lane) for his alms, but what is the idea of sitting down in the street or lane? There are allusions to many cases of the Blessed One accepting invitations from the householders and taking meals in their houses in the *Sūtra-piṭaka,* especially in the *Mahāparin.-S.* It is unlikely that 'antargṛha' simply means 'in the village' or 'on the street', and not 'in the house'.

We find that some of the translators also committed mistakes by interpreting the original terms very literally, e.g. 'bījagrāmabhūtagrāma' (=vegetation and a group of beings) where the word 'bhūta' has been interpretated as 'ghost' or 'spirit' as e.g. (to destroy) the village of ghost and spirit' etc.[193]....It is obvious that they must have lost sight of the exact meaning.

Besides, there are so many cases which bear the stamp of such great variations which fall within one of the categories of explanations treated above.

---

191. Gilg., vol. III, pt. 3, p. 22.
192. See also B.C. Law, Buddhist rules of decorum: Bhārata-kaumudi, p. 384.
193. Pmk., V.11, (Sarv.) of the texts compared below.

VI. THE ŚAIKṢA DHARMAS

Regarding the antiquity of the Śaikṣa dharmas, we have discussed the problems elsewhere in the course of our studies, and also the striking dissimilarity of arrangement between the Mahāsg. and other schools. The nature of these rules is essentially concerned with the daily conduct and decorum of the Bhikṣus such as—walking, moving to and fro, looking, dressing, contracting and stretching and so forth.[194] They do not come under any penal section, inasmuch as there will not be any sanction or punishment for their breaches or violations. The violation of any of them by a Bhikṣu is not considered to be a criminal act but simply bad manners. Its origin might have been the Four Iriyāpathās viz., walking, standing, sitting and lying (Gamanaṃ, ṭhānaṃ, nissajjaṃ and seyyaṃ[195]) and in the course of time, they developed to such an extent that they passed beyond the mark of 100 rules as shown in almost all the texts, except the Mahāsg. Pāli and Upālipariprcchā. The manner of its growth as we find in the later texts, especially the Sarv., is that, new rules branch out from the principal ones for instance.

From Mahāsg. Pāli and Upāli.-p. Śk. 1. 'To wear the inner-garment all round', the Sarv. has made another 11 rules.

Not to wear the inner-garment high, low, in disorder, like an axe, like a tāla-tree, like an elephant-trunk, like two ears, like a pig-head, like a farina-ball, in fine foldings and of fine yarn[196] (1-11), excluding the original one, that is, the 12th in the Sarv The other additions and omissions in all the different schools may be accounted for as of a local nature. The addition of the 'Stūpa' section in the Dharmag. School is most remarkable.

We give below either a translation or the original text of the Śk. rules, that are not found in the concordance Table IV.vii, and are of a special interest for each or some of the texts concerned:

Skt. VII.39-40. Na paryastikākṛta...To be applied to both 'to enter' and 'to sit' (cf. Mahāvyut. 20).

Skt. VII.43-44. Na vinyastikākṛta...To be applied to both 'to enter' and 'to sit' (cf. *ibid.* 19).

Skt. VII.57-58. Na viḍaṃgikayā...To be applied to both 'to enter' and 'to sit' (cf. *ibid.* and *Tib.* 39).

194. Cf. M.I., p. 57 (Satipaṭṭhāna-sutta).
195. S. v. p. 78.
196. See Appendix IV.vii.

Skt. VII.79. Na pātrāvalehakaṃ...To be applied to both 'to enter' and 'to sit' (cf. *ibid.* 62).

Skt. VII.99. Na paryastikākṛtaśya...To be applied to both 'to enter' and 'to sit' (cf. *ibid.* 86).

Skt. VII.100. Nātyastikākṛtaśya...To be applied to both 'to enter' and 'to sit' (cf. *ibid.* (?)).

Skt. VII.101. Na vinyastikākṛtaśya...To be applied to both 'to enter' and 'to sit' (cf. *ibid.* 85).

A few of the above terms are in no way clear to us. Even the fragments of the Sarv. edited and studied by Jean Filliozat and Hōryū Kuno do not carry us very far.[197]

Pāli VII.11. To go amidst the houses without loud laughter.

Pāli VII.12. To sit amidst the houses without loud laughter.

Pāli VII.26. To sit amidst the houses without walking on the heels and toes.

Pāli VII.28. To pay attention to the bowls while receiving an alms.

Pāli VII.29. To take alms with equal curry (samasūpakaṃ).

Pāli VII.31. To eat alms placed in the bowl with an alert mind.

Pāli VII.35. To eat alms without placing down the top.

Pāli VII.42. Not to put the whole hand into the mouth while eating.

Pāli VII.44. Not to toss the food into the mouth while eating.

Pāli VII.50. Not to smack (capu-capu) the lips while eating.

Pāli VII.54-55. To eat without licking the bowl and lips.

Pāli VII.68. Not to preach to a person who sits on a seat, whilst the Bhikṣu is on the ground.

Dharmag. VII.5-6. To enter and to sit in the layman's house without wrapping his neck with the robe.

Dharmag. VII.9-10. Not to enter and to sit in the layman's house by jumping.

Dharmag. VII.24-25. Same as Pāli VII.11-12.

Dharmag. VII.28. To receive soup to the level of the bowl.

Dharmag. VII.35. Should be watchful at the bowl while eating (cf. Pāli VII.28).

Dharmag. VII.39. Same as Pāli VII.44.

Dharmag. VII.43. Not to cause the food to enter the mouth as if by inhailing.

197. JA, vol. ccxxx, pp. 25-7, 1938.

Dharmag. VII.46. Not to scatter food with hand.

Dharmag. VII.53. Not to preach to a person who wraps his neck with cloth.

Dharmag. VII.60. Not to sleep or remain in the stūpa[198] except on watch.

Dharmag. VII.61. Not to hide treasures and other articles, in the stūpa, except for preservation.

Dharmag. VII.62. To enter the stūpa without wearing shoes.

Dharmag. VII.63. To enter the stūpa without taking shoes in hand.

Dharmag. VII.64. To go around the stūpa without wearing shoes.

Dharmag. VII.65. To enter the stūpa without wearing sandals (Pu-la).

Dharmag. VII.66. To enter the stūpa without holding sandals in hand.

Dharmag. VII.67. Not to take meals at the foot of a stūpa, and leave the remnant of food and grass on the ground and go away. Thus the ground may be spoiled.

Dharmag. VII.68. Not to carry a corpse passing by a stūpa.

Dharmag. VII.69. Not to bury a corpse under a stūpa.[199]

Dharmag. VII.70. Not to cremate a corpse at the foot of a stūpa.

Dharmag. VII.71. Not to cremate a corpse towards the direction of a stūpa.

Dharmag. VII.72. Not to cremate a dead body around a stūpa, so that the bad smell may not be whiffed into it.

Dharmag. VII.73. Not to carry the dead body's robe passing by a stūpa, except for the pupose of washing, dyeing or spraying a scent.

Dharmag. VII.74. Not to ease oneself at the foot of a stūpa.

Dharmag. VII.75. Not to ease oneself towards the direction of a stūpa.

Dharmag. VII.76. Not to ease oneself around the stūpa so that the bad smell may not spread all over the place.

Dharmag. VII.77. Not to carry the Buddha's image to the privy.

Dharmag. VII.78. Not to chew a tooth-stick (a willow-twig) at the foot of a stūpa.

Dharmag. VII.79. Not to chew a tooth-stick towards the direction of a stūpa.

---

198. From 60 to 85 of this text, we don't find any such rules in any other text. 'Stūpa' here means the Stūpa of the Buddha.

199. Dhv., ch. 21, VII.69 means it to be in the stūpa.

Dharmag. VII.80. Not to chew a tooth-stick around a stūpa.

Dharmag. VII.81. Not to spit and discharge mucus at the foot of a stūpa.

Dharmag. VII.82. Not to spit and discharge mucus towards the direction of a stūpa.

Dharmag. VII.83. Not to spit and discharge mucus around a stūpa.

Dharmag. VII.84. Not to sit stretching one's feet towards a stūpa.

Dharmag. VII.85. Not to place a (small) stūpa downstairs whilst one is living upstairs.

Dharmag. VII.88. Not to preach to a person who is on the seat whilst he is not.

Dharmag. VII.93. While walking on the road, hands should not be interlaced.

Dharmag. VII.95. Not to carry a bowl fitted to a network on the shoulder with a stick.

Mahīś. VII.6. No to wear the inner-garment like a mango tree.

Mahīś. VII.27-28. Not to enter and to sit in the layman's house without the knowledge of the people.

Mahīś. VII.31-32. To enter and to sit in the layman's house without (hands) being placed on the cheeks.

Mahīś. VII.35-36. To enter and to sit in the layman's house without looking high up.

Mahīś. VII.45-46. Same as Dharmag. VII.24-25.

Mahīś. VII.49-50. To enter and to sit in the layman's house maintaining a good order.

Mahīś. VII.61. Same as Dharmag. VII.43.

Mahīś. VII.67. Not to smell the food by shrinking the nose (shu-pi).

Mahīś. VII.71. Not to get food by stretching the arm.

Mahīś. VII.76. Same as Dharmag. VII.39.

Mahīś. VII.78. Not to be in a dissatisfied and fault-finding mood while eating.

Kāśy. VII.10. Not to look at the robe left and right, except for the sake of proper-dressing.

Kāśy. VII.11. Go straight to the layman's house.

Kāśy. VII.18. Not to put on the robe covering the entire shoulder.

Kāśy. VII.20. Same as Dharmag. VII.24.

Kāśy. VII.23. To enter without putting the hands on the sides.

Kāśy. VII.24. Same as Dharmag. VII.9.

Kāśy. VII.30. To enter without inclining the body.

Kāśy. VII.31. To enter without placing the hands on each others' shoulders.

Kāśy. VII.32. To enter after being invited.

Kāśy. VII.33. Not to lie down (in the house).

Kāśy. VII.34. See the beds (seats) and sit.

Kāśy. VII.35. Not to sit with full force.

Kāśy. VII.36. To sit without embracing the bowels(?)

Kāśy. VII.37. To sit without the legs hanging.

Kāśy. VII.38. To sit wihtout letting the legs being widely placed.

Kāśy. VII.42. Not to stretch forth the hand to ask for food, when it has not been brought yet.

Kāśy. VII.44. Not to cover the rice with soup.

Kāśy. VII.47. To receive soup by holding the bowl uprightly.

Kāśy. VII.49. Not to puff the rice with the mouth.

Kāśy. VII.50. Not to spit on the food.

Kāśy. VII.55. Not to mould the food into the shape of a leaf while eating.

Kāśy. VII.57. Not to lick the bowl while eating.

Kāśy. VII.58. Not to eat with the hand supporting the (mouth).

Kāśy. VII.59. Not to eat with the hand supporting the bowl.

Kāśy. VII.60. Not to make a sound while çrunching the cakes.

Kāśy. VII.61. Not to make the food in the shape of a stūpa.

Kāśy. VII.67. Not to spoil one's neighbour's robe while eating.

Kāśy. VII.70. Not to place the bowl on the ground.

Kāśy. VII.71. Not to stand while washing the bowl.

Kāśy. VII.72. Not to keep the bowl in such a place that is likely to cause it to fall or being considered as dangerous.

Kāśy. VII.73. Not to wash the bowl in a dangerous place

Kāśy. VII.75. Not to preach to a person who is lying down while he himself is standing.

Kāśy. VII.79. Not to preach to a person who is walking in front whilst he himself is at the back.

Kāśy. VII.82. Not to preach to a person who sits in a palanquin.

Kāśy. VII.88. Not to preach to a person who wears a cap.

Kāśy. VII.89. Not to preach to a person who is with a garland.

Mahāsg. VII.6-17. Same as Pāli VII.11-12.

Mahāsg. VII.9. Same as Pāli VII.25.

Mahāsg. VII.20. To sit in the house without embracing the knees.

Mahāsg. VII.23. To sit in the house without moving the hands and the legs.

Mahāsg. VII.36. Not to lick the fingers while eating.

Mahāsg. VII.38. Same as Dharmag. VII.43.

Mahāsg. VII.55. Not to preach to a person who is placing his legs one upon the other.

Upālip. VII.5-6. To enter and sit in the house scoldingly.[200]

Upālip. VII.23-24. To monkey with the hands and feet while entering and sitting in the house.

Upālip. VII.26. To look towards the left and right while receiving food.

Upālip. VII.29. To snatch away food and heap it up.

Upālip. VII.32. Taking much soup.

Upālip. VII.37. Same as Pāli VII.42.

Upālip. VII.39. Same as Mahiś. VII.61.

Upālip. VII.40. Same as Pāli VII.54.

Upālip. VII.42. Same as Mahiś. VII.67.

Upālip. VII.44. To vomit while eating.

Upālip. VII.46. To let the bowl loose while eating.

Upālip. VII.48. To mix rice with ghee and eat.

Upālip. VII.57. Preaching to a person who is seated on a couch whilst he himself is on the floor (cf. Pāli VII.68).

Mūlasarv. VII.14. Same as Mahīś. VII.36.

Mūlasarv. VII.19. Cf. Kāśy. VII.31.

Mūlasarv. VII.21. Not to walk on the toes (cf. Pāli VII.26).

Mūlasarv. VII.22. Same as Kāśy. VII.24.

Mūlasarv. VII.24. Not to protrude the body while entering the house.

Mūlasarv. VII.28. Not to make a row by standing shoulder to shoulder.

Mūlasarv. VII.30. Not to sit in the layman's house when one is not requested to do so.

Mūlasarv. VII.31. One should not sit in the house without good observation.

Mūlasarv. VII.32. Same as Kāśy. VII.35.

Mūlasarv. VII.34. Not to place the inner ankles one upon the other.

Mūlasarv. VII.35. Not to place the outer ankles one upon the other.

Mūlasarv. VII.36. Not to draw back the feet rapidly.

Mūlasarv. VII.37. Not to stretch forth the feet too much.

Mūlasarv. VII.38. Not to show the body.

Mūlasarv. VII.42. Not to extend the bowl forwards before the arrival of food (cf. Kāśy. VII.42 and Mahīś. VII.71).

---

200. The word 'not', should be added to each of the sentences, though in the text it is not clearly stated.

Mūlasarv. VII.43. Not to place the bowl on the food.

Mūlasarv. VII.45. Not to make too small handfuls of rice.

Mūlasarv. VII.53. To warm the food with puffings.

Mūlasarv. VII.55. Same as Kāśy. VII.49.

Mūlasarv. VII.56. Same as Mahīś. VII.78.

Mūlasarv. VII.60. Same as Kāśy. VII.61.

Mūlasarv. VII.62. Same as Kāśy. VII.57.

Mūlasarv. VII.64. Not to shake the bowl.

Mūlasarv. VII.69. Not to keep the remainder of food inside the bowl.

Mūlasarv. VII.70. Not to place the bowl on the ground without any support.

Mūlasarv. VII.71-72. Same as Kāśy. VII.71-72.

Mūlasarv. VII.73. Not to draw water against the current.

Mūlasarv. VII.83. Not to preach to the person who rests his hands on the shoulders.

Mūlasarv. VII.84. ...not to the elephant-riders.

Mūlasarv. VII.86. ...Same as Kāśy. VII.82.

Mūlasarv. VII.87. ...not to the chariot-riders.

Mūlasarv. VII.90. Same as Kāśy. VII.88.

Mūlasarv. VII.91. ...not to crown-wearers.

Mūlasarv. VII.92. ...not to the person who wears a top-knot like that of the Buddha.

Mūlasarv. VII.94. ...not to the person who is decorated with flowers on the head.

Tib. VII.15. Going amidst the houses looking only as high as a yoke.

Tib. VII.17. Going amidst the houses wihout making any grimaces.

Tib. VII.18. Going amidst the houses wihout pressing my head to my shoulders.

Tib. VII.19. Going amidst the houses without folding together the hands upon my neck.

Tib. VII.20. Going amidst the houses without folding together the hands upon my arms.

Tib. VII.21. Same as Mūlasarv. VII.22.

Tib. VII.22. Going amidst the houses without stretching my limbs.

Tib. VII.24. Going amidst the houses not to lean on my breast.

Tib. VII.29. Going amidst the houses without putting together my arms.

Tib. VII.31. While amidst the houses, not to sit down on a couch without being bidden.

Tib. VII.32. Same as Mūlasarv. VII.31.
Tib. VII.33. Same as Mūlasarv. VII.32.
Tib. VII.35. To sit without placing the thighs one upon the other.
Tib. VII.36. To sit without placing the ankles one upon the other.
Tib. VII.37-38. Same as Mūlasarv. VII.36-37.
Tib. VII.39. To sit not to make the private parts visible.
Tib. VII.41. Not to cover the meal (cf. Kāśy. VII.44).
Tib. VII.44. Same as Mūlasarv. VII.42.
Tib. VII.45. Not to cover the sauce with rice.
Tib. VII.47. Same as Mūlasarv. VII.43 but adds: hard and soft.
Tib. VII.48. To eat the meal in a proper manner.
Tib. VII.49. Same as Mūlasarv. VII.45.
Tib. VII.56. Not to make a hu-hu noise (cf. Mūlasarv. VII.53).
Tib. VII.57. Not to make a phu-phu noise (cf. Mūlasarv. VII.54).
Tib. VII.59-60. Not to prefer one kind of corn, and one kind of taste to another.
Tib. VII.62. Not to lick the palate.
Tib. VII.65 and 67. Same as Mūlasarv. VII.62 and 64 respectively.
Tib. VII.68. Same as Mūlasarv. VII.60.
Tib. VII.71. Same as Kāśy. VII.67. (But here more detailed.)
Tib. VII.73. Not to pour out the remains of a meal from the bowl.
Tib. VII.74. Same as Mūlasarv. VII.70.
Tib. VII.75. Same as Mūlasarv. VII.72. (But here it is more detailed such as on a precipice, in an abyss or on a steep declivity.)
Tib. VII.76. Same as Mūlasarv. VII.71.
Tib. VII.77. Same as Kāśy. VII.73.
Tib. VII.78. Same as Mūlasarv. VII.73.
Tib. VII.86. Not to preach to a person who is embracing another.
Tib. VII.87. Same as Mūlasarv. VII.83, but we find 'neck' here instead of 'shoulder'.
Tib. VII.88. Not to preach to a person who folds his arms.
Tib. VII.89. Not to preach to a person who wears braided hair.
Tib. VII.90. Same as Mūlasarv. VII.90.
Tib. VII.94. Same as Mūlasarv. VII.84.
Tib. VII.96. Same as Mūlasarv. VII.86.
Tib. VII.97. Same as Mūlasarv. VII.87.
Tib. VII.103. Not to preach to a person who holds a battle-axe.
Tib. VII.104. Not to preach to a person who puts on a coat of mail.

Mahāvyut. VII.15. Yugamātradarśinaḥ (cf. Tib. VII.15).
Mahāvyut. VII.19. Nodvyastikayā (cf. Tib. VII.19).
Mahāvyut. VII.20. Paryastikayā. (cf. Mūlasav. VII.19).

Mahāvyut. VII.21. Noṭṭaṅkikayā (cf. Mūlasva. VII.21).

Mahāvyut. VII.22. Nojjaṅkikayā[201]—without pulling the robe while going.

Mahāvyut. VII.23. Nollaṅghikayā (cf. Mūlasarv. VII.23).

Mahāvyut. VII.31. Nānanujñāta (cf. Mūlasarv. VII.30).

Mahāvyut. VII.32. Nāpratyavekṣāsaṇaṃ (cf. Mūlasarv. VII.31).

Mahāvyut. VII.33. Na sarvakāyaṃ samavadhāya (cf. Mūlasarv. VII.32).

Mahāvyut. VII.35. No sakthani sakthy ādhāya (same as Tib. VII.35).

Mahāvyut. VII.36. Na gulphe gulpham ādhāya (same as Tib. VII.36).

Mahāvyut. VII.37. Na saṃkṣipya pādau (same as Tib. VII.37).

Mahāvyut. VII.38. Na vikṣipya pādau (same as Tib. VII.38).

Mahāvyut. VII.39. Na vidaṅgikayā (same as Tib. VII.39).

Mahāvyut. VII.45. Nānāgate khādanīye bhojanīye pātraṃ upanāmayiṣyāmaḥ (same as Tib. VII.44).

Mahāvyut. VII.47. Satkṛtya piṇḍapātaṃ paribhokṣyāmaḥ (cf. Tib. VII.48).

Mahāvyut. VII.48. Nātikṣuṇakair ālopaiḥ (cf. Tib. VII.49).

Mahāvyut. VII.53. Na cuccukārakaṃ.

Mahāvyut. VII.55. Na thutthukārakaṃ (cf. Tib. VII.56).

Mahāvyut. VII.56. Na phutphukārakaṃ (cf. Tib. VII.57).

Mahāvyut. VII.59. Navarṇakārakaṃ (same as Mūlasarv. VII.56).

Mahāvyut. VII.60. Na gallāpahārakaṃ—not changing the cheeks (Körös-Mahāvyut. I, p. 229).

Mahāvyut. VII.61. Na kavaḍacchedakaṃ—not cutting in several mouthfuls.

Mahāvyut. VII.62. Na jihvāsphoṭakaṃ (same as Tib. VII.62).

Mahāvyut. VII.64. Na pātrāvalehakaṃ (same as Tib. VII.65).

Mahāvyut. VII.66. Na pātrāsamdhunakaṃ (same as Tib. VII.67).

Mahāvyut. VII.67. Na stūpākṛtim avamṛdya piṇḍapātaṃ paribhokṣyāmaḥ (same as Tib. VII.68).

Mahāvyut. VII.69. Na sāmiṣeṇodakenāntarikaṃ bhikṣuṃ sprakṣyāmaḥ (same as Tib. VII.71).

Mahāvyut. VII.72. Na pātreṇa vighasaṃ chorayiṣyāmaḥ (same as Tib. VII.73).

Mahāvyut. VII.73. Nānāstīrṇapṛthivīpradeśe pātraṃ sthāpayiṣyāmaḥ (same as Tib. VII.74).

---

201. Cosma de Körös' STEV: Mahāvyut., I, p. 227, 'Nor as if I would measure (with my hand).'

Mahāvyut. VII.74. Notthitāḥ pātraṃ nirmādayiṣyamaḥ (same as Tib. VII.76).

Mahāvyut. VII.75. Na taṭe na prapāte na prāgbhāre pātraṃ (same as Tib. VII.75).

Mahāvyut. VII.76. Na nadyāhāryahāriṇyāṃ pratisrotapātreṇodakaṃ grahīṣyāmaḥ (same as Tib. VII.78).

Mahāvyut VII.85. Na viyastikākṛtayāglānāya dharmaṃ deśayiṣyāmaḥ (same as Tib. VII.87).

Mahāvyut. VII.86. Na paryastikākṛtayāglānāya dharmaṃ deśaiṣyāmaḥ (same as Tib. VII.88).

Mahāvyut. VII.87. Noṣṇisaśirase dharmaṃ deśayiṣyāmaḥ (same as Tib. VII.89).

Mahāvyut. VII.88. Na kholaśirase...(same as Tib. VII.90).

Mahāvyut. VII.89. Na mautīśirase...(same as Tib. VII.91).

Mahāvyut. VII.91. Na hastyāruḍhāya...(same as Tib. VII.94).

Mahāvyut. VII.93. Na śibikāruḍhāya...(same as Tib. VII.96).

Mahāvyut. VII.94. Na yānāruḍhāya...(same as Tib. VII.97).

Mahāvyut. VII.101. Na saṃnaddhāya...(same as Tib. VII.104).

Below is a Table showing the number of the Śaikṣa rules found in various texts, which are either in agreement or disagreement with the Sarv. School:[202]

	In agreement	*In disagreement*	*Total*
Skt.	103	10	113
Pāli	61	14	75
Dharmag.	59	41	100
Mahīś.	84	16	100
Kāśy.	60	36	96
Mahāsg.	57	9	66
Upālip.	57	15	62
Mūlasarv.	62	36	98
Tib.	52	56	108
Mahāvyut.	63	42	105

Thus, we have a complete view of the Śaikṣa dharmas of all the schools that are not included in the concordance Table in our Appendix IV.vii. This gives us a very distinct idea of the relatively closer relation, between the schools. This is due to their common origin which however is not of a great antiquity as noted earlier. It may be noted in passing

202. Because our comparison has taken the Sarv. Text to be the base throughout.

that, considering the dates of the translations of the Mūlasarv. into Tibetan[203] and Chinese, one will naturally not attach much importance to the claim of that school, although its title (Mūlasarvāstivādin) signifies a high antiquity.

VII. PRĀTIMOKṢA, EXTERNAL INFLUENCES, AND FUNCTION

The tradition of observing the Darśapūrṇamāsa[204] Sacrifice and the sacred day Upavasatha connected with it, on the full and new moon days, by the Brāhmaṇas and Śramaṇas of ancient India is undoubtedly of great antiquity. At such celebrations, the people would generally gather[205] together and the ascetics used to preach and expound their tenets to them. It served two purposes, social intercourse on the one hand and religious propagation on the other. It is quite possible that the Buddhists derived their inspiration for their fortnightly recitation[206] of the Prātimokṣa rules from such practices, though the function in the latter case is entirely different. The Buddhist Uposatha devotes itself exclusively to the sphere of examining the Bhikṣus' conduct and judgment would be delivered thereby by the Saṅgha, if it was found that anybody had committed any of the grave offences prescribed in the *Prātimokṣa-sūtra.* Such half monthly recital was at first meant for the purification of the Bhikṣus. Whether they were pure or not, each and everyone should be present at the function[207] and give his answer either by keeping silent, which is a sign of 'pure' conduct, or informing the Saṅgha outright as to what he had done. But it underwent a change, even during the lifetime of the Founder of Buddhism viz. that an impure Bhikṣu was not allowed to attend[208] such meetings and therefore the person in question had to be dragged out from the assembly. Besides the usual congregation at prescribed intervals, it also could be held at a juncture, when the reunion[209] of the Saṅgha after a schism took place. That is to say it served the purpose of social rehabilitation of the Order as well.

Before entering into details of the external influences on the Pmk. text, we would very much like to see what the original Pmk., as a text,

---

203. At the end of the 9th century A.D. JASB, 1915, p. 30: By I-Tsing, 710 A.D.
204. Śatapatha-Brāhmaṇa, II.1.4, I.1; SBE, vol. XIII, p. x.
205. HIL, vol. II, p. 23 and n. 3.
206. King Bimbisāra recommended such practice to the Buddha on the models of the Paribbājakas; Mv., II.1.3.
207. Mv., II.3.2.
208. Cv., ix.2.1-2; T., I, p. 478.
209. Mv., II.36.4, n. 3.

looked like. From the data found in the *Dīgha-Nikāya* and at the end of each of the Pmk. texts compared, it appears that the content of the Pmk. was a very simple[210] one, for instance:

"Khantī paramaṃ tapo titikkhā
Nibbānam paramaṃ vadanti Buddhā. . . . . .
Sabba-pāpassa akāranaṃ, kusalassa upasampadā
Sacitta-pariyodapanaṃ, etaṃ Buddhāna sāsanam."

These verses are said to be the 'Prātimokṣa' uttered by Vipassi, one of the seven past Buddhas. The other six 'Prātimokṣa' belonging to different Buddhas are of the same type. Moreover, the recital of the Pmk. by his disciples is alleged to be once in six years. Such statements simply show that before the custom of the half-monthly recital had been finally established, the Saṅgha had to be contented with such moral instruction as: 'To avoid all evil and perform all good', though the past seven Buddhas may be imaginary. Traces of the original simple form of Pmk. may be said to be still visible in the introductory and concluding verses, like the above, found in various versions, e.g. Skt. Sarv. added to the main body of rules.[211]

The practices of ancient Indian sages and Śramaṇas before the emergence of Buddhism had a direct influence[212] on the formulation of the Buddhist moral conduct for the Bhikṣus. Gautama Buddha, of course, was a reformer in some respects but as the conventional conception of morality had been so well established before his time, that he had simply to accept their fundamental principles, and cast new rules in order to suit the requirements of his disciples, under unusual circumstances. Amongst the important cardinal rules in Buddhism in general, and in Prātimokṣa in particular, the observance of Brahmacaryā or celebacy, and the Five Precepts of good conduct were adopted from the Brāhmaṇical Code beyond any shadow of doubt. They have been accepted not merely by the Buddhists, but by the Jains as well. To serve as an illustration, we give below the 5 rules that are observed by each of the religious groups:

(A) Brāhmaṇical[213]

1. Abstain from injuring the living beings.

---

210. Mahāpadāna-sutta, 3, 28; D., vol. ii, p. 49; T., I, p. 10.
211. Cf. Dutt's EBM, p. 87.
212. Oldb. Life, p. 332.
213. Baudhāyana II.10.18; see Bühler's translation; SBE, vol. xiv, p. 275; Jacobi's Introduction to the Jaina Sūtras; SBE, vol. xxii, pp. xxii-iv.

2. Truthfulness.
3. Abstain from appropriating the property of others.
4. Continence.
5. Liberality.

(B) Buddhist

1. Not to destroy life.[214]
2. Not to steal.
3. Abstain from comitting adultery.[215]
4. Not to tell lies.[216]
5. Abstain from intoxication of liquor.[217]

(C) Jain

1. Not to destroy life (Ahiṃsā).
2. Not to speak a lie (Sunṛta).
3. Not to take what is not given (Asteya).
4. Abstain from sexual intercourse (Brahmacaryā).
5. Renounce all interest in worldly things (Aparigraha).

Besides, we find a large number of rules of the Pmk. bearing a striking resemblence to that of the Sacred Laws mentioned in the works of Āpastamba and Gautama as well as in the Jaina Sūtras. Both the Buddhists and the Jains might have directly borrowed some rules from the ancient Brāhmaṇical Law Codes to suit their own purpose. In fact, there was hardly any hard and fast rule regarding the morality and decorum between the various religious groups. To behave properly and walk in the path of good manner, is a common duty of all ascetics, except in a few rare cases such as e.g. a sect of the Jains preferring to do away with clothes on account of their peculiar conception of emancipation and other practices. Whatever rules of good conduct, a student, a snātaka, an ascetic or a hermit were expected to observe (cf. Āpastamba and Gautama), a Buddhist had also to follow them in general. We see the following classification of 1. eating, 2. drinking, 3. attitude towards women, 4. respects to the Guru or teacher, and 5. other precepts of decorum in both the Āpastamba and Gautama, imprinted on the structure (especially in the Śaikṣa dharmas) of the Pmk. The comparison below will testify to the truth of our observation:

214. Laws of Manu: SBE, vol. xxv, p. 476; The Sacred Laws of the Āryas: SBE, vol. ii, p. 188.
215. The Institutes of Vishnu: SBE, vol. vii, p. 136 (a crime in the 4th degree).
216. The Sacred Laws of the Āryas: SBE, vol. ii, p. 290, sq.
217. *Ibid.*, pp. 63, 74, 188.

1. ***Rules Regarding Eating***
   (a) *Āpa.*, p. 11. To beg food with a vessel.[218] The Buddhists[219] also beg food in the same manner.
   (b) *Āpa.*, p. 13. Begging is not for one's own sake (cf. Sarv. VII.84).
   (c) *Āpa.*, p. 59. Not to bite off with his teeth (cf. Sarv. VII.72).
   (d) *Āpa.*, p. 62. Not to eat food stored for one night or turned sour (cf. Sarv. V.38).
   (e) *Āpa.*, p. 149. To make a lump of food just swallowable (cf. Sarv. VII.69).
   (f) *Āpa.*, p. 150. Not to make a noise while eating (cf. Sarv. VII.73).
   (g) *Āpa.*, p. 149. Not to scatter away anything (food) (cf. Sarv. VII.80).
   (h) *Āpa.*, p. 150. Not to shake the right hand (cf. Sarv. VII.81).

2. ***Rules Regarding Drinking***

Āpa., p. 63.; *Gau.*[220], p. 287. All intoxicating drinks are forbidden (cf. Sarv. V.79).

3. ***On Attitude Towards Women***
   (a) *Āpa.*, p. 8. To preserve chastity (cf. Sarv. I.1).
   (b) *Āpa.*, p. 26.; *Gau.*, p. 188. Not to touch a woman (cf. Sarv. II.2).
   (c) *Āpa.*, p. 11. To talk with a woman as much (only) as his purpose requires (cf. Sarv. VII.5).

4. ***On Paying Respects to the Guru***
   (a) *Āpa.*, p. 24. If the master stands, he shall not sit (cf. Sarv. VII.93).
   (b) *Āpa.*, p. 24. If the master[221] sits, he shall not lie down (cf. Sarv. VII.94).
   (c) *Āpa.*, p. 53. Not to salute with his head wrapped up or with shoes on (cf. Sarv. VII.95.104).

5. ***Other Rules of Decorum***
   (a) *Āpa.*, p. 25; *Gau.*, p. 194. Not to cut the leaves of flowers, of herbs or trees; to avoid the destruction of seeds (cf. Sarv. V.11).
   (b) *Gau.* p. 223. Not to ease oneself at beautiful spots[222] (cf. Sarv. VII.110).

---

218. Āpastamba: SBE, vol. II, p. 11.
219. E.g. Gil. vol. III, pt. 3, p. 17.
220. Gautama: SBE, vol. II.
221. The Pmk. has put 'Bhikṣu' to replace the 'master'.
222. Cf. Jaina Sūtras: SBE, vol. xxii, pp. 181-182.

The other undesirable elements[223] that should be eradicated are: Anger, exaltation, grumbling, covetousness, perplexity, doing injury, hypocrisy, lying, gluttony, calumny, envy, lust, secret haterd, neglect to keep the senses in subjection...(Āpa., p. 187) and also to avoid perfumes, garlands, ointments, playing musical instruments, singing etc... (Gau., p. 187). These have their counterparts in the Buddhist literature and in the *Vinaya-piṭaka*. It would betray one's sound reasoning, if one denies the fact that pre-Buddhistic[224] traditions of moral conduct had no hand in the formation of the Buddhist Religious Law. Further more, a good deal of similar decorum regarding sitting, walking, lying down, looking, eating, being courteous, speaking, dressing, begging and so forth, can also be compared with Śāṅkhyāyana's *Gṛhya Sūtra*[225] and the *Ācārāṅga Sūtra* of the Jains. It goes without saying that Jainism being a contemporary of Buddhism, the existence of the Brāhmaṇical Laws had to be presupposed in their case also. However, it should be borne in mind that the Buddhists took only such rules that would suit them best, and added a considerable number of rules for their particular requirements. They have their own ways of punishment and atonement attached to every principal rule and classified according to the nature of the offences under a particular heading such as Pārājika etc.... This is not so in the Brāhmaṇical Laws. This may be said without exaggeration that the orderly arrangement of the cases of commissions, omissions and exemptions the Pmk. has advanced a step further than their predecessors. With the untiring efforts of the commentators and compilers of the Vinaya works on the Buddhist Law, it reached in its own time the zenith of perfection in the history of Law-making in ancient India. Moreover, the punishment in the Pmk. are of a more practical nature, than the Brāhmaṇical ones, at least in some cases. For instance, the penalty for breaking the Vow of Chastity is excommunication in the Pmk., whereas the same, prescribed by Gautama[226] is that the guilty person has to offer an ass to Nirṛiti on a cross-road and put on the skin of an ass, with hair turned outside! He should also hold a red earthen vessel in his hands and beg from seven houses, proclaiming his deeds. This merely amounts to branding him as an undesirable in the society.

---

223. Gṛhya Sūtra, IV.12.26: SBE, xxix, p. 126.
224. The Āpastambīya school is dated back in the 600 or 700 B.C. See G. Bühler's Introduction to *Āpa.*: SBE, vol. ii, p. xix.
225. SBE, vol. xxix, iv, p. 107 ff; SBE, vol. xxii, I and 1 (see also B.C. Law's Buddhist rules of decorum, Bhārata-Kaumudī, Lucknow, pp. 393-402).
226. Gautama: SBE, vol. ii, p. 289.

Among other factors which furthered the cause of framing the Pmk. rules, the opinion of the public was the most influential one. We find innumerable cases in the Vinaya that the establishment of a new rule, was usually a result of yielding to the criticism of the people regarding the behaviour of the Bhikṣus. This included some less critical rules, like those about wearing the robes and taking meals[227] etc. From these facts one may judge, that the growth of the Pmk. has been nourished by two vital streams: one is the Brāhmaṇical tradition, and the other is the public censure or opinion.

The important point, in which the Buddhist Church differs from other religious groups in ancient India, is that, it is a well-organised democratic body. All the Bhikṣus are equals, though morally, the younger and the junior have to show respect to their elders. But that should not be understood in the sense of Brāhmaṇical relationship between a tutor and the taught. The founder of Buddhism, at the moment of his attaining the Mahā-parinirvāṇa, instructed his disciples to take refuge in the Dharma and Vinaya[228] as their teacher, after his demise. The Pmk. thereby played a very important role of a constitution for the whole of the Buddhist Church, so far as the daily administration and the conduct of the Bhikṣus are concerned. It is also an obvious fact, that the persons who joined the Buddhist Church were both elites and persons of undesirable characters. Some came with the supreme ideal of Nirvāṇa and others purely for a comfortable living as we find it constantly mentioned in the Vinaya how notoriously the Chabbaggiya Bhikṣus behaved themselves. There might have never existed the so-called 'group of six Bhikṣus' in reality, but we believe, there must have been persons in the Saṅgha who did represent such characters and a major portion of the Pmk. rules was originally framed on their account. Considering the maintenance of unity of the Saṅgha, with such a multi-coloured multitude, it is out of sheer necessity that there emerged into existence the rules and regulations embodied in the Pmk., though shadowed by a traditional background. A classification of the rules that govern the action of the Bhikṣus is shown below:[229]

1.	Relating to the opposite sex	18
2.	Relating to food, drink, medicine etc.	23

227. See Sarv. the section on dressing and taking food; EBJ, pp. 55-57.
228. MPS, ch. VI.1; SBE, vol. xi, p. 112.
229. The division into which the rules are classified may be the same, but the degree of their offence is different, i.e. some are light and others grave.

3.	Relating to robes and various personal belongings	40
4.	Relating to housing, association, living and bathing etc.	10
5.	Relating to wrong views, schisms and misbehaviour	23
6.	Relating to Saṅgha-karma, recitation of the Vinaya etc.	17
7.	Relating to trade, accepting money etc.	8
8.	Relating to killing, stealing and associating with the army or thieves	11
9.	The Śaikṣa dharmas or rules of decorum	113
	Total[230]	263

From the above list, one will certainly frame a fair and clear idea as to the extent to which the Pmk. serves as an authority and functions as a governing instrument. To carry out its authority, it has been armed with definite powers to impose punishment and penalty that have been laid down in every rule, except in the sections of III—Ani.; VIII—Adhik. dharmas. The Buddhists do not inflict upon anybody any corporal punishment nor impose any fine, their punishments are comparatively very light, viz.:

(i) Excommunication for the violation of Pj.
(ii) Mānatta[231] and parvāsa for the violation of Saṃ.
(iii) Forfeiture and formal confession for the violation of Np.
(iv) Formal confession for the violation of Pā.
(v) Formal confession for the violation of Pd.

Besides, there are other later additions of offences and penalties in the Vinaya-piṭaka, namely: Thullaccaya,[232] Dukaṭa, Tajjanīya-kamma,[233] Nissaya-kamma,[234] Pabbājanīya-kamma,[235] Patisāranīsa-kamma,[236] Ukkhepanīya-kamma,[237] and Pakassanīya-kamma.[238] They may be called supplementary regulations of the Pmk. They serve their purposes under particular circumstances. Regarding the detailed procedure as to how these various karmas and punishments are to be carried out, one may

230. This is based on the text of the Sarv. See Appendix I.
231. For details, see EBJ, p. 107.
232. Its punishment is like that of the Brahmadaṇḍa, being described in the MPS, VI.4.
233. Cv., I.5.
234. *Ibid.*, I.6.
235. *Ibid.*, I.13.6-7.
236. *Ibid.*, I.22.
237. Its punishment is like the Tajjanīya-kamma.
238. Cv., VII.3.

refer to the *Cullavagga* and *Mahāvagga* of the *Vinaya.*

Thus, the function of the Pmk. is clear enough that it legally governs the actions of the Bhikṣus (and the Bhikṣuṇīs) maintains peace and unity in the Saṅgha and has the right to impose penalties on the culprits. Religiously, it retains the ancient traditional custom of observing the new and full moon day celebrations.

VIII. CONCLUSION

We have had a lengthy discussion on the important aspects of the *Prātimokṣa* including its position and relation with the Hindu Law Books, its antiquity, its growth and development as shown in the various Buddhist schools, its references to the Buddhist Councils, its function and other significance. It may be observed that adequate evidence and testimonies have been presented here, in order to reveal the 'truth' underlying their plausible reliability and historicity. As a book of 'Law', the Pmk. has its unique value both from the historical and literary points of view. It is true, that the text itself is primarily concerned with the Buddhist Saṅgha, and is not so voluminous or of a wider scope, as those of the *Gṛhya Sūtra, Ācārāṅga Sūtra* and other Brāhmaṇical legal codes. But the unique position it has achieved in providing a truly historical background to each of the rules. But the unique position it has achieved in providing a truly historical background to each of the rules with a hair-splitting analysis, so that it determines the offences, exemptions and punishment accordingly. On the basis of the *Prātimokṣa,* the rich literature of Vinaya of various Buddhist schools was developed. Indeed, this excellent work as a Code of Conduct for the Bhikṣus occupies a prominent position among the Law Books in ancient India. Further, it furnishes us with invaluable data for framing a magnificent picture of the economic and social conditions during the period in which it arose. The essential portions of the texts must have established when the Buddha was still alive[239] that is to say about 450 B.C. and not later.[240] The most ancient among the texts compared, seems to be the text of the Mahāsaṅghika School, which is worthy to be specially mentioned and recommended as such.

239. To give up the minor and lesser rules as stated in the MPS, VI.3, is a good evidence.

240. Cf. IB, p. 43.

II

COMPARISON OF THE PRĀTIMOKṢA TEXTS OF VARIOUS VERSIONS BELONGING TO VARIOUS SCHOOLS

Prātimokṣa Sarvāstivāda

NIDĀNA

May the venerable Saṅgha hear me!

The first month of winter, except one night has already passed. Now there remains one night and three months only, O venerable sirs, the messenger of old age and death is approaching nearer and the doctrine of the Buddha is about to terminate. You should, for the sake of attaining enlightenment, be diligent and exertive with a concentrated mind. Why? Because by doing so, the Buddhas attained even their highest enlightenment, not to speak of other Dharmas which lead to the path of virtue! The persons who have not yet received the higher ordination are out and now the Saṅgha is in harmony, what should we do first?—One replies: observe Uposatha and recite the rules—O venerable sirs, let us enquire into the lustful thoughts and purity of the Bhikṣus who are absent:

1. With folded palms, we pay pure
   Homage to the Śākya Siṃha
   I wish now to recite the Vinaya Rules,
   The Saṅgha should listen to them attentively.
2. Even if it be the smallest offence,
   There should be great fear in the heart.
   One should confess it whole-heartedly when one is guilty,
   And should never do it again.
3. If one lets loose the horse-like mind
   Galloping on the evil path,
   It is rather difficult to control.
   To be earnest in the practice of Śīla,
   Spoken by the Blessed One,
   Is just like one's paying much attention
   To the tightening up of the bridle.

4. The good will be able to believe and
   Practise the instructions uttered
   By the Blessed Tathāgata.
   That is, both the man and the horse
   Have been well-trained and
   They are able to defeat the army
   Of evil dispositions (*Kleśa*).
5. If one does neither accept His command
   Nor become fond of Śīla,
   That means that neither the man nor the
   Horse is properly trained,
   And they will be annihilated by the
   Army of evil dispositions.
6. If one takes care of the Śīla,
   Just as a yak[1] is fond of its tail;
   And also let the mind be well-concentrated.
7. Be always earnest in day and in night,
   For the sake of seeking the True wisdom.
   Such a man will, in the doctrine of the Buddha,
   Be able to attain a pure life.

May the venerable Saṅgha listen to me!

Today, the 15th of the (lunar month) is the day for Uposatha[2] and recitation of the Prātimokṣa. If it is the time for the Saṅgha and if it be convenient to them, they may celebrate the Uposatha and recite the Prātimokṣa with a concentrated mind and speak thus:

> O venerable sirs, we shall now together celebrate the Uposatha and recite the Prātimokṣa. The Saṅgha should listen to it very attentively.
>
> Whosoever has committed any fault, let him confess it. If there is no fault, let him remain silent. It is by that silence that we know the venerable sirs to be pure.
>
> As a Bhikṣu gives an answer if a question is put to him separately, so each Bhikṣu is to give an answer when a question is repeated three times in such an assembly of Bhikṣus. Whosoever Bhikṣu in such an assembly, thus questioned for the third time, does not confess a fault of which he has recollection, is guilty of

1. Vis. Vim., p. 15; Visd., I.198.
2. See Mv. II.

uttering a deliberate lie. The offence of uttering a deliberate lie has, O venerable sirs, been declared by the Blessed One to be an obstacle on the way. When a Bhikṣu remembers the fault committed by him and wishes to be free from it, he should confess it. By making a confession, he will reside at ease. But if he hides it, his offence will be graver.

Venerable sirs, the Introduction (*Nidāna*) of the Prātimokṣa is now recited.

Thus do I question you, venerable sirs, "Are you pure in this matter?"

A second and third time may I question you, "Are you pure in this matter?"

The venerable ones are pure in this matter, therefore they keep silence. This should be so:

Skt. The verse portion of the Nidāna here is bridged up with broken lines. We do not find the 7 complete verses as in the Chinese Sarv. but it seems to have contained the same number of verses.[3]

Pāli. The verses and the prose portion preceding the verses in the Sarv. are not found here.

The whole Pāli Nidāna corresponds to the last prose portion of the Sarv.

Dharm. This text begins with 12 verses in praise of the virtue and the goodness of the Śīla. It states that those who practise the Rules will gain priceless merit, otherwise they will suffer from fearful consequences.

These verses are however quite different from those in the Sarv. The prose portion of the Nidāna is substantially the same as that of the Sarv., but we find in it the addition of a remarkable sentence: "Who sends the Bikṣuṇī here to receive instructions?" This is not found in the Sarv.

Mahīś. The verse and prose portions are the same as those of the Sarv. At the beginning of the prose section, however, there appears: "...the first month of Spring..."

Kāśy. We have altogether 18 verses here, the first two seem to be composed by the ancient editors themselves. In them it is stated that it is a rare merit to be able to hear the *Prātimokṣa Sūtra* and the Saṅgha will be happy, if they observe the Śīla.

In the remaining 16 verses, it gives the total number of persons

3. JA, 1913, p. 477, note 1.

who had attended the assemblies of each of the past Seven Buddhas in connection with their pronouncing the Prātimokṣa. It also mentions the name of Śākyamuni and says that he preached the teachings of Śīla to innumerable assemblies and peoples.

The prose portions are the same as that of Sarv.

Mahāsg. The following six conditions to be remembered given at the beginning of the text, are not found in the Sarv.:

1. To remember the date correctly of the new moons and full moons etc.
2. In the morning to perform the ceremony of alms-giving.
3. To remember daily the number of years since one's higher ordination.
4. To remember which robes one should wear and which donors had given them.
5. To remember not to eat separately.
6. One should know whether he is ill or not.

Other portions are the same as the Sarv.

Upālip. As this text has assumed the form of a Sūtra, although it is virtually a sort of commentary of the Prātimokṣa, its contents are supposed to be the utterances of the Buddha; we find therefore that there is hardly anything in common with other texts except the outlines of the names of offences.

The main purpose of this book is to mention the specific offences under certain rules and to impose punishments according to circumstances under which anybody may have committed an offence.

Mūla-Sv. The 6 verses at the commencement of the text praising the value of the Śīla and illustrating the term 'happiness' are not in the Sarv. At the beginning of the prose section we have '...some parts of the Spring have passed and some still remain.....'. At the end of the prose section, we have: ...who sends the Bhikṣuṇīs to seek for instructions?.... (cf. Dharm. above).

Further, there are 5 verses somewhat resembling the 7 verses in the Sarv., but are not quite the same.

Other portions are the same as the Sarv.

Tib. We find 22 verses in all in this text. From verses 12 to 17, it agrees with the first 6 verses in the Mūla-Sv. and from 18 to 22, it agrees with the remaining 5 verses.

In other texts there is no trace of the Tib. verses 1 to 11. The time is described as: '....some seasons of the year are over and some are to come....'

Later on we have: '...today is the 14th[4] or 15th day of the lunar month....'

The other portions are like those of the Sarv.

I. THE FOUR PĀRĀJIKA DHARMAS[5]

Sv. I.1

O venerable sirs, here are four Pārājika Rules as known from the Prātimokṣa recited each half-month.

Whosoever Bhikṣu has entered into the Bhikṣus' system of self-training and rule of life, and has not thereafter withdrawn from the training, or declared his weakness, shall perform the act of sexual intercourse with any one, down even to an animal, this Bhikṣu has fallen into a Pārājika, he should not be in communion with others.

Skt. 1. ...Maithunaṃ dharmaṃ pratiṣevitāntatas tiryagyonigatayāpi sārdham...

The same,[6] but the Ms. is incomplete.

Pāli 1. ...Methunaṃ dhamaṃ paṭisevcyya antamaso tiracchāna-gatāyāpi...

Dh. 1, *Mhs.* 1 and *Ksy.* 1. The same.

Msg. 1. The following is an addition:

> This rule was laid down with reference to Sthavira Yaśakalanda-putra by the Blessed One, while he was staying at Vaiśāli. It was laid down in the afternoon of the 12th day of the 5th fortnight of the 5th year in the Winter, after the Buddha's enlightenment. At that time, the shadow, cast down, on the ground, of a man sitting in the Eastern direction, was equal to the height of one-man-and-a-half.

One should follow it, when it has been established. That is called 'to follow and obey the Dharma'. Rest is the same.

---

4. Why is Uposatha held on the 14th of a lunar month? Satis Chandra Vidyabhusana was of the opinion: 'If there is a junction of three lunar days (*tithi*) on one solar day, the middle one is not recognized. Hence when the 15th lunar day is unrecognized, the Prātimokṣa is to be recited on the 14th.' See JASB, vol. XI, nos. 3 and 4 (N.S.), p. 39, note 1.
5. Henceforth the following principal abbreviations are followed in the text:
   Sv. Sarvāstivāda; Msv. Mūlasarvāstivāda; Dh. Dharmaguptaka;
   Msg. Mahāsaṅghika; Mhs. Mahīśāsaka; Ksy. Kāśyapīya;
   Mpt. Mahāvyutpatti.
6. This abbreviated expression adopted in the following means that the content of the text are substantially the same as those of the Sarv.

Msv. 1. Last line translated as: ...'not to live together with others'.
Tib. 1. The same.
Mpt. 1. Abrahma-caryaṃ.

Sv. I.2

Whatsoever Bhikṣu shall taken from a village or from a forest, anything not given—which is counted as a theft for which a King or a King's (officers) would seize the thief, and slay, or bind or banish or impose a fine, saying, 'Oh thou art a fool, (lit. a child) thou art stupid and thou art a thief'—the Bhikṣu who in that manner takes the thing not given, has fallen into a Pārājika, he should not be in communion with others.

Skt. 2. '....etaṃ gṛhītvā hanyād vā badhnīyād vā pravrājayed vā...' Ms. incomplete.

Pāli 2. 'gāmā vā araññā vā adinnaṇ theyyasaṃkhātaṃ ādiyeyya...'
Omits: 'to impose a fine' and 'King's Officers'.

Dh. 2. The phrases: 'King or King's (Officers)'; 'to banish'; and 'to impose a fine' are omitted here.

Mhs. 2. For differences see *Dh.* 2 above. The content is the same but the language slightly abridged.

Ksy. 2. The following phrases in their respective context:

'...King or minister...banish him out of the country or torture him with all kinds of sufferings...you take things not given...' are not the same as in Sv.

Msg.. 2. Omits: 'to impose a fine'. The following is added:

This rule was laid down with references made to Elder Dhanika, son of a potter (Kumbhakāraputra), King Bimbisāra and Pāṃśukulika Bhikṣu by the Blessed One, while he was staying at Rājagṛha. It was laid down in the afternoon of the 10th day of the second fortnight of the 6th year in the Winter, after the Buddha's enlightenment. At that time, the shadow, cast down, on the ground, of a man sitting in the Eastern direction, was equal to the height of two men and a half.

One should follow it, when it has been made.
This means 'to follow and obey the Law'. The rest is the same.

Msv. 2. The phrases in their respective context: '...a King or a minister...or scolds by saying "O man! you are a thief, you are stupid, you are a fool to have committed such a theft"...' do not agree with Sv.

Tib. 2. The phrases: ...a King or a minister would seize him and kill, imprison or banish him saying "Thou art a thief, thou art stupid, thou art dishonest," do not agree with Sv.

Mpt. 2. Adattādānaṃ.

Sv. I.3

Whatsoever Bhikṣu shall knowingly deprive of life a human being or a man-like being, with his own hand, or with a knife, or shall seek out an assassin for him, or shall instigate him to self-destruction, or utter the praises of death saying thus: 'O man, what is the use of this sinful life? It is better for you to die than to live.' In following his inclination of taking delight in death, instigating him to kill himself and to speak in praise of self-destruction to him, so that the man dies as a consequence thereof, this Bhikṣu has fallen into a Pārājika.

Skt. 3. ...Manuṣyaṃ svahastena saṃcintya jīvitād vyaparopaye... Ms. incomplete.

Pāli 3. Sañcicca manussaviggahaṃ jīvitā voropeyya...

Omits: 'With his own hand or with a knife.'

The last portion differs slightly.

Dh. 3. The phrases: '...destroy the life of a human being...take a knife and give it to another person to kill...' do not agree.

Omits: 'As a consequence thereof.'

Mhs. 3. The following differences in phrases may be noted:

> 'to kill the life of a human being or a man-like being or to urge himself to do it...to have harboured such thoughts and to kill accordingly...'

Ksy. 3. Differences in phrases, as follows:

> '...to kill...with a sword or to seek a person who holds a sword...this bad and sinful life...by following his desire and the thoughts that occurred to his mind and with various arguments to instigate...'

Msg.. 3. Different phraseology: '...to destroy the life of a human being with a knife, or by handing it over to an assassin...if he dies on no other account but this...'

Omits: 'With various arguments.' The following is added:

> This rule was laid down with reference to many convalescent Bhikṣus in connection with Mṛgavana, the heretic, by the Blessed One, while he was staying at Vaiśāli. It was laid down in the morning of the 9th day of the 3rd fortnight of the 6th year in the Winter, after the Buddha's enlightenment. At that time, the shadow,

cast down, on the ground, of a man sitting in the Northern direction, was equal to the height of one man and a half.

One should follow it, when it has been made. This means 'to follow and obey the Law'.

Msv. 3. Different phraseology: 'to destroy the life of a human being or a human embryo by his own hand, or with a sword, or give a sword to others to do it or by seeking an assassin...this sinful, burdensome, impure and evil life...; to follow his own thoughts and to praise with words of self-destruction to others...'

Tib. 3. 'A human being only.'

Omits: 'With his own hand or with a knife.'

'...or procures a weapon for his death,' do not agree.

Adds: 'impure and wretched (life)'. '...the Bhikṣu who thus causes the death of a human being incurs a Defeat...' This seems to be a repetition of 'as a consequence thereof,' in the Sv.

Mpt. 3. Vadhaḥ.

Sv. I.4

Whatsoever Bhikṣu, without possessing any knowledge and without seeing the extraordinaty qualities, shall regard himself as if he had known and had seen or had accomplished the insight of the noble ones saying 'Thus do I know', 'Thus do I perceive', and at some subsequent time whether on being questioned or without being questioned, this Bhikṣu, shall be desirous of being cleansed from his fault, and shall say, 'When I knew not I said that I knew; when I saw not, I said that I saw—telling a fruitless falsehood'; then, unless he so spoke through undue confidence, he too, has fallen into a Pārājika. He should not be in communion with others.[7]

Venerable sirs, the four Pārājikas have been recited. When a Bhikṣu has fallen into one or the other of these, he should not be in coresidence and communion with the Bhikṣus as before. So after, he has committed an offence of Pārājika, he should not be in communion with others.

Now, I ask the venerable ones 'Are you pure in this matter?'

A second and a third time I ask, 'Are you pure in this matter?'

The venerable ones are pure herein, therefore, do they keep silence. This should be so:

Skt. 4. Ms. incomplete.

---

7. Sv-Vibhāṣā, ch. 2: The language here is a bit different. It tells us that the Bhikṣu does the boasting because he was desirous of obtaining offerings and presents.

Pāli 4. Uttarimanussadhammaṃ...

Omits: 'as if he had seen and had known'.

Dh. 4. '...I have entered into the conditions of the noble, the wise and the victorious.....'—do not agree.

Omits: as in Pāli 4 above.

Mhs. 4. Omits: 'Without possessing anything...as if he had seen and known.'

Ksy. 4. 'Without having the wisdom of the noble ones to see the supreme conditions' differs slightly from the Sv.

Omits the quotation as shown in Mhs. 4 above.

Msg. 4. 'Whatsoever Bhikṣu having neither seen nor known (any higher qualities) shall declare himself that he has attained the extraordinary noble dharma and his knowledge or insight is excellent and supreme...' do not agree. The following is added:

> This rule was laid down with reference to the Bhikṣu in a village and the Bhikṣu of undue confidence, by the Blessed One, while he was staying at Vaiśāli. It was laid down in the afternoon of the 13th day of the 14th fortnight of the 6th year in the Winter, after the Buddha's enlightenment. At the time, the shadow, cast down, on the ground, of a man sitting in the Eastern direction, was equal to the height of three men and a half.

One should follow it, when it has been made. This means 'to follow and obey the Law'.

Msv. 4. 'Whatsoever Bhikṣu indeed without possessing any knowledge or omniscience, and also knowing that he has not attained the estraordinary qualities, the supreme enlightenment, the insight and the living at-ease of the solitary saints shall declare himself....'O Brethren, when I knew not...' do not agree.

This text has been greatly enlarged.

Tib. 4. '...Without possessing a clear and perfect knowledge speaks of himself, "I possess superhuman knowledge, I am an elect, I am a specialist, I know this, I see this, without such practice something is not known and something is not seen".' Also "O Brethren, when I knew not..."

Mpt. 4. Uttaramanuṣyadharmapralāpaḥ.

II. THE THIRTEEN SAṂGHĀVAŚEṢA DHARMAS

Sv. II.1

Venerable sirs, here are the 13 Saṃghāvaśeṣa (Pāli. sanghādisesa) Dharmas as known from the Prātimokṣa recited each half month.

Whatsoever Bhikṣu shall purposely have an emission of semen, except in a dream, that is a Saṃghāvaśeṣa.

Skt. 1. ...Sañcintya śukravisarga...
Pāli 1. ...Sañcetanika sukkavissajjī...
Dh. 1. Different phraseology '...purposely handle the genitals and cause an emission of semen...'
Mhs. 1. Different phraseology '...purposely have an emission of impurities...!'
Ksy. 1. 'Purposely have an emission of semen by remembering (a certain object)' do not agree.
Msg. 1. The same.
Msv. 1. The same:[8] language is different.
Tib. 1. The same.[9]
Mpt. 1. Śukravisṛṣṭiḥ.

Sv. II.2

Whatsoever Bhikṣu being perverted by passion, shall come into bodily contact with a woman, by taking hold of her hand, or arm or hair or by touching any part of her body, either up or down, for its smoothness and softness—that is a Saṃ.

Skt. 2. ...Mātṛgrāmena sārdhaṃ kāyasaṃsargaṃ samāpadyeta ....substantially...the same.
Pāli 2. ...Mātugāmena saddhiṃ kāyasaṃsargaṃ samāpajjeyya...
Dh. 1. '...with lustful desires to touch the body of a woman...'
Mhs. Omits: 'Either up or down.' Other portions are the same.
Ksy. 2. '...With impure mind to touch and experience such touch...'. Omits: 'Smoothness...etc.', so also in Msg. Saṃ 2., and in Msv. Saṃ 2.
Msg. 2. '...to take delight in such touch...' not agree see Ksy. 2 above.
Msv. 2. '...with a stained and lustful mind...to enjoy while touching...'. See Ksy. 2 above.
Tib. 2. '...with a perverted mind...takes hold of her hand or shoulder or braid of hair, or touches any other parts of her body for enjoyment...' do not agree but cf. Skt.
Mpt. 2. Kāyasaṃsargaḥ.

---

8. A summary (*uddāna*) of the following 13 Rules is given in both the texts: Emission of semen, contact, discourse, bodily service, intermediation, house, monastery, groundless, a mere trifle, causing dissension, taking sides, corrupting family, and harsh speech.
9. *Ibid.*

Sv. II.3

Whatsoever Bhikṣu being perverted by passion, shall address a woman with obscene, evil and vicious words as those of a young man to a maid—that is a Saṃ.

Skt. 3. ...Mātṛgrāmaṃ duṣṭhulayā vācā ābhāṣeta...

Pāli 3. ...Mātugāmaṃ dutthullāhi vācāhi obhāseyya...

The English translation 'Exciting to passion...' in SBE, vol. XIII, p. 7, for 'Methunūpasaṃhitāhi' is not quite correct.

Dh. 3. 'Whatsoever Bhikṣu, being lustful shall speak obscene, and wicked words to a woman, and utter those obscene and wicked words in whatever way he likes—that is a Saṃ' do not agree.

Mhs. 3. '...to speak by following the path of lust.'

Ksy. 3. '...like a man and a woman speak to each other.'

Msg. 3. '...to speak wicked words in front of a woman by following the path of lust as those of a young man to a maid.'

Msv. 3. '...with a stained and lustful mind to speak lewd, unlawful and obscene words with a woman as a husband to a wife.'

Tib. 3. '...holds a vicious discourse with a woman regarding sexual intercourse....'

Mpt. 3. Maithunābhāṣaṇaṃ.

Sv. II.4

Whatsoever Bhikṣu, being perverted by passion, shall magnify, in the presence of a woman (the merit of) service with the body to himself, saying 'O sister, to offer coition to the Bhikṣus like us who have been observing the Śīla, abstinence from coition and cultivating good deeds, is the supreme service or offering'—that is a Saṃ.

Skt. 4. ...Mātṛgrāmasyāntike ātmana kāyaparicaryām saṃvarṇayet... Ms. incomplete.[10]

Pāli 4. Mātugāmassa santike attakāmaparicaryāya vaṇṇaṃ bhāseyya ...mādisam sīlavantaṃ.....

'Mādisam'—one like me, differs from the Sv. as 'to the Bhikṣus like us'.

Dh. 4. Idea is the same; language is different.

Mhs. 4. '...the Bhikṣus like us who have been observing...cultivating

10. We find 'in a woman's presence to praise himself (or his body)' in Dh. Saṃ. 4; Mhs. Saṃ. 4; Ksy. Saṃ. 4 and Msv. Saṃ. 4, which is slightly different from the Skt. text.

good deeds' in the Sv. is not to be found here.

Ksy. 4. "...You should offer me coition, this is the best kind of offering."

Msg. 4. The same: 'Samaṇa' for 'Bhikṣu'.

Msv. 4. 'to one like me'...

Adds: 'If a Bhikṣu speaks thus.'

Tib. 4. ...(he) extolling the woman's service with the body' at the end of the Rule, is slightly different.

Mpt. 4. Paricaryāsaṃvarṇanaṃ.

Sv. II.5

Whatsoever Bhikṣu shall act as a go-between, conveying the words of a man to a woman or those of a woman to a man, either for becoming a wife or for the purpose of adultery, even for a moment of coition—that is a Saṃ.

Skt. 5. The same; Ms. incomplete.

Pāli 5. Saṃcarittam samāpajjeyya...

'Antamaso tam-khaṇikāya pi' has been translated as 'or even for a harlot,' in SBE, vol. XIII. Can it be a wrong interpretation based on the word 'Gaṇikā'?

Dh. 5. '...even for a moment' and 'of coition' is omitted here.

Mhs. 5. '...shall act as a go-between, or for the purpose of adultery by conveying the words of...even for a moment of coition.'

Ksy. 5. The same.

Omits: 'of coition' and the text has 'for a moment' only.

Msg. 5. '...shall act as a messenger to make matches or unions between men and women...even for a moment.'

Msv. 5. The same as Ksy. Saṃ. 5.

Tib. 5. '...conveying the words of...acts as an intermediary for a wife, a paramour or even for a harlot...'[11]

Mpt. 5. Saṃcaritraṃ.

Sv. II.6

If a Bhikṣu, being independent of a layman and begging materials together, is desirous of building a hut for himself, he must observe the proper measurements. And herein this is the proper measurement—the house must be of twelve Sugata's spans in length and seven of those spans in breadth inside. He must also bring other Bhikṣus and show them

11. Tha. na. thaṅ. literally means: 'Even for a moment'.

the site which is without danger and free from obstacle—and those Bhikṣus must show him a site free from danger and without obstacle. If the Bhikṣu being independent of a layman and begging materials together builds a hut for himself on a dangerous and obstructive site, and also does not bring the Bhikṣus and show them the site or exceeds the meaure—that is a Saṃ.

Skt. 6. ...Asvāmikaṃ ātmoddeśikaṃ pramāṇikaṃ kuṭiṃ kārayīta... Ms. incomplete.

Pāli 6. ...Kuṭim assāmikaṃ...kāreyya...

The sentences: '...the Bhikkhus must be brought to the place to approve the site...and with an open space around it...' show a slight difference.

Dh. 6, *Msg.* 6. The same.

Mhs. 6. Omits: 'inside...seven spans in breadth'.

'...and the Bhikṣus should show the site free from danger and accompanied with a walking space; if he does not bring the Bhikṣus for finding the site or exceeds the measure...'

Ksy. 6. '...he should bring other Bhikṣus to see the site, and those Bhikṣus should observe that the site is free from danger...'

Msv. 6. 'this Bhikṣu should bring other Bhikṣus to see the site; and those Bhikṣus should observe that the site is in accordance with the Dharma, pure, free from dispute and possesses a space for walking...'

Tib. 6. 'for the inspection of the site, he must bring a community of monks who should see that the site is suitable, is not exposed to danger and is easy of access...'

The composition here is more or less resembling that of Msv. Saṃ. 6.

Mpt. 6. Kuṭikā.

Sv. II.7

If a Bhikṣu, being dependent on a layman, desirous of building a big house for himself, he must bring other Bhikṣus and show them the site which is without danger and free from obstacle; and those Bhikṣus must show him a site free from danger and without obstacle. If the Bhikṣu being dependent on a layman builds a big house for himself, and also would not bring the Bhikṣus and show them the site—that is a Saṃ.

Skt. 7. ...Vihāraṃ kārayamāṇaḥ sasvāmikaṃ ātmoddeśikaṃ...Ms. incomplete.

Pāli 7. Sassāmikaṃ mahallakaṃ vihāraṃ...kāreyya. For other slight differences see Pāli Saṃ. 6, above.

Dh. 7, *Msg.* 7. The same.

Mhs. 'If a Bhikṣu, being dependent on someone is building a house for himself, he should bring other Bhikṣus to find out the site. Those Bhikṣus should show him the site which is free from danger and possesses a walking space. If he does not bring other Bhikṣus to find out the site that is a Saṃ.'—do not agree.

Ksy. 7. '...if the Bhikṣu having first of all prepared the ground for constructing a big house...'—do not agree.

Msv. 7. For the differences see Msv. Saṃ. 6, above.

Tib. 7. 'If a monk seeks to build for monks a large monastery in which there shall be a resident layman...'[12]

For other differences see Tib. Saṃ. 6, above.

Mpt. 7. Mahallakaḥ.

Sv. II.8

Whatsoever Bhikṣu,[13] being in anger and malice, disliking a pure and faultless Bhikṣu, shall defame him, with the intention of destroying his pure conduct (Śīla), on a groundless charge of having committed a Pārājika offence—and then sometime later, either when he is pressed or not pressed, the case turns out to be groundless, that Bhikṣu is on that account (to be considered as being) in a fit of anger. If he speaks to other Bhikṣus: 'I spoke so, because I was in anger'—that is a Saṃ.

Skt. 8. ...Apārājikīyaṃ bhikṣuṃ pārājikena dharmeṇānudhvaṃsayed....

This rule is closer to the Chinese *Sv. Vibhāṣā* than to the Sv. text.

Pāli 8. Amūlakena Pārājikena dhammena anuddhaṃseyya...

Omits: 'Disliking a pure and faultless Bhikṣu.'

The last portion differs greatly from the Sv.

Dh. 8. 'Disliking a pure and faultless Bhikṣu'; is not to be found here, also in Mhs. Saṃ. 8.

---

12. This interpretation is rather difficult to comprehend, for, we understand, firstly there was no such practice that a layman should live together with the Bhikṣus in a monastery and secondly Ch. 4 says: 'Yu chu' or 'being dependent on a layman' means 'there is a donor who builds the house'.

13. The Svv., ch. 4, Saṃ. 8, has the following:
"Whatsoever Bhikṣu, being in malice and anger, shall charge a Bhikṣu, through the desire to spoil his Brahmacaryā, a groundless offence of Pārājika of which, the latter is blameless, and if after sometime whether this Bhikṣu is questioned or not questioned, the charge turns out to be groundless, he is taken to have said so, because he was in anger and malice, that is a Saṃ."

Adds: 'If a Bhikṣu speaks so' at the end of the rule.

Mhs. 8. 'If a Bhikṣu, being in malice and anger and behaving himself unbecomingly, shall...' See Dh. 8 above.

The language of the last portion here differs from Sv.

Ksy. 8. ...'to charge a pure and blameless Bhikṣu with a...being asked or scolded or not asked...'

Msg. 8. ...'being in anger, malice and displeased...'

Omits: 'Speaks to the Bhikṣus.'

Msv. 8. '...being persistent in anger charges a pure Bhikṣu with.' The last portion is not quite the same as that of Sv.

Tib. 8. The same in content, but differs in language.

Mpt. 8. Amūlakaṃ.

Sv. II.9

Whatsoever Bhikṣu, being in anger, malice or displeased shall defame another Bhikṣu with the desire of spoiling his pure conduct by a groundless charge of having committed a Pārājika offence of which the latter is blameless, and shall moreover, pick up some point or other that really rests on something of a different kind, if after sometime, either when he is pressed[14] or not pressed, the case turns out to be that he has picked up some point or other that really rests on something of a different kind,—this Bhikṣu is to be regarded as being in a state of anger. It he speaks to other Bhikṣus: "I spoke so, because I was in anger," —that is a Saṃ.

Skt. 9. ...Kañcid eva leśamātraṃ dharmaṃ upādāya apārājikīyaṃ bhikṣuṃ pārājikena dharmeṇānudhvaṃsayed...

Pāli 9. ...Kañci desaṃ lesamattaṃ upādāya pārājikena dhammena anuddhaṃseyya...

The sentence: 'Appeva nāma naṃ imasmā brahmacariyā cāveyyaṃ' is in the indirect speech in the Sv.

Language differs in the latter portion.

Dh. 9. '...being covered by anger and hatred...'

Omits: 'This Bhikṣu therefore was in a state of anger,' and 'if he speaks to other Bhikṣus'.

Mhs. '...being in malice and anger and behaving himself unbecomingly...'

'...whether he is asked or not asked, if he says: "I have, in this case, taken some point or other that rests on something of a different kind.

14. The Svv., ch. 4 says: "He is asked or not asked."

And because I was in a state of anger, so I made the blunder"—do not agree.

Ksy. 9. '...to harass a pure and blameless Bhikṣu with a groundless charge of having committed a Pārājika offence by taking points of a different kind but having a similar nature...and the Bhikṣu said: "I was angry, therefore, I told a lie"...'—do not agree.

Msg. 9. '...taking some minor point of a different kind but not a Pārājika...'

Language differs in the later portion.

Msv. 9. '...being persistent in anger charges a pure Bhikṣu...'

Tib. 9. In the Sv. we find: 'I may thus remove him anyhow from the course of purity,' is, both here and in Tib. Saṃ. 8, above, in the indirect speech.

The latter part here is inflated and the language also differs.

Mpt. 9. Laiśikāṃ.

Sv. II.10

Whatsoever Bhikṣu endeavours to cause a division in the Saṅgha which is in harmony or persists in emphasising the points calculated to cause a division, that Bhikṣu should be admonished by the Bhikṣus: "O venerable sir, do not endeavour to cause a division in the Saṅgha which is in harmony, and also do not persist in emphasising the points calculated to cause a division. Sir, you should have communion with the Saṅgha, because, the Saṅgha being in harmony, there will be happiness and absence of disputation. They will live happily and peacefully, with one-mind and under one doctrine, just as the combination of water and milk. Sir, you abandon your expedients to cause a division in the Saṅgha." If the Bhikṣu being thus admonished by other Bhikṣus, still persists in doing so and does not give it up, he should be admonished a second and a third time. If he abandons his expedients, it is well; but if he does not—that is a Saṃ.[15]

Skt. 10. ...Samagrasya saṃghasya bhedāya parākramet...

Pāli 10. ...Saṅghassa bhedāya parikkameyya...

'Be, sir, at one with the community, for the community being at unity, in harmony, wihout dispute, dwells pleasantly under one authority' is not the same as the Sv.

Dh. 10. '...being desirous of breaking the Saṅgha that is in

15. The language in the Svv. ch. 4, is a bit different but more clear, 'to scold' for 'to admonish'.

harmony, or persisting in emphasising the points... "Sir, you should not cause a schism in the Saṅgha, not try to break the Saṅgha and not to persist in raising the points that cause a division in the Saṅgha. Sir, you should be at one with the Saṅgha, be happy and free from dispute, be like the combination of water and milk while you follow the teaching of the same master, so that there will be benefit, peace and bliss in the Buddhist doctrine...'—do not agree.

Mhs. 10. Omits: 'Persists in emphasising the points calculated to cause a division in the Saṅgha.'

'...live together happily and peacefully for expounding the teachings of the Teacher...'

Ksy. 10. Language at the end differs slightly.

Msg. 10. '...to follow the doctrine like the combination of water and milk; to preach according to the Dharma, there will be enlightenment, peace and happiness...'

Msv. 10. The Bhikṣu is addressed here in the form of 'Āyuṣman'.

'...so that the teaching of the Great Master may be brightened and promoted and last long with peace and happiness...'

Language at the end is a bit different.

Tib. 10. '...the community being in harmony there will be no innovations and they being in peace there will be no disputation; combining with one another, as milk combines with water, they do brighten the doctrine of the Buddha and live in happiness...'

Language at the end is not the same.

Mpt. 10. Saṃghabhedaḥ.

Sv. II.11

The Bhikṣu who endeavouring to cause a division in the Saṅgha, has other Bhikṣu, one or two or many who are his friends agreeing with his disagreeable words, and these partisan Bhikṣus speak to other Bhikṣus: 'Venerable sirs, do not admonish this Bhikṣu for anything regarding this matter. Why so? because, this Bhikṣu speaks according to the Dharma, he speaks according to what is good, he never speaks what is not Dharma and what is not good; he knows what to speak and not otherwise. Whatever has been spoken by him is approved by us, whatever he wishes to adopt, we also wish to adopt.' Then let those partisan Bhikṣus be admonished by the Bhikṣus thus:

> 'Say not, venerable sirs, that "this Bhikṣu speaks according to the Dharma, that he speaks according to what is good, that he never speaks what is not Dharma and what is not good, that he knows what to speak and not otherwise, that whatever has been spoken by

him is approved by us, that whatever he wished to adopt, we also wish to adopt". Sirs! do not take delight in helping the schism of the Saṅgha, you should gladly help in furthering the harmony of the Saṅgha. Why? Because the Saṅgha being in harmony, there will be happiness and absence of disputation. They will live with one mind under one doctrine, just as the combination of water and milk. Sirs, you should abandon these partisan disagreeable words. 'If those Bhikṣus when they have been thus spoken to by the Bhikṣus, should persist as before, those Bhikṣus should be admonished a second and third time. If they give up their course, it is well, but if they abandon it not, that is a Saṃ.'

Skt. 11. 'Tasya ced bhikṣor bhikṣavaḥ syur anuvartino vyagravādina eko vā dvau vā sambahulā vā te tam bhikṣūn evam vadeyuḥ... dharmavādī ca sa bhikṣur vinayavādī ca...'

'Vinayavādī ca' is not in the Sv., but has 'he speaks according to what is good' instead.

Pāli 11. ...Anuvattikā vaggavādakā...

'One or two or three' only, 'many' is not here.

'Vinayavādī is not the same.

The words spoken by the partisan Bhikṣus and the reply made by other Bhikṣus are not quite the same; we find more words in the Sv.

Dh. 11. '...has one or two or three even up to countless.... He speaks "according to the Dharma and according to the Vinaya. Whatever he speaks is the delight of our mind and our mind agrees with it," then the other Bhikṣus advise them not to speak so, "because that Bhikṣu does neither speak according to the Dharma nor the Vinaya"...'

Mhs. 11. 'If there be two or three or many Bhikṣus who help to cause a division in the Saṅgha.'

'Vinaya' for 'what is good.'

Adds: Why? Because this Bhikṣu speaks what he does not know, and does neither speak according to the Dharma nor according to the 'Vinaya'.

For other minor differences see Ṁhs. Saṃ 10, above.

Ksy. 11. '...two or three or many...' "This Bhikṣu has no evil intention, because...whatever he speaks is according to our desire, joy and agreement; and whatever he desires, takes delight in or agrees to, we do also in the same manner..."

Adds: Why, because whatever this Bhikṣu speaks is neither according to the Dharma, nor according to the Vinaya and he speaks 'what he does not know'.

Language at the end differs slightly.

Msg. 11. '...one or two or many who speak in the same tone and hold the same view with the desire to cause a division in the Saṅgha...'

Adds: 'Do not speak good or bad of this Bhikṣu', and 'why, because whatever he speaks is neither according to the Dharma, nor according to the Vinaya'.

For other differences see Msg.. Saṃ. 10, above.

Msv. 11. 'one or two or many'..."...that Bhikṣu speaks according to the Dharma and the Vinaya and he also speaks the truth. What he likes I also like..."

Adds: Why? Because that Bhikṣu does not speak according to the Dharma or the Vinaya, nor does he speak the 'truth'.

For other differences see Msv. Saṃ. 10, above and 12 below.

Tib. 11. '...one, two or more'..."O Brethren, do not say anything good or bad to this dissentient monk. Why so? Because...receiving well the Law and precepts, he holds them carefully and observes them and he speaks with knowledge and not without it. Since he speaks only when he is so desired, it is our desire that he should speak."

Adds: 'O sirs, this dissentient monk speaks not according to the law...do not sirs, desire him to speak.'

For other differences see Tib. Saṃ. 10, above.

Mpt. 11. Tadanuvartakaḥ.

Sv. II.12

If a Bhikṣu or Bhikṣus[16] taking residence in a city[17] or in a village practise evil deeds and corrupt (other) families, and such deeds are seen, heard and known, let those Bhikṣus be spoken to by the other Bhikṣus thus: "Venerable sirs, the act of your practising evil deeds and corrupting other families has been seen, heard and known; sirs, you should not stay here and go away now from this place." If those Bhikṣus should reply to the Bhikṣus thus: "Venerable sirs, the Bhikṣus are in the path of longing, malice, fear and ignorance. Why? Because, there are Bhikṣus who having committed a fault of a like nature, some of whom are sent away, and some not sent away." Then those Bhikṣus should be spoken to by the Bhikṣus thus: "Say not so, venerable sirs! that the Bhikṣus are in the path of longing, malice, fear and ignorance, and that they send not some away from the Bhikṣus for their having committed a fault of a like

16. The Skt. is in the singular form. We find the text at times in the singular and at times in the plural form.

17. The word 'city' is not in the Svv., ch. 4 and the language at the end is slightly different.

nature, while they send others away.[18] Why? Because the Bhikṣus are not in the path of longing, malice, fear and ignorance. The act of your practising evil deeds and corrupting other families has been seen, heard and known. Sirs, do abandon the words such as 'in the path of longing, malice, fear and ignorance' you should not stay here and go away now from this place." If those partisan Bhikṣus being thus admonished by the Bhikṣus should persist in doing as before and would not give it up, those Bhikṣus should be admonished by the Bhikṣus a second time, and a third time. If they abandon the cause, it is well; if they do not,—that is a Saṃ.

Skt. 12. Sa ca syāt kuladūṣakaḥ pāpasamācāras...

'Grāmam vā nigamaṃ vā viharet' (cf. Sv., 'city and village').

The words 'seen, heard and known' have been used after 'kulāni duṣṭāni' and 'pāpasamācāraḥ' separately.

Pāli 13. ...Kuladūsako pāpasamācāro...

The construction here is more or less like that of the Skt.

Omits: 'known'.

The words 'Chandagāmino, dosagāmino, mohagāmino, bhayagāmino', have been translated into English as: Walking in longing, in malice, in delusion and in fear.

'Alaṃ te idhāvāsena'—you have dwelt here 'long enough' is different from the Sarv.

Dh. 12. We have only "seen as well as heard", and the use is in the same manner as the Skt.

"Now you may leave this village and do not stay here."

Mhs. 13. Ksy. 12., Msg. 13., Msv. 12.—The same.

The use of 'seen', heard and known' is as in Skt.

The Msg. omits 'known'.

Msv. 12. 'If they[19] being thus admonished by the Bhikṣus abandon their course, it is well; but if they do not, the Bhikṣus should earnestly advise them a second and a third time and according to the teachings should command them to give it up. If they give it up, it is well, if they do not,—that is a Saṃ.'

Tib. 12. '...You have dwelt here long enough.'

Rest is the same; language differs slightly.

Mpt. 12. Kuladūṣakaḥ.

---

18. The Eng. translation of the Pāli Pāṭimokkha says: "and they send not some away for a fault of a like nature while they send others not away". The last 'not' in the sentence is obviously a misprint. See SBE, vol. XIII, p. 13, and the Pāli is: 'Tādisikāya āpattiya ekaccaṃ pabbājenti ekaccaṃ na pabbājenti.'

19. This is also applicable to the last portion of Saṃ. 10 and 11 of Msv. above.

Sv. II.13

Should a Bhikṣu possess a bad temper and is difficult to be spoken to; and when he is spoken to by the Bhikṣus in accordance with the Dharma and Vinaya,[20] touching the rules of the Prātimokṣa concerning which he has been guilty, will not allow anything to be said to him and thus he will say: "Venerable sirs, say nothing to me, either good or bad! and I will say nothing, either good or bad, to you. You need not, venerable sirs, advise me anything!" Let that Bhikṣu be admonished by the Bhikṣu thus: "Sir, the Bhikṣus speak in accordance with the Dharma and Vinaya touching the rules of the Prātimokṣa concerning which you have been guilty. Do not make yourself a person, who cannot be spoken to; make yourself rather, sir, a person to whom we can speak. Speak to the Bhikṣus, Sir, in accordance with the Dharma and Vinaya; and the Bhikṣus, sir, will speak in accordance with the Dharma and Vinaya to you. Why so? Because thus has the Saṅgha of the Tathāgata grown large; that is to say, by mutual converse, by mutual advice, so that one may save the other from falling into sin. Sir, do give up the practice of being a person who cannot be spoken to." If that Bhikṣu being thus admonished by the Bhikṣus should persist as before and would not give it up, he should be admonished by the Bhikṣus a second time and a third time. If he can abandon the course, it is well, if he does not—that is a Saṃ.

Skt. 13. '...Mā mām āyuṣmantaḥ kiñcid vadantu kalyāṇaṃ akalyāṇaṃ vā.' Ms. is not quite complete.

Pāli 12. ...Dubbacajātiko hoti—

'In accordance with the Vinaya' is not found here. We find 'Sahadhammikaṃ' only; cf. Skt. 'Saha dharmeṇa saha vinayena ca'...

'Touching the precepts handed down in the body of recited law'—do not agree.

'By mutual converse, by mutual help', not 'mutual advice', as in the Sarv.

Omits: 'So that one saves the other from falling into sin.'

Dh. 13. Omits: '...concerning which he has been guilty.'

'...and thus by one admonishing the other, one instructing the other and one confessing to the other, the disciples of the Buddha will be increased.'

Omits: 'So that one saves the other from falling into sin.'

Mhs. 12. Adds: 'While learning the teaching and precept along with other Bhikṣus he often commits offences.'

---

20. Literally it means 'goodness'.

Omits: 'Make yourself rather, sir, a person to whom we can speak.'

'...thus mutually instruct, mutually confess and become (good) disciples of the Tathāgata.'

Ksy. 13. 'If a Bhikṣu while following the precepts of Vinaya in learning the doctrines of the Buddha, turns down others' advice by uttering abusive words (ngo-k'ou)...Why so? Because, thus the disciples of the Tathāgata, the Arhat and the well-enlightened One will grow and increase, they will admonish one another, instruct one another, speak to one another and mutually confess...'

Msg. 12. ....'The Bhikṣu speaks improper words according to his desire, when other Bhikṣus professing the same faith of doctrine advise him in accordance with the Dharma and Vinaya...'—do not agree.

'...you must accept the instruction made by the Bhikṣus in accordance with the Dharma and Vinaya' is different from the Sv.

Omits: 'Sir, do give up the practice of being a person who cannot be spoken to.'

Msv. 13. 'If a Bhikṣu possessing a bad temper refuses to accept the advice given by the Bhikṣu in accordance with the Dharma and Vinaya in regard to the Prātimokṣa spoken by the Buddha...'—do not agree

'O brother, you should not refuse to accept advice' is different from the Sv. Do not make yourself a person who cannot be spoken to 'make yourself rather, sir, a person to whom we can speak.'

Omits: 'Mutually converse...so that one saves the other from falling into sin,' and 'do give up the practice of being a person who cannot be spoken to'.

Tib. 13. 'If a monk of harsh speech, when spoken to by a community of monks about matters of training in accordance with the Law and precepts delivered by the Buddha...'—do not agree.

'O brethren, refrain from speaking to me, I too shall refrain from speaking to you—here is in fact nothing to be spoken about'—do not agree.

'...about matters of training' for the Sv.: 'touching the rules of Prātimokṣa concerning which he has been guilty'—do not agree.

'...thus grown up the monkhood established by our fully enlightened Lord, the Blessed Tathāgata, the Vanquisher of enemies,'—do not agree.

Mpt. 13. Daurvacasyam.

Sv.

O venerable sirs, I have recited the thirteen offences of Saṃghāvaśeṣa. Of these the first nine become sins at once, while the remaining four do not become sins until the end of the third admonition.

If a Bhikṣu, commits any of these sins, for as many days must that Bhikṣu, even against his will, remain in probation.[21] When the probation is over, that Bhikṣu must, for six further days and nights, in the Saṅgha, undergo the Mānatvam discipline.[22] When the Mānatvam is done, there comes the ceremony āvṛṃhaṇa (Pāli: Abbhāna) or pardoning of offence. The mind of the Bhikṣus will be happy when everything is carried out according to the Law. Thereupon that Bhikṣu must be reinstated in some place where the community of Bhikṣus form a body of twenty. If a community of Bhikṣus forming a body of less than twenty, even by one, should reinstate that Bhikṣu, he is not reinstated, and that community is blameworthy. This is the proper course in that case.

In respect of these (rules) I ask the venerable ones, 'Are you pure in this matter?'

A second and a third time, I ask the venerable ones, 'Are you pure in this matter?'

The venerable ones are pure herein; therefore do they keep silence. Thus do I observe.

Skt. ...Ṣaḍrātraṃ manatvaṃ...A portion of the Ms. is missing.

Pāli. 'Six nights of mānatta discipline.'

Omits: 'The mind of the Bhikṣus will be happy when everything is carried out according to the Law.' It is also not found in Dh., Mhs., Ksy., Msg., and Msv.

Dh. Mhs., Ksy., Msg., Msv. The same. 'Six nights' only, without 'days' as in the Sv.

III. TWO ANIYATA DHARMAS

Sv. III.1

Here are venerable sirs, the two Aniyata Dharmas as known from the Prātimokṣa recited each half month.

Whatsoever Bhikṣu shall take a seat with a woman in a solitary protected place suitable for carrying out lustful desires; when a female devotee, trustworthy of speech charges him with one or other of the three offences, viz., either under the Pārājika, or under the Saṃghāvaśeṣa or under the Pātayantika rules, if that Bhikṣu acknowledges: 'I sat in such

21. Paryuṣita or to live in a separate residence, see Cv., II.1-3.
22. 'Penance' for the regulation of this, see Cv., II 6-8.

a place', then let him be dealt with according to the circumstances reported for a Pārājika, or for a Saṃghāvaśeṣa or for a Pātayantika; or let that Bhikṣu be dealt with under other rules under which the female devotee, trustworthy in speech, shall lay it to his charge.

This is the first Aniyata Dharma.

Skt. 1. Mātṛgrāmeṇa sārdham ekaikena rahasi praticchanne āsane niṣadyāṃ kalpayed...

Pāli 1. Mātugāmena saddhim ekāya raho āsane nisajjaṃ kappeyya...

'Upāsikā disvā'...seen by a female devotee.

Dh. 1. Adds: 'and speak words not in accordance with the Law', 'or let that Bhikṣu be dealt with under other rules'.

Mhs. 1. Omits: 'Or let that Bhikṣu be dealt with under other rules under which, the female devotee...shall lay it to his charge.'

Ksy. 1. 'Or let that Bhikṣu be dealt with under other rules' differs slightly from the Sv.

Msg. 1. 'Under other rules'. It is not clearly stated here.

Msv. 1. At the beginning there is a gāthā summarising the two rules called indeterminate.

Tib. 1. A summary[23] at the beginning.

The ending portion differs slightly in language.

Mpt. Nil.

Sv. III.2

Whatsoever Bhikṣu, shall take a seat with a woman in an open place not suitable for carrying out lustful desires but convenient for addressing a woman with wicked and obscene words; and if a female devotee, trustworthy of speech charges him with one or other of the two offences, viz., either under Saṃghāvaśeṣa, or under Pātayantika rules, if the Bhikṣu acknowledges: 'I sat in such a place', then let him be dealt with according to the circumstances reported for a Saṃghāvaśeṣa or for a Pātayantika; or let that Bhikṣu be dealt with under rules which the female devotee, trustworthy of speech, shall lay it to his charge.

O venerabe sirs, I have recited the Two Aniyata Dharmas. Now, I ask the venerable ones: 'Are you pure in this matter?'

A second and a third time I ask the venerable ones: 'Are you pure in this matter?'

The venerable ones are pure herein, therefore do they keep

23. This is the summary:
'Sitting in a solitary protected place.'

silence. Thus do I observe.

Skt. 2. Na ca rahasi praticchanne āsane niṣadyāṃ kalpayet...
The same.
Pāli 2. Na paṭicchanaṃ āsanaṃ hoti, ekāraho nisajjaṃ kappeyya...
'Seen by a believing woman', the word 'seen', is not in Sv.
Dh. 2. 'To sit alone with a woman' and 'or under other rules' are not clearly stated here as they are in the Sv.
Mhs. 2. 'Sit alone with a woman.'
Omits: 'Or let that Bhikṣu be dealt with under other rules which, the female devotee...shall lay it to his charge.'
Ksy. 2. 'Or under rules' differs slightly from Sv.
Msg. 2. 'Under other rules' is not clearly stated here.
Msv. 2. The same.
Tib. 2. '...sits together with a woman in a solitary place, which is however not suitable for carrying out of lustful desires...'
The ending portion differs slightly in language.
Mpt. Nil.

IV. THE THIRTY NIḤSARGIKA PĀTAYANTIKA DHARMAS

Sv. IV.1

Here are, venerable sirs, the thirty Niḥsargika Pātayantika (Pāli: nissaggiya pācittiya) Rules as known from the Prātimokṣa each half month.

When the three robes[24] have been made ready and taken up at the time of receiving the Kaṭhina[25] robe by the Bhikṣu, an extra robe may be kept up to the end of a period of ten days. If he goes beyond that, that is a Niḥsargika Pātayantika.

Skt. 1. 'Niṣṭhitacīvareṇa bhikṣuṇā uddhṛte kaṭhine daśarātraparaman cīvaraṃ dhārayitaviyam...'
Pāli 1. Atirekacīvaraṃ...
Not 'three robes' here.
Dh. 1. 'If the robes for the Bhikṣu are ready and the Kaṭhina robe

24. The Svv. ch. 5 says: 'If the robes for the Bhikṣu are ready and the Kaṭhina robes have been given, the Bhikṣu may keep an extra robe up to a period of ten days...'

25. The Kaṭhina robe is usually made for the Bhikṣus in the course of a single day and night by themselves. And it is presented mostly during the end of Vassā between the full moon of Āśvinī and Kārtika.

is out (offered), he may keep an extra robe which is considered as a gift of impurity (pu chin shih) up to a period of ten days...'

Mhs. 1. '...the three robes are ready and the Kaṭhina robe has been given...'

Ksy. 1. 'If the robes for the Bhikṣus are ready and the Kaṭhina robe is out (i.e. offered) an extra robe...'

Msg. 1. '... and the Kaṭhina robe has been given...' same as Ksy. Np. 1, above-mentioned.

Msv. 1. 'An extra robe, may be retained (not)[26] without discrimination, up to a period of ten days...'

[27]*Tib.* 1. 'A monk, after a set of Kaṭhina robes has been obtained and made ready for him...'

Mpt. 1. Dhāraṇaṃ.

Sv. IV.2

When the three robes have been made ready and taken up at the time of receiving the Kaṭhina robe by the Bhikṣu, if a Bhikṣu remains without any of his three robes while sleeping elsewhere, even for a single night, unless with the permission of the Saṅgha...that is a Np.

Skt. 2. Trayāṇāṃ cīvarāṇāṃ ekatamāc cīvarād vipravased...'to sleep elsewhere'

Pāli 2. Ticīvaraṃ vippavaseyya...

Omits: 'To sleep elsewhere.'

'Be without his three robes.'

The language at the beginning differs slightly.

Dh. 2. '...and the Kaṭhina robe is out.'

Other portions are the same.

Mhs. 2. '...and the Kaṭhina robe has been given...'

Other portions are the same.

Ksy. 2. '...the Kaṭhina robe is out...'

Msg. 2. '...and the Kaṭhina robe has been given...'

---

26. The Msvv., ch. 16, says that during the limited period, the Bhikṣu who received a robe on behalf of another Bhikṣu, should make a distinction between what is his own and that which belongs to another. In this Comm. we read the following:

'If the robes are made ready and the Kaṭhina robe has been offered (out), an extra robe may be kept with discrimination up to a period of ten days, if he keeps it without making a distinction,' that is a Np. "In the actual text of Msv., the word 'not' is a mistake."

27. A summary (*Uddāna*) of the following ten rules is added here (Msv. I): "Retaining, leaving, keeping as a deposit, washing, accepting, begging, sufficient for upper and lower garments, price, taking each separately and sending."

Omits: 'Even for a single night.'

Msv. 2. '...the Kaṭhina robe is also out...' 'To sleep outside the boundary...except Saṅghakarma.'

Tib. 2. '...after a set of Kaṭhina robes has been...made ready for him, leaves in joke even for one night any one of the robes...'

Omits: 'To sleep elsewhere.'

Mpt. 2. Vipravāsaḥ.

Sv. IV.3

When the three robes have been made ready and taken up at the time of (receiving the) Kaṭhina robe (Chia-cheh-i) by the Bhikṣu, if he gets a robe[28] out of season, it may be accepted by him should he be in need of it. But he should get it made (as a robe of a Bhikṣu) at once and keep it.[29] If it is sufficient, it is well, if not, it may be kept up to the end of a month by that Bhikṣu should he have any hope that the deficiency may be supplied. If he keeps it beyond the time of one month...that is a Np.

Skt. 3. The same; Ms. incomplete.

Pāli 3. Akālacīvaraṃ uppajjeyya...

Dh. 3. '...the Kaṭhina robe is out...'

'Having accepted it, he should quickly make it into a robe.' Also see note 31, above.

Mhs. 3. 'The Kaṭhina robe has been given...'

Omits: 'Keep it.'

Ksy. 3. '...having accepted it, he should make it into a robe at once.'

Omits: '...should he have any hope that the deficiency may be supplied.' Also see note 29, above.

Msg. 3. '...the Kaṭhina robe has been given...'

'Having accepted it...'

Other portions are the same.

Tib. 3. '...if another set of robes be offered to him out of seasons... After it has been accepted, andy deficiency thereof (in point of length, etc.) should be made up at once...'[30]

Mpt. 3. Nikṣepaḥ.

---

28. This appears to be rather a piece of cloth than a ready-made robe.
29. 'To keep it' is not found in Dh., Mhs., and Ksy.
30. Instead of "turning it into a robe" as in Dh. Ksy. etc.

Sv. IV.4

Whatsoever Bhikṣu shall receive a robe from a Bhikṣuṇī not related to him, except in exchange, that is a Np.

Skt. 4. Ajñātyā bhikṣuṇyāḥ santikāc cīvaraṃ pratigṛhṇīyād.

Pāli 5. Cīvaraṃ paṭigaṇheyya...

For Skt. 'Bhikṣuṇyāḥ santikāt' we have here 'Bhikkhuniyā hatthato' ...from the hand of a Bhikkhuṇī.

Dh. 4, *Mhs.* 4, *Msg.* 4. The same.

Ksy. 4. The translation is not quite clear. The word 'except' seems to have been dropped either due to a misprint or through the carelessness of the translator.

Msv. 5, *Tib.* 4. The same.

Mpt. 5. Pratigrahaḥ.

Sv. IV.5

Whatsoever Bhikṣu shall cause his old robes to be washed, dyed or beaten by a Bhikṣuṇī not related to him, that is a Np.

Skt. 5, *Dh.* 5, *Mhs.* 5, *Ksy.* 5, *Msg.* 5. The same.

Skt. 5. Ajñātyā bhikṣuṇyā purāṇascīvaraṃ dhāvayet...

Pāli 4. Purāṇacīvaraṃ dhovāpeyya vā rajāpeyya vā ākoṭapeyya vā...

Msv. 4, *Tib.* 4. The same.

The English version of the Tibetan text puts 'to be ironed'(!) for 'Ḥchag tu ḥjug na.'

Mpt. 4. Dhāvanam.

Sv. IV.6

Whatsoever Bhikṣu shall ask a householder or a householder's wife, not related to him, for a robe, and if he gets it except at the right season—that is a Np.

Here the right season means when he has been robbed of his robe or when his robe has been lost, burnt or carried away by water. This is the right season here.

Skt. 6. Ajñātiṃ gṛhapatiṃ vā gṛhapatipatnīṃ vā cīvaraṃ vijñāpayed...

Pāli 6. Aññātakaṃ gahapatiṃ vā gahapatāniṃ vā cīvaraṃ viññāpeyya...

Omits: The Skt. 'Abhiniṣpanne cīvare...' If he gets the 'robe', as well as 'has been burnt or carried away by water.'

Dh. 6, *Mhs.* 6, *Ksy.* 6, *Msg.* 6, *Msv.* 6 and *Tib.* 6. Omits: 'If he gets it.'

Mhs. 6. '... the other time' means, "when his robe is lost". Nothing further has been mentioned here.

Msv. 6., *Tib.* 6. Adds: 'Carried away by wind.'

Mpt. 6 Yācñā.

Sv. IV.7

If a Bhikṣu has been robbed of his robe, or his robe has been lost, burnt or carried away by water, he asks a householder or a householder's wife, not related to him, for the same. If the householder or the householder's wife not related to him offers him a choice (from among the materials) of many robes, he may take it, if he so desires, but he should, at the most, accept the materials for making an upper and a lower garment only. If he accepts the offer beyond this limit—that is a Np.

Skt. 7. ...Bhikṣuṇā sāntarottara paramamtataś cīvaraṃ pratigṛhitavyaṃ...'

Pāli 7. ...Santaruttaraparamaṃ cīvaraṃ sāditabbaṃ...

The first half of Sv. is not found here.

Dh. 7, *Ksy.* 7. '...this Bhikṣu should accept the robe with contentment'. See also under Tib. 7.

Mhs. 7. Adds: 'If the robe is destroyed.'

'The Bhikṣu should accept two robes only.' See Tib. 7 below.

Ksy. 7. Omits: 'Choice'.

Msg. 7. The words: 'Robbed of, destroyed, burnt, carried away by water' are not here. See Tib. 7 below.

Msv. 7. Adds: 'Carried away by wind.'

'If he needs it.'

Tib. 7. '...should take materials sufficient to make an upper and a lower garment of due measurement...'

The following texts Dh. 7, Mhs. 7, Ksy. 7, Msg. 7, and Tib. 7... omit 'Should he so desire.'

Mpt. 7. Sāntarottaraṃ.

Sv. IV.8

If the price for a robe has been set apart for a particular Bhikṣu by a householder or a householder's wife, not related to him, saying, 'I shall get such a robe with such an amount of robe-fund and give them to such and such a Bhikṣu,' if that Bhikṣu before the offer has been made to him, goes to the place of the householder or the householder's wife, and desirous of getting something fine, on a certain pretext saying thus: 'It is good indeed that you have set apart such an amount of robe-fund for buying such a robe for me'—for something fine, and if he obtains that robe—that is a Np.

Skt. 8. ...Cīvaracetanakāny upaskṛtāni....

'Evaṃ nāmānaṃ bhikṣuṃ ācchādayiṣyāmīti'—I shall give it to the Bhikṣu of such a name.

'Āyuṣmata' not in Sv.

Pāli 8. ...Cīvaracetāpanaṃ upakkhaṭaṃ hoti....

'Itthaṃ nāmaṃ bhikkhuṃ' as in Skt.

Omits: 'On a certain pretext' and 'if he obtains that set of robes'.

Dh. 8. Omits 'not related to him'.

'...take such (amount) of robe-fund and give it to a certain Bhikṣu'.

Omits: 'On a certain pretext'.

Adds: 'O good householder...'

Mhs. 8. 'If the householder and the lady of the householder discuss together with the purpose of setting apart a cetain amount of robe-fund for making a robe for a certain Bhikṣu...."Do you set apart such an amount of robe-fund for preparing a robe for me?" "Yes," replies (the householder). "It is good indeed", says a Bhikṣu, "O householder and wife of the householder, you may make such a robe for me"—that is a Np.'

Ksy. 8. ...The construction here is more or less like that of Mhs. Np. 8. The difference is: 'Take this robe-fund and give it to such a Bhikṣu; make such a good-coloured robe for me.'

Msg. 8. ..."It is good indeed, O Householder, that you buy for me a robe of such colour[31] with such an amount of robe-fund..."

Msv. 8. '...together (arrange) set apart an amount of robe-fund and buy such a pure (proper) robe for the timely use of such a Bhikṣu...when he is informed by others, he goes to their house saying thus: "O gentle one, you may buy me such a pure robe for my timely use, with the robe-fund that you have set apart"....

Tib. 8. Omits: 'On a certain pretext.'

"......and clothe me with the same in due time..."

Mpt. 8. Caitanakāni.

Sv. IV.9

If the price for a robe has been set apart for a Bhikṣu by each of

31. This may be a literary translation of Skt. 'Evaṃrūpaṃ'.

(two) householders or by each of (two) wives of householders, saying: "We shall buy such robes with such an amount of robe-fund and give them to such and such a Bhikṣu," if that Bhikṣu, before the offer has been made to him, goes to the place of the householders or that of the wives of the householders, on a certain pretext, saying thus: "It is good indeed that you have set apart such an amout of robe-fund, you combine (the efforts) as one and buy me a robe"...for getting something fine, and then if he obtains that robe—that is a Np.

Skt. 9. ...Dvābhyāṃ ajñātibhyāṃ gṛhapatibhyāṃ gṛhapatipatnībhyāṃ vā pratyekacīvaracetana kāny upaskṛtāni...

The Sv. does not state clearly as to the setting apart of the robe-fund by two persons.

Pāli 9. Ubhinnaṃ...paccekacīvaracetāpannaṃ upakkhaṭā hoti....

"We will each get a set of robes...."

Adds: 'Go and give directions as to how to make the robes.'

For other non-corresponding parts, see Pāli Np. 8 above compared.

Dh. 9. 'Two householders or two householders' wives.'

For other differences, see Dh. Np. 8 above.

Mhs. 9. '....."O householders or ladies of the householders, you may together make a robe for me"...'

The other parts are like that of Mhs. Np. 8 above compared.

Ksy. 9. 'If among two householders, each is arranging an amount of robe-fund for a Bhikṣu...'

'... "Do you two really desire to make a robe for me"....!'

Construction is different.

Msg. 9. For portions not corresponding and for additions see Dh. Np. 8 above.

Msv. 9. Except 'each' and 'together buy me such a pure robe', the other portion is the same as stated in Msv. Np. 8.

Tib. 9. '... by a layman and the same has been done by his wife... "of such and such a name when he arrives" ..."with that let each of you purchase such and such a set and folding the two sets together make them one and clothe me with the same...'

'On a certain pretext.'

Mpt. 9. Pratyekaṃ.

Sv. IV.10

If a King, or a Minster[32] or a Brāhmaṇa or a householder sends

32. Literally it means; 'minister of a king' from Skt.: Rājamahāmātra.

through a messenger the price of a set of robes for a particular Bhikṣu, and if this messenger after going to the Bhikṣu's place thus speak to that Bhikṣu: "O venerable sir, do you know that this robe-fund has been sent by the King or the Minister or the Brāhmaṇa or the householder? Sir, do accept it." Then the Bhikṣu should answer the messenger thus: "It is the custom of the Bhikṣus, that they should not accept the price of robes. But when we are in need of robes, if we get the suitable (pure) cloth, we may take it and promptly make a robe with it and keep it as well." If then that messenger speaks to the Bhikṣu: "O sir, have you got any agent who often serves the Bhikṣus?" Then the Bhikṣu who is in need of the robe should point out to him the agent, such as the guard of the monastery or a householder and tell him: "These are the people who often manage affairs on behalf of the Bhikṣus." When the agent is shown, the messenger speaks to him thus: "O good agent, you buy such a set of robes with such an amount of robe-fund and give it to such and such a Bhikṣu; when that Bhikṣu is in need of it he will come to you and you give it to him." Having requested and instructed the agent either personally or by sending a man, the messenger returns to the Bhikṣu and informs him: "O venerable sir, I have requested and instructed the agent who was pointed out, that when you are in need of robes, you might go and take it from him and he is sure to give it to you." This Bhikṣu being desirous of getting the robe should then go to the agent to ask him for it and speak thus: "I need the robe, I need the robe." In the second and the third time he should also beg for it in the same manner. If he succeeds in obtaining the robes, it is well. Should he not succeed in obtaining them, let him up to the fourth, fifth, or sixth time go and stand silently in front of the agent. If while so standing silently in front of him up to the fourth, fifth, or sixth time, he should succeed in obtaining the robe, it is well. Should he not succeed in thus obtaining it, but by exerting himself beyond that limit to get the robe, if he were to obtain it—that is a Np. But if he should not succeed in obtaining it, let him either go himself or send a messenger to the place whence the robe-fund was brought to him, and say thus: 'The robe fund, which you sent for such and such a Bhikṣu, has in no wise benefited that Bhikṣu. You should know this and not let your money go to ruin.'

This is the proper course in the matter.

Skt. 10. Dūtasya haste cīvaracetanakāni preṣitāni...
'Anukampām upādāya' is not in Sv.
'iyaṃ tatra sāmīcīḥ' agrees with the Sv.
Pāli 10. ...Dūtena cīvaracetāpanaṃ pahiṇeyya...
'Rājabhoggo' for 'minster'.

The words spoken by the King etc. "'Iminā' cīvaracetāpanena cīvaraṃ cetāpetvā itthaṃ-nāmaṃ bhikkhuṃ cīvarena acchādehī'ti" are not in the Sv.

The words spoken by the messenger to the Bhikṣu in requesting the Bhikṣu to accept the robe-fund and those of the Bhikṣu's reply are not corresponding.

'This man, my friend, is the Bhikṣu's agent' is slightly different.

Omits the words spoken by the messenger to the agent.

The words spoken by the messenger to the Bhikṣu about the arrangement he made with the agent do not quite correspond with the Sv. See Dh. 10, below.

Dh. 10. Adds: 'Or the wife of the householder.'

The construction and language mostly correspond to those in Pāli Np. 10, above.

"You get back your money and do not let it go to ruin."

'Having requested and instructed the agent personally or by sending a man' is absent; also not in the Pāli No. 10, Mhs. Np. 10, and Ksy. Np. 10.

Mhs. 10. '...the King or the great minister sends you this robe-fund...'.

The Bhikṣu's reply to the messenger differs slightly.

'The guard of a monastery....etc.' absent.

'O venerable sir, I have given (the money) to the agent pointed out by you; when you need the robe, you may go and take it.'

'You better get your (money) back and don't let it be lost.' See Dh. 10, above.

Ksy. 10. Adds: 'A gṛhapati or a merchant or the wife of a gṛhapati.'

'Take this robe-fund and give it to such and such a Bhikṣu,' is absent.

'Sir, kindly accept this robe fund.'

'Sent by King...etc' absent.

Omits: 'Who often serves the Bhikṣu.'

'A garden-keeper'. The original word 'Arāma' is capable of being interpreted both as a garden as well as a monastery. This term also occurs in Msg. Np. 10 (Pāli: ārāmika).

'These people...' absent.

Adds: 'This is so and so's robe-fund for making robes for such a Bhikṣu.'

'Let him be reminded' absent in Sv.

'I have given the robe-fund to such an agent. When you need the robe, you go there and you will get it.'

'Let the donor be informed about it and let him withdraw the donation.'

Msg. 10. 'By a King or a minister' only.

'The messenger thus requested the agent.'

The language and construction correspond to those in Sv.

Msv. 10. Omits: 'Who often serves the Bhikṣu' and 'these people....'

'I have given the robe-fund to the agent pointed out by you; when you get the suitable (pure) robe, you should accept it.'

Tib. 10. Adds: 'Or a towns man or a villager, or a rich man or a trader.'

The following lines do not correspond.

'Do you know....'

'... to look to your requisites.'

'O agent, my friend, attend to me.'

'...and clothe with the same ... when he arrives.'

'...having spoken everything elegantly and shown everything accurately...'

The language here is also slightly different.

Mpt. 10. Preṣaṇaṃ.

Sv. IV.11

Whatsoever Bhikṣu shall have a rug or a mat (to sit on?) made with new silk—that is a Np.

Skt. 11. Navakauśeyasaṃstaraṃ kāraye (sic)...

Pali 11. Kosiyamissakaṃ santhataṃ kārāpeyya....'Nava' absent.

Dh. 11. '...prepare a rug (or a bedding)[33] mixed with silk from wild silk-worms.'

Mhs. 21. '...make a rug or a bedding with new silk.'

Ksy. 11. Adds: 'If causes other persons to make it and get it done.'

Msg. 13. '...make a new mat or a rug with silk mixed with pure black wool of goat.' This seems mixed up with Msg. 11.

Msv. 11. '...make a mat or rug with new Kauśeya silk.'

Tib. 11. 'gets[34] a new mat made with silk.'

Mpt. 11. Kauśeyam.

33. Wo-chü—a thing to lie on.
34. Both in Msv. and Tib., there is a summary in verse of the following: 'A piece of silk entirely of wool, two parts, six years, a full span, journey, washing, gold and silver, silver (coin), and buying and selling.'

Sv. IV.12

Whatsoever Bhikṣu shall have a rug or a new mat made of pure black wool of goat—that is a Np.

Skt. 12. Śuddhakāḍānāṃ eḍakalomnāṃ 'new' absent.
Pāli 12. Suddhakāḷakānāṃ eḷakalomānaṃ...'new' absent.
Dh. 12. '...with new, pure black wool of goat...'
Msg. 11, *Mhs.* 23, *Msv.* 12, *Tib.* 12. The same.
Ksy. 12. Adds: 'Or ask others to make.'
Mpt. 12. Suddhakālakānāṃ.

Sv. IV.13

If a Bhikṣu is desirous of making a mat or a rug, two parts thereof should be taken of pure black wool of goat, the third part of white wool and the fourth part of wools of inferior quality. If a Bhikṣu should have a new rug made without taking two parts of pure black wool, the third of white, and the fourth of inferior quality[35]—that is a Np.

Skt. 13. (i) Dvau bhāgau Suddhakāḍānāṃ...
(ii) Tṛtīyaṃ avadātānāṃ...
(iii) Caturthaṃ gocarikānāṃ...
Pāli 13. (i)...Dve bhāgā Suddhakāḷakānaṃ...

For 'gocariya' the Eng. translation has been given as: '...of the colour of oxen (reddish brown),' SBE, vol. XIII, p. 25. (cf. Dh. 13 and Tib. 13), below.

Dh. 13. '...the fourth part of grey (black-white mixed) colour...'
Mhs. 23, *Msg.* 12. The same.
Msv. 13. '...make a new rug of wool...the fourth part of coarse quality...'
Tib. 13. '...the fourth part of motley-coloured...
Mpt. 13. Dvibhāgḥ.

SV. IV.14

If a Bhikṣu be desirous of making a new rug, his old rug must have been used for six full years. If he should have another new rug made within six years, whether he has left or not the old one, unless with the permission[36] of the Saṅgha—that is a Np.

35. 'Hsia'—inferior or of less value. The Svv., ch. 7, says: "Hsia means the wool or hair of the head, of the stomach or of the leg."
36. Literally it means: 'Except by the Saṅghakarma.'

Skt. 14. ...saṃstaraṃ ṣaḍ varṣāṇi dhārayitavyaṃ...The following words are not in the Sv:

'...kalyāṇakāmatām upādāya.'

Pāli 14. Santhataṃ chabbassāni dhāretabbaṃ...

The Skt. words: 'Akāmaṃ' and 'kalyāṇakāmatām upādāya' absent in Pāli.

Language differs slightly.

Dh. 14. '...if within less than six years, he makes another new one and does not give up the old one...'

Mhs. 24, *Dh.* 14, *Ksy.* 15, *Msg.* 14. '...having had a new rug made, he should use it for six years...'

Ksy. 15. Omits: 'Whether he has left or not the old one.'

Msv. 14. '...has had a rug or mat made, should use it, even against his wish, for six years. If he makes another new one in less than six years, and does not give up the old one...'

Tib. 14. '...who has got a mat made, should use it even against his wish, for six years...'

The word 'new' is absent.

Mpt. 14. Ṣaḍvarṣāṇi.

Sv. IV.15

If a Bhikṣu be desirous of making a new seat-rug (*niṣīdana*), a piece (of the breadth) of the Sugata's span must be taken from each of the four sides of the old seat rug in order to disfigure the good colour (of the new one). If the Bhikṣu does not take a piece of the breadth of the Sugata's span from each of the four sides of the old seat-rug to disfigure the colour but to make it look good—that is a Np.

Skt. 15. Navaṃ bhikṣuṇā niṣīdanasaṃstaraṃ....durvarṇī karaṇāya...

Pāli 15. Nisīdanasanthataṃ dubbaṇṇakaraṇāya...Skt. 'navaṃ' and 'Kalyāṇakāmatām upādāya; absent here. See Dh. 15 below.

Dh. 15. Adds: 'One span in length and in breadth.'

'Sugatavitastir' absent here.

Omits: 'From each of the four sides'; the same case with Pāli 15, Mhs. 25, Ksy. 14, Msg. 15, Msv. 15 and Tib. 15.

Omits: 'to make it look good' this is also not found in Mhs. 25, Ksy. 14, Msv. 15, Msg. 15 and Tib. 15.

Mhs. 25. '...makes a new seat-rug with pure black wool of goat.' See Dh. 15 above.

Skt. 'Sāmantakāt' absent here.

Ksy. 14. '...should take a piece, about the size of a square hand from the old rug and stitch it on the new one, otherwise, that is a Np.' See Dh. 15 above.

Msg. 15. '...makes a new rug or carpet or niṣīdana, that should be covered with a piece of a square span of the Buddha's span from the old one...' See Dh. 15 above.

Msv. 15. '...one Buddha's span in length and in breadth should be taken from the strong portion of the old one...' See Dh. 15 above.

Tib. 15. '...gets a new piece of carpet made into a seat for himself...patch the same with a piece...taken from all parts of the old one...'. See Dh. 15 above.

Mpt. 15. Vitastiḥ

Sv. IV.16

If a Bhikṣu while walking on the road, gets some goat's wool, let him accept it if he likes; and having accepted it, he should carry it in his own hand, if there is no carrier found up to a distance of three leagues (*Yojanas*). If he carries it further—that is a Np.

Skt. 16. Triyojanaparamaṃ svayaṃ hastavyāny asati hārake... 'Pratigṛhya' not in Sv.

Pāli 16. Triyojanaparamaṃ sahatthā haritabbāni...

Dh. 16. The same.

Mhs. 26. Omits: 'If there is no carrier'; the same case with Msg. Np. 16.

The translation is very incomplete and ambiguous.

Ksy. 16. The same; language differs slightly.

Msg. 16. The language here is much simpler than the Sv. See Mhs. 26 above.

Msv. 16. The same.

Tib. 16. '...while he is on a journey...'

'Three mile' is an incorrect English interpretation of 'three yojana'.

Mpt. 16. Adhvorṇoḍhiḥ.

Sv. IV.17

Whatsoever Bhikṣu gets goat's wool washed, or dyed, or combed by a Bhikṣuṇī who is not related to him—that is a Np.

Skt. 17. Ajñātikāṃ bhikṣuṇīm eḍakalomāni dhavayed vā...

Pāli 17. Aññātikāya bhikkhuniyā eḷakalomāni dhovāpeyya...

Dh. 17, *Mhs.* 27, *Ksy.* 17, *Msg.* 17, *Msv.* and *Tib.* 17. The same.

Mpt. 17. Ūrṇāparikarmaṇaḥ.

Sv. IV.18

Whatsoever Bhikṣu shall receive gold or silver with his own hand, or get someone to receive for him or allow it to be kept as a deposit[37] for him—that is a Np.

Skt. 18. Svahastaṃ rūpyam udgṛhnīyād...'gold' is not here.
Pāli 18. Jātarūparajataṃ ugganheyya...
Skt. 'svahastaṃ...with his own hand' absent here.
Dh. 18. Adds: 'Or money.'
'Or who receives it for him by obeying his intructions'[38] absent.
Mhs. 30. Adds: 'Or money.'
'Or with the intention that he is going to take it'
Ksy. 20. 'If a Bhikṣu receives precious articles—that is a Np.'
Msg. 18. For 'gold and silver' we note here the Chinese translations of the Pāli. Jātarūparajata by 'sheng she shih she —'the growing colour and the resembling colour'.
'Or has an attachment for it.'
Msv. 18. Adds: 'Or money etc.'
Msv. 18, *Tib.* 18. Omits: 'Or allow it to be kept for him.'
Mpt. 18. Jātarūparajata sparśanam.

Sv. IV.19

Whatsoever Bhikṣu shall buy various kinds of articles with gold and silver—that is a Np.[39]

Skt. 19. Nānāprakāraṃ rūpyavyavahāraṃ samāpadyeta...'gold' absent here.

Pāli 19. Nānāprakāraṃ rūpiyasaṃvohāraṃ samāpajjeyya....

Dh. 19. 'Whatsoever Bhikṣu shall engage in various kinds of selling and buying of gold, silver and other precious articles—that is a Np.'

Mhs. 29. '...shall perform different kinds of buying and selling with gold, silver and money...'

Ksy. 19. '...undertakes trade in various precious articles...'

Msg. 20. '...engage in the trade of gold and silver...' See Msg. Np. 18.

Msv. 19. '...different kinds of emptying out and taking in for profit...'

Tib. 19. '...performs the various transaction in silver (coin).'

---

37. Literally it means: 'Or instruct other persons to take it for him.'
38. This sentence is not in the Dhv., ch. 8. It adds: 'Or keep it on the ground' instead.
39. The following texts hardly agree with one another. The proper meaning of the Skt. or the Pāli text is: 'Would engage in various transactions of silver.'

Mpt. 19. Rūpikavyavahāraḥ.

Sv. IV.20

Whatsoever Bhikṣu shall engage in any one of the various kinds of buying and selling—that is a Np.

Skt. 20. '...Nānāprakāraṃ krayavikrayaṃ samāpadyeta...'
Pāli 20. '...Nānāppakārakaṃ kayavikkayaṃ samāpajjeya...'
Dh. 20, *Ksy.* 18, *Msg.* 19, *Msv.* 20, *Tib.* 20. The same.
Mhs. 28. Adds: 'For profit.'
Mpt. 20. Krayavikrayaḥ.

Sv. IV.21

A Bhikṣu may keep a spare bowl up to the limit of ten days. If he exceeds that—that is a Np.

Skt. 21. Atiriktaṃ pātraṃ dhārayitavyam...
Pāli 21. Atirekapatto dhāretabbo...
Dh. 21, *Ksy.* 21. '...an extra bowl (which is considered) a gift of impurity may be kept up to the limit of ten days...'
Mhs. 20, *Msg.* 21, *Msv.* 21, *Tib.* 21.[40] The same.
Mpt. 21. Pātradhāraṇaṃ.

Sv. IV.22

Whatsoever Bhikṣu shall ask for a new bowl when his old one[41] is broken in less than five places for the sake of having something fine—that is a Np.

The bowl of this Bhikṣu must be forfeited by him to the Bhikṣu-saṅgha; and whosoever in that company of Bhikṣus shall have the worst bowl, to him it shall be given and he should be instructed thus: "This, Bhikṣu, is thy bowl, it must be kept until it breaks." This is the right course in this case.

Skt. 22. Pātre ūnapañcabandhane anyaṃ pātraṃ vijñapayet...
Pāli 22. Ūnapañcabandhanena pattena aññaṃ navaṃ pattaṃ

---

40. There is a verse summarising the following ten rules:
'Two rules regarding the bowl, two rules regarding the weaver, gift taken back, the last month of Autumn, being in a solitary residence, the materials for robes, appropriation, and keeping in store.'
This verse is however, preceding to Np. 21 in the Msv. and Tib. versions.
41. Literally it means: The one he has been using.

cetāpeyya...

Skt. 'sati paribhogīye' and 'kalyāṇakāmatāṃ upādāya' are absent here.

Dh. 22. '...the broken bowl, broken in less than five places and not leaking...and the Saṅgha in turn, give him the worst one and command him to keep it till it breaks.'

Here the construction is different.

Mhs. 19, *Ksy.* 22. '...the one he has been using' absent here.

Ksy. 22. Omits: 'and not leaking'.

'O you Bhikṣu without a bowl, you should accept this and keep it well, until it breaks...'

Msg. 22. The same.

The vocative is 'Āyuṣman' not 'Bhikṣu'.

Msv. 22. '...can still be used..."We give you this bowl in return you should not keep it aside, or make any distinction or give it to another person but should use it carefully and reflect upon it till it breaks"...'

Tib. 22. '...and still can be used.'

'It must not be given away or abandoned...'

Here the Msv. and the Tib. versions do not agree.

Mpt. 22. Pātraparīṣṭiḥ.

Sv. IV.23

Whatsoever Bhikṣu shall himself ask for yarn, and have it woven into cloth by employing a weaver not related to him—that is a Np.

Skt. 23. Yācitaṃ sūtraṃ vijñāpya...vāyayet...

Pāli 26. ...Sāmam sūttaṃ viññāpetvā...vayāpeyya...

Skt. 'ajñātinā' and 'yācitaṃ' are not in the Pāli.

Dh. 23, *Ksy.* 23, *Msg.* 26. The same.

Mhs. 11. 'Not related to him' absent here.

Omits: 'employing a weaver'.

Msv. 23. '...gets, by begging, a bundle of wool and sends the same to...into a garment and obtains the garment...'

Mpt. 23. Vāyanaṃ.

Sv. IV.24

In case, a householder, or the wife of a householder, not related to the Bhikṣu, shall have the cloth woven for him by weavers; and if that Bhikṣu, before the offer has been made to him, being desirous of having a good robe, goes to the weaver on a certain pretext, and says to him: "Do you not know that this cloth which you are making is for me? Weave it nicely, make it long and broad. I shall give you some little tip (article)." If that Bhikṣu having himself requested and instructed the weaver or by sending a messenger[42] to him, should later on give him something such as a meal, or an utensil, or even a price equal to that of a meal, for getting the cloth, and if he obtains it—that is a Np.

Skt. 24. Tantravāyena cīvaraṃ vāyayet...

'Not related to him' is absent here as well as in the Mhs. Np. 12, Msg. Np. 27.

The Sv. 'on a certain pretext' may have been translated from 'kañcid eva vikalpam āpadyeta'.

'For having a good robe' is absent here, also we don't find it in Pāli Np. 27, Dh. 24, and Mhs. 12.

Pāli 27. Tantavāyehi cīvaraṃ vāyāpeyya...

The instructions given by the Bhikṣu as to how the cloth should be woven: 'Āyataṃ ca...vitthataṃ ca suvītaṃ ca, suvilekhitaṃ ca, suvitacchitaṃ ca karotha...make it long, broad, thick, well-woven, evenly woven, with evenliness, and well-carded,' are not corresponding to the Skt. and Sv.

We do not have Skt.: 'Piṇḍapātaṃ vā piṇḍapātamātraṃ vā piṇḍapātasaṃvaraṃ vā' here, but only 'antamaso piṇḍapātamattaṃ pi.'

Skt.: 'Cīvarasyābhiniṣpattaye abhiniṣpanne cīvare' is not found here. See Skt. 24, above.

Dh. 24. Pāli 'aññatako' is absent here.

This corresponds to the Pāli very closely including the seven adjectives of how the cloth should be made; but adds: 'If he gets the cloth,' at the end of this rule which is absent in Pāli but present in the Sv. See Skt. 24, above.

Mhs. 12. Omits: 'Or a utensil.' See Skt. 24, above.

Ksy. 24. Or the wife of the householder' absent.

'Went to the weaver's place by keeping in mind (that is so).'

'I shall give you some price of the cloth'.

'Even a meal' only.

Msg. 27. 'I shall give you a price in money or a price in food, and if he obtains the cloth by so requesting...' See Skt. 24, above.

Msv. 24. '... a fancy comes to his mind' for 'on a certain pretext'.

'You should weave it nicely, well-carded, well-selected, very strong and well-beaten.'

Tib. 24. 'If a layman[43] or a laywoman sends for a weaver not

---

42. To give such instruction is not found in all other texts.
43. See So-sor-thar-pa: JASB, 1915, p. 50.

related to them to make a garment for a monk...'

The version here is wrongly interpreted, for there is no question whatsoever as to whether the weaver is related to his employer or not; the question arises if the donor is not related to the Bhikṣu.

'...make it long and broad, thick and well-woven' is not quite the same.

Mpt. 24. Ūyamānavardhanaṃ.

Sv. IV.25

Whatsoever Bhikṣu, when he has given a robe to another Bhikṣu, shall, thereafter, being angry, malicious or displeased with him, take it away or has it taken away, saying 'O Bhikṣu, give me back the robe, it is not given to you'—that is a Np.

This Bhikṣu should let the robe be forfeited to the Bhikṣu-Saṅgha.

Skt. 25. Pātraṃ vā cīvaraṃ vā dattvā...ācchindyat...

The 'bowl' is not in the Sv. and Pāli.

Pāli 25. Sāmam cīvaraṃ datvā...acchindeyya...

We have 'kupito anattamano' instead of Skt. 'ābhiṣaktaḥ kupitaḥ caṇḍikṛtonāptamanāptamanāḥ.'

And Skt.: 'Ānayabhikṣo cīvaraṃ na te bhūyo dadāmīti,' and 'bhikṣuṇā sa vastuśeṣo niḥsṛṣṭavyo bhavati, cāsya' are not here.

See Skt. 25, above.

Dh. 25. The last paragraph of the Sv. is not here and the language differs also.

Mhs. 13. The paragraph of the Sv. is not here.

Ksy. 25 and *Msg.* 24. The words spoken by the Bhikṣu and also the last paragraph are not found here.

Msg. 24. Adds: 'If he gets the robe.'

Msv. 25. '...being angry, scornful and disgusted with...If the robe is taken away from his person and he himself uses it—that is a Np.'

Tib. 25. '...and if the second monk on account of his possessing an extra robe returns the set....'; the later portion does not agree.

Mpt. 25. Dattvādānaṃ.

Sv. IV.26

If a Bhikṣu gets a robe as a gift on a special occasion ten days before the end of the rainy season, he may accept it with his own hand if he needs a robe. And he may keep it till the robe time. Should he keep it beyond that—that is a Np.

Skt. 27. Daśāhānāgatayaṃ pravāraṇāyāṃ[44]...

Ms. is incomplete.

Pāli 28. Dasāhānāgataṃ kattika-temāsi-puṇṇamaṃ[45]..... accekacīvaraṃ uppajjeyya.

Dh. 28, *Ksy.* 26. '...ten days before the end of the third month of the Summer.'

'...with his own hand, if he needs a robe' is not here, also is not in Msg. Np. 28 and Msv. Np. 26.

Mhs. 18. Adds: 'Chien-hou... former and latter to 'ten days before the end of the rainy season.' We may interpret this as 'about'.

Msg. 28. The Msgv. ch. 11. says: 'Ten days before the end of the third month of Summer.' This is different from the text here. See Dh. 28, above.

Msv. 26. '...the three months of the rainy season started sometime ago and ten days before its completion....'

See Dh. 28, above.

Tib. 26. '...the last month of Autumn not yet being complete by ten days.'

Mpt. 26. Kārttikātyayikaṃ.

Sv. IV.27

When the three months of the Summer are over, but the eighth month is not yet complete, due to intercalation, if a Bhikṣu's residence is in the forest and his mind is driven away by doubt, fear and danger, he may, if he desires, leave one or other of his three robes in a hut (inside a village); and if there be any ground he may go away from the boundary of (his residence) and sleep without them up to the sixth night. Should he exceed that limit—that is a Np.

Skt. 28. Bahiḥ[45] sīmāṃ gantuṃ ṣaḍrātraparamaṃ....

Ms. incomplete.

Pāli 29. Tiṇṇam cīvaraṃ...antaragare nikkhipeyya...

The first portion of the Sv. concerning time, does not agree with this text and the language is also slightly different.

Dh. 29. '...for spending the rainy season up to the 15th of the eighth month.'

'Intercalation' is absent here and also in the Mhs. Np. 16.

Mhs. 16. Adds: 'Spending the rainy season.'

---

44. The no. 26 given in 'Concordance du texte Sanskrit avec le Pāli' in JA, 1913 is incorrect. Similarly this applies to no. 27 of the *Skt.* below.

45. This refer to Pavāraṇā, the ceremony at the end of Vassa.

'Put each of the robes in the house of a householder inside the boundary.' Also see Dh. 29, above.

Ksy. 28. The time and month are not mentioned here at all.

Msg. 29. 'During the three months of Summer, when the last month of the three has not yet reached.' The translation here does not express itself very clearly and the sentence: 'If there be any ground' has been misplaced.

Adds: 'Except by Saṅghakarma.'

Msv. 27. Time and month are not mentioned here, but it adds the sentence: 'After the rainy season is over.'

Adds: 'If there are many Bhikṣus.'

'To leave the boundary of the forest-residence' is different. This is also the case with Tib. Np. 27.

Tib. 27. There is no mention of month. See Msv. 27, above.

Adds: 'If the rainy season has been at an end.'

Mpt. 27. Saptarātravipravāsaḥ.

Sv. IV.28

When a month of the Spring season is still left, let the Bhikṣu beg a robe for the rainy[46] season; and when half a month of the Spring season is left, let him use it. If the Bhikṣu begs a robe for the rainy season when more that a month has yet to run, or if he uses it when more than half a month of the Spring season has yet to run—that is a Np.

Skt. 26. Varṣāśāṭicīvaraṃ[47] paryeṣitavyaṃ....

'Grīṣma—hot season' not 'Spring' as in the Sv.

Ms. is incomplete.

Pāli 24. Vassikasāṭikacīvaraṃ pariyesitabbaṃ...

'Māso seso gimhānaṃ' not 'Spring'.

Dh. 27. 'Use and bathe (with the robe).'

Other portions are the same.

Mhs. 17. The same.

Ksy. 27. '...after half a month, he should use it, if he uses it, before that...' The idea here is not completely expressed.

Msg. 25. The construction here is very close to the Pāli version, especially its: 'katvā nivāsetabbaṃ'. But the language of the latter portion is condensed.

Msv. 28. The last sentence here is not quite intelligible, because it

46. It literally means: A robe for bathing in the rainy season.

47. The no. 28 given in the 'Concordance du texte Sanskrit avec le Pāli' in JA, 1913 is incorrect.

says: 'If he still uses it after that half month....'

Tib. 28. 'Hot season', not 'Spring'—other portions are the same.

Mpt. 28. Vārṣāśatyakālaparīṣṭidhāraṇaṃ.

Sv. IV.29

Whatsoever Bhikṣu, knowing that the donor[48] is desirous of dedicating articles to the Saṅgha, shall cause it to be diverted to himself—that is a Np.

Skt. 29. Jānam saṃghikaṃ lābhaṃ pariṇataṃ...

Pāli 30. Jānam saṅghikaṃ lābhaṃ pariṇataṃ...

Dh. 30, *Mhs.* 14. The same.

Ksy. 29, *Msg.* 30, *Msv.* 29. '...knowing other persons offering articles to the Saṅgha...'

Tib. 29. '...knowingly appropriate for his own use a property intended for the community of monks...'

Mpt. 29. Pariṇāmanaṃ.

Sv. IV.30

The Blessed One allowed the sick Bhikṣus to take four kinds of medicines possessing digestive[49] power, to wit, ghee, oil, honey and molasses. The sick Bhikṣu may enjoy them and store them up to the seventh day for use. If he keeps them beyond seven days—that is a Np.

Venerable sirs, the Thirty Niḥsargika Pātayantika Rules have been recited.

Now, I ask the venerable ones, 'Are you pure in this matter?'

A second and a third time I ask the venerable ones, 'Are you pure in this matter?'

The venerable ones are pure herein; therefore do they keep silence. Thus I observe.

Skt. 30. Yāni bhaiṣajyāni anujñātāni...sarpis, tailaṃ, madhuh, phāṇitaṃ...sannidhi...

Pāli 23. Yāni...bhesajjāni...sappi, navanītaṃ, telaṃ, madhu, phāṇitaṃ...sannidhikārakaṃ...

'Navanītaṃ' is not in the Skt. and Sv.

Skt. 'Bhagavatāglānānāṃ bhikṣuṇām...'allowed by the Buddha' is not here.

---

48. This sentence does not quite correspond to the Skt. and Pāli.

49. These words are added to the translation and are not found in the Skt. or other versions.

Dh. 26. 'If a Bhikṣu fell ill, he may use ghee, oil, butter, honey and molassess up to seven days...'

Mhs. 15. Omits: 'Allowed by the Blessed One' and 'may enjoy and store them up.'

Ksy. 30. Adds: 'Butter.'

'By the Buddha' is not here.

Msg. 23. Adds: 'Butter and cream.'

The Msgv. ch. 10, says: 'By mixing or touching the cream, ghee, butter, oil, honey and molasses.' That is somewhat new to other texts.

'Chih' literally 'fat', is here translated by us as 'cream'.

Msv. 30. 'Ghee, oil, honey and sugar (=perhaps also 'molasses').'

'All these may be used freely,' is different.

Tib. 30. 'The medicine prescribed by the Blessed Buddha for the benefit of sick monks are these, viz., butter, oil, honey and sugar....'

Mpt. 30. Saṃnidhikāraḥ.

V. THE NINETY PĀTAYANTIKA DHARMAS

Sv. V.1[50]

O venerable sirs, here are ninety Pātayantika (Pāli: Pācittiya) Rules as known from the Prātimokṣa recited each half-month.

Whatsoever Bhikṣu tells a lie knowingly—that is a Pātayantika.

Skt. 1. Saṃprajānamṛṣavādāt....

Pāli 1. Saṃpajānamusāvāde...

Not 'three robes' here.

Dh. 1, *Mhs.* 1, *Ksy.* 1, *Msg.* 1, *Msv.* 1, *Tib* 1. The same.

Mpt. 1 Mṛṣā.

Sv. V.2.

Whatsoever Bhikṣu speaks in abusive language—that is a Pā.

Skt. 2. ...Apakarṣavādāt...

Pāli 2. Omasavāde...

---

50. Both the Msv. and Tib. have two summaries in verses:
(1) General Summary—'Knowingly, seed, not deputed, again and again, water, house, deliberately, many invitations, robber and entertainment.'
(2) 'Telling a lie, speaking evil, slandering a monk, quarrelling, preaching, reciting, depravity, supernatural power, to make known and destroying the minute ones.'

Dh. 2. 'To insult another Bhikṣu with various kinds of abusive language.'

Mhs. 2. 'Abuse other Bhikṣus.'

Ksy. 3, *Msv.* 2. 'Abusive language.'

Msg. 2. 'To abuse others by calling their caste names.[51]

Tib. 2. 'To speak evil of a man.'

Mpt. 2. Ūnavādaḥ.

Sv. V.3

Whatsoever Bhikṣu slanders[52] another Bhikṣu—that is a Pā.

Skt. 3. Bhikṣupaiśunyāt...

Pāli 3. Bhikkhupesuññe...

Dh. 3, *Ksy*, 2, *Msg.* 3. 'Words of a capricious tongue.'

Mhs. 3. The same.

Msv. 3. 'To speak words that will break a good relationship (between two parties).'

Tib. 3. Language is different.

Mpt. 3. Bhikṣupaiśunyaṃ.

Sv. V.4

Whatsoever Bhikṣu shall stir up for a decision again a matter which he knows to have been settled[53] by the Saṅgha in accordance with the Dharma—that is a Pā.

Skt. 4. Punaḥkarmaṇy utkoṭayet...

Pāli 63. Puna kammāya ukkoṭeyya....

The Skt. 'Saṅghena...' is not here.

Dh. 66, *Mhs.* 5, *Ksy.* 4. The same.

Msg. 4. 'If a Bhikṣu knowing that the Saṅgha has already settled a dispute according to the Dharma and according to the Vinaya, shall stir it up again and say: 'This Karma cannot be counted, it should be done once more.' If it is simply on this account, not otherwise—that is a Pā.

Msv. 4. Adds: 'The harmonious Saṅgha.'

'...the dispute is already settled and disposed of. If he stirs it up

51. The Msgv. ch. 12 says that to ashame a Bhikṣu by calling his former caste or professional names such as: 'You are a Caṇḍālika, a barber, a weaver, a potter or a cobbler.'
52. Literally it means: To make other Bhikṣus quarrel by his double tongue or backbiting.
53. See Mv. IV.16.25.

again in the Karma...' is not quite the same.

Tib. 4. '...revives a quarrel with a peaceful monk knowing that the latter has settled a dispute in accordance with the precepts...'

Omits: 'By the Saṅgha.'

The language is not the same.

Mpt. 4. Khoṭanaṃ.

Sv. V.5

Whatsoever Bhikṣu shall preach the doctrine, in more than five or six words, to a woman—that is a Pā, except when there is an intelligent person (present).

Skt. 5. Mātṛgrāmasya...dharmaṃ deśayed anyatra vijñupuruṣat....

Pāli 7. Mātugāmassa dhammaṃ deseyya aññatra viññunā purisaviggahena....

Dh. 9, *Ksy.* 5, *Msg.* 5, *Msv.* 5, *Tib.* 5. The same.

Mhs. 4. '...except when there is a man who understands what are good words and what are bad...'

Mpt. 7. Ṣaṭpañcikayā vācā dharmadeśanāyāḥ.

Sv. V.6

Whatsoever Bhikṣu shall teach clause by clause the metrical (*chanda*) Gāthā to the persons who have not yet recieved the higher[54] ordination—that is a Pā.

Skt. 6. Padaśo dharmaṃ vācayet...

Pāli 4. Padaso dhammaṃ vāceyya...

Skt: 'Pudgalena sārdham' is not here.

Dh. 6, *Ksy.* 6. '...to recite together with the persons...'

Mhs. 6. '...to teach the sūtra to and recite together with...'

Msg. 6. '...to teach the person...to preach the Padaśo dharma.'

Msv. 6. '...recite jointly and teach the doctrine to...'

Tib. 6. '...recite sermons jointly with one who is not ordained.'

Mpt. 6. Samapadoddeśadānaṃ.

Sv. V.7

Whatsoever Bhikṣu speaks of his own superhuman power e.g. in

54. The Svv. ch. 9 reads: 'If a Bhikṣu teaches the Padaśo dharma to unordained persons,—that is a Pā... Padaśo dharma means the doctrine of the Buddha whether complete or incomplete in sentences, in meaning and in words.'

seeing[55] or knowing, in the presence of a person not yet ordained and say: 'Thus I know and thus I see,' even if it be true—that is a Pā.

Skt. 7. Ārocayed bhūtam.
Ms. is incomplete and it does not give the important portion here.
Pāli 8. Uttarimanussadhammam āroceyya...
Skt.: 'Pudgalasyānike' is not here.
Omits: 'about himself...in the presence of'.
Dh. 8. 'Speaks to...' and 'about himself' absent.
Mhs. 8. The same.
Ksy. 7. Like the Pāli.
Msg. 7. 'Speaks to...' and 'even if he speaks the truth'.
Msv. 8. 'If a Bhikṣu really possessing superhuman powers speaks about it to persons who are not yet Upasampanna—that is a Pā.'
Tib. 8. This more or less resembles the Msv. Pā 8.
Mpt. 7. Uttaramanuṣyadharmārocanaṃ.

Sv. V.8

Whatsoever Bhikṣu knowing the grave offence of another Bhikṣu tells it to a person who has not yet received the higher ordination, except when there is the permission of the Saṅgha—that is a Pā.

Skt. 8. Jānaṃ duṣṭhulam āpattim...ārocayet...
Pāli 8. Duṭṭhullam āpattim...āroceyya...
Skt. 'jānan' absent here.
The words 'aññatra bhikkhusammutiyā' are not translated in the English translation in the SBE, vol. XIII, p. 53.
Dh. 7, *Mhs.* 9, *Ksy.* 8, *Msg.* 8, *Msv.* 7. The same.
Tib. 7. '...about the depravity of another monk...'
Omits: 'Except the Saṅghakarma or the permission of the Saṅgha.'
Mpt. 5. duṣṭhulārocanaṃ.

Sv. V.9

Whatsoever Bhikṣu having previously gladly consented to, says thereafter thus: 'The Bhikṣus have for the sake of friendship, given away the property of the Saṅgha to their own man'—that is a Pā.

Skt. 9. Ime bhikṣavo sāṃghikam lābham pariṇāmayanti...
Pāli 81. Bhikkhu saṃghikam lābham pariṇāmenti...
The first portion here is quite different from that of the Skt.

55. This clause is not found in other texts.

Nothing has been mentioned in the Skt. about the article which the Bhikṣu has consented to give away, but here we find 'cīvaraṃ datvā having given away the robe'. And instead of Skt: 'Pūrvasamanujñako bhūtvā' we have 'Samaggena saṅghena' here.

Dh. 74. '...having together agreed with the (saṅgha) or together performed the Karma...'

Mhs. 80. 'If a Bhikṣu says thus: ......'

Ksy. 9. 'If a Bhikṣu knowing others to be offering articles to the Saṅgha gives them to his own friend—that is a Pā.' It also gives a quite different meaning.

Msg. 9. 'Whatsoever Bhikṣu having at the beginning consented to the distribution of articles that belong to the Saṅgha, says later on thus:...'

Msv. 9. '...the Āyuṣmans give away the benefit of the Saṅgha to others according to their friendship...'

Tib. 9. '... having previously done what was befitting...'

Mpt. 9. Saṃstutiḥ.

Sv. V.10

Whatsoever Bhikṣu, when the Prātimokṣa is being recited, says: "What is the use of reciting each half[56] month the minute little precepts in the Prātimokṣa! On account of reciting them, the mind of the Bhikṣus become regretful, ruinous, upset, heated, sorrowful, unhappy and rebellious against the rules." To speak such disdainful words about the precepts—that is a Pā.

Skt. 10. Kiṃ punar ebhiḥ kṣudrakānukṣudrakaiḥ śikṣāpadair uddiṣṭair...

Ms. is not quite complete.

Pāli 72. Kiṃ panimehi khuddānudhuddakehi sikkhāpadehi uddiṭṭehi...

This corresponds to the Skt.

Dh. 72. This agrees with the Pāli.

Mhs. 10. Omits: 'When the Prātimokṣa is being recited.'

'While the precepts are being recited that make people feel uneasy and vexed.'

Ksy. 10, *Msv.* 10. 'When the Prātimokṣa is being recited at each

56. The translation is greatly enlarged, for we don't find 'each half month...in the Prātimokṣa' and 'on account of reciting them, the mind of the...' in Skt. as well as the adjectives regarding the state of the mind of the Bhikṣus are not so many. We find: 'Kaukṛtyāya. vilekhāya, vihiṃsanāya...' only.

half month, says thus: .....

Adds: 'No other cause than this,' at the end.

Msg. 10. 'When the Prātimokṣa...by the Saṅgha' only.

Msv. 10. The later portion here is very close to the Sv., but the adjectives are not as many as the latter.

Tib. 10. This version here is seriously misinterpreted.

Besides, it is quite different even from the Msv. To have a clear view, we therefore quote the enitre rule below:

> 'Whatever monk, when the So-sor-thar-pa is being recited, says: "O Brethren, what is the good of reciting each half-month the minute little precepts regarding the regrets of monks" (Tib. V.62) etc....(he) thus destroying the minute precepts, commits a sin...'

See JASB, 1915, So-sor-thar-pa, p. 54.

Mpt. 10. Vitaṇḍanaṃ(?)

Sv. V.11

If a Bhikṣu destroys grass and trees—that is a Pā.

Skt. 11. Bījagrāmabhūtagrāmapātanāt...

Pāli 11. Bhūtagāmapātavyatāya...

Dh. 11. 'To destroy the village of ghost and spirit.'

Starting right from here, we find that all the following versions have misunderstood the correct meaning of 'Bhūtagrāma.' They have 'ghost' or 'spirit' for 'bhūta' and 'village' for 'grāma'.

Mhs. 11. 'If a Bhikṣu attacks the village of ghost himself, or causes it to be attacked......'

Msg. 11, *Ksy.* 11. '...destroys seeds and village of the ghost....'

The Skt. 'bījagrāma' is here, represented by 'seeds'.

Msv. 11. 'If a Bhikṣu destroys seeds and a village of living beings himself, or casuses them to be destroyed....'

Tib. 11. 'Destroying[57] or causing to be destroyed an accumulation of seeds and a residence of living beings....'

The Msv. and Tib. have got the meaning most correctly.

Mpt. 11. Bījagrāmabhūtagrāmavināśanaṃ.

Sv. V.12

If a Bhikṣu derides or abuses others—that is a Pā.

---

57. Both the Msv. and the Tib. have a summary of the following 10 ruels in verses: 'Seed, deriding, instruction, couch, mattress, expulsion, encroachment by one coming later, movable, sprinkling and rebuilding.'

Skt. 12. Avadhyānakṣepaṇāt...
Pāli 12. Aññavādake...
Dh. 12. '...to vex others by making a false statement.'
Mhs. 12. Omits: 'to prevaricate to others.'
Ksy. 13. 'Not to accept admonishing.'
Msg. 12. 'To vex others by using improper language.'
Msv. 13. 'To prevaricate to others for disobeying their words.'
Tib. 13. 'Not to listen to precepts.'
Mpt. 13. Ājña(anya?) viheṭhanaṃ.

Sv. V.13

If a Bhikṣu worries other Bhikṣus—that is a Pā.

As the materials are insufficient, we are unable to make the normal comparison here.

Sv. V.14

Whatsoever Bhikṣu who has put out, or got another to put out, in the open, the furniture[58] of the Saṅgha such as a chair, a bedstead, a mat or a carpet for sitting or lying on it. If he does not while going away, put it back or cause it to be put back—that is a Pā.

Skt. 14. Ms. is incomplete. We find at the end the words: 'noddharen noddhārayed vā' which agrees with 'to put or cause to put it back'.

Pāli 14. Saṅghikaṃ mañcaṃ vā...ajjhokāse santharitvā vā santharāpetvā vā....

Omits: 'for sitting or lying on'.

Dh. 14. 'Taking the rope-bedstead, wooden cot, mat or sitting carpet...'

Mhs. 14. 'Articles for sleeping purposes' only.

Adds: 'Without informing others to take it back' and 'if he sees such an article lying in the open and without picking it up...'

This addition seems to mean that if other Bhikṣus saw articles lying in such a condition and if they do not restore them to their original place, to them there will be a Pātayantika offence.

Ksy. 14. 'Putting the articles for sleeping purposes in the open....'

This is much shortened in form.

Msg. 14. 'In the dwelling place of the Saṅgha.'

Msv. 14. 'Spread the covering-articles, bed and seats...and without[59] giving information, if there is a Bhikṣu, except when there are other

58. Literally it reads: 'Articles for the purpose of sleeping down.'

59. This portion is also added to the Msv. 15, below.

causes...'

Tib. 14. 'Takes a couch, chair, stool, blanket, pillow or mat...unless there is a reason to do the same...'

Mpt. 14. Mañcaḥ.

Sv. V.15

Whatsoever Bhikṣu has put or got another to put out a bedstead in the dwelling place of the Bhikṣus for sitting or lying on it, if while going away, he does not put it back or cause it to be put back—that is a Pā.

Skt. 15. Sāṃghike vihāre śayyāṃ saṃstīrya vā saṃstārayed vā...

Pāli 15. Saṅghike vihāre seyyaṃ saṃtharitvā vā saṃtharāpetvā vā....

'Anāpucchaṃ vā' is not in the Skt.

Dh. 15. 'Spreading bed and sitting carpet...'

Mhs. 15. Adds: 'Without informing others to take it up.'

Ksy. 15, *Msv.* 15. 'To spread grass or leaves in the residence of the Saṅgha...' This is quite different. See note 1 on Sv. V.14.

Msg. 15. 'Inside the house of the Saṅgha spreading bed and carpet.'

Tib. 15. 'To spread out a mattress of grass or leaves in a monastery...unless there is a reason to do the same.

Mpt. 15. Saṃstraḥ.

Sv. V.16

Whatsoever Bhikṣu, being angry or displeased with another Bhikṣu shall drive him out or cause him to be driven out of the residence of the Bhikṣus and shall say to him thus: 'You[60] get out, go away beyond sight, and you should not stay here.' If there is no other cause than this—that is a Pā.

Skt. 16. Vihārād bhikṣuṃ niṣkarṣen niṣkaraṣayed vā cara pareṇa...

Pāli 17. Bhikkhuṃ saṅghikā vihārā nikaḍḍheyya vā nikaḍḍhāpeyya vā...

Skt.: 'Mohapuruṣa naśya tvaṃ na tvayeha vastavyaṃ' is not here.

Dh. 17. Omits the 'address' portion.

Mhs. 16. The same.

Ksy. 16. 'If a Bhikṣu being previously angry and vexed pulls out another (Bhikṣu) out of the room—that is a Pā.'

Msg. 16. 'Even say: "You get out." only.'

---

60. Skt. 'Mohapuruṣa' is absent here.

Msv. 19, *Tib.* 16. Omits the address portion.

Mpt. 16. Niṣkarṣaṇam.

Sv. IV.17

Whatsoever Bhikṣu, in a dwelling place of the Bhikṣus, knowing the other Bhikṣu have already spread their beds, shall spread his bedding or cause it to be spread there by force and think thus: "Those who don't like it, they may go away'. If there is no other cause than this—that is a Np.

Skt. 17. Paścād āgatyānupraskandya śayyāṃ kalpayed...

'Cause others to spread.'

Pāli 16. Jānaṃ pubbūpagataṃ bhikkhuṃ anupakhajja seyyaṃ kappeyya...

Skt. 'paścād āgatya' is not here.

Dh. 16, *Ksy.* 16. "If he dislikes the narrow space, he should go away in order to avoid me."

Language is lightly different.

Mhs. 17, *Ksy.* 16. Omits: 'In the dwelling place of the Bhikṣus.'

Msg. 17. '...coming after others, shall spread his bedding to disturb them with the intention to make them go away.'

Msv. 17. '...purposely makes vexation by sitting or lying on those beds (of other Bhikṣus).'

"If they find it intolerable, they should avoid me by quitting" not quite the same.

Tib. 17. '...comes after another monk into a monastery belonging to a community of monks, lies down or sits down knowingly encroaching upon the space occupied by the monk who arrived before him and thinks that he will go away if he is inconvenienced...'

Mpt. 17. Anupraskandyapātaḥ.

Sv. V.18

Whatsoever Bhikṣu shall forcefully sit down or lie down in the upper story of a dwelling place of the Bhikṣus, on a bedstead or chair with sharp-pointed legs—that is a Pā.

Skt. 18. '...Uparivehāyasikūṭikāyām āhāryapādake pīṭhe vā mañce vā balena niṣīded vā nipadyed vā...'

Pāli 18. ...Uparivehāsakuṭiyā āhaccapādakaṃ mañcaṃ vā pīṭhaṃ vā abhinisīdeyya vā abhinipajjeyya vā...

Dh. 18, *Ksy.* 18, *Msg.* 18. Omits: 'forcefully'.

Dh. 18, *Ksy.* 18. 'The leg of a rope-bed is broken.'

Mhs. 18. The same.

Ksy. 18. Adds: 'Without the support of the hand.'

Msv. 18. '... to sit down on a bed and other articles with broken legs without restraint...'

Tib. 18. '...lies down or sits down with his whole weight on a couch or stool, the legs of which are known to be movable...'

Mpt. 18. Āhāryapādakārohī.

Sv. V.19

Whatsoever Bhikṣu knowing there are creatures in the water shall sprinkle it on grass or on clay or shall cause others to do the same—that is a Pā.

Skt. 19. Saprāṇakenodakena siñcet secayed vā...

Pāli 19. Sappāṇakaṃ udakṃ siñceyya siñcāpeyya vā...

Dh. 19, *Ksy.* 19, *Msg.* 19. The same.

Mhs. 20. Adds: 'Or use it for drinking or cooking purposes.'

Msv. 19. Adds: 'Or mix it up with cow-dung.'

Tib. 19. '...on grass, dung or dust...' This is not quite the same.

Mpt. 19. Saprāṇikopabhogaḥ.

Sv. V.20

Whatsoever Bhikṣu, being desirous of constructing a big house may build it from the border of the ground of doors and windows gradually upwards two or three times in order to make it strong.[61] If he builds beyond these limits—that is a Pā.

Skt. 20. Mahallakaṃ vihāraṃ kārayatā...

Ms. is not complete.

Pāli 20. Mahallakaṃ vihāraṃ kārayamānena...

The following words: 'Yāva dvārakosā aggalaṭṭhapanāya āloka sandhiparikammāya...' correspond to Skt. 'Yāvad dvārakośārgaḍas-thāpana ālokasaṃtabhūmi...'

For clarification of different readings, we reproduce the Eng. translation here:

'In case a Bhikkhu is having a large dwelling-place put up, he may have the work rectified, in a place where straw is scarce, round the

61. This differs from the Svv. and it does not express itself very clearly. The Svv. ch. 11, reads: 'If a Bhikṣu being desirous of building a big house, he should build walls, erect pillars, have doors, windows, prepare the ground and cover it with (materials) three times...'

doors, and where the bolts are put in, and the openings for light are set, and till the roof has been twice or thrice covered in. Should he go beyond that, even in such a place that is a Pācittiya.'

See SBE, vol. XIII, p. 35.

Dh. 20. '...should have doors, windows and other decorations, and should instruct someone to cover the roof with straw twice or thrice. If he does beyond that limit...'

Mhs. 19. '...should build it from the ground and leave a space for doors and windows. He should make it strong and cover the roof twice or thrice.'

Ksy. 20. '...he should supervise himself the covering of the roof twice or thrice up to the window. If it goes beyond that...'

Msg. 20 '...having put the doors and windows, cover it twice or thrice and should stay in a place where straw is scarce, if, he goes beyond the limit...'

Msv. 20. '...between the wooden boards of a door should put a bolt as well as to the windows. He should make arrangement of drainage. If the wall is built with wet mud, it should be two or three layers up to the roof. If he does beyond the limit...'

Tib. 20. '...after examining the door frame, bolts and windows for the supply of light etc., may build with brick and mud twice or three times...'

Mpt. 20. Dvau vā trayo vā chadanaparyāya dātavyaḥ.

The present rule, as we have seen is so variously expressed that there seems hardly anything in common in all the texts, each has its own peculiarities.

Sv. V.21

Whatsoever Bhikṣu, not thereto deputed by the Saṅgha, shall give admonition to the Bhikṣuṇīs—that is a Pā.

Skt. 21. Asaṃmataḥ saṃghena bhikṣuṇīr avavādet...

Pāli 21. Asaṃmato bhikkhuniyo ovadeyya...

Dh. 21, *Mhs.* 21, *Ksy.* 21, *Msg.* 21. The same.

Msv. 21. Adds: 'Except when he has attained the Conquering Dharma.'[62]

Tib. 21.[63] Adds: 'Unless he possesses virtues befitting such

62. The Svs. ch. 10 says: 'One who has obtained the Arhatship.'

63. In both the Msv. and Tib. versions, there is a summary in verse of the following ten rules: 'Not deputed, the sun having set, rice, robe given, robe made up, by appointment, boat, sitting in a solitary place, standing in a solitary place and procured by a nun.'

deputation.'

Mpt. 21. Asaṃmatāvavādaḥ.

Sv. V.22

If a Bhikṣu even when thereto deputed by the Saṅgha to give admonition to the Bhikṣuṇīs after the sun has set—that is a Pā.

Skt. 22. Astaṃgamanakālasamayād bhikṣuṇīr avavādet...
Pāli 22. Atthaṃagate suriye bhikkhuniyo ovadeyya...
Dh. 22, *Mhs.* 22, *Ksy.* 22, *Msv.* 22, *Tib.* 22. The same.
Msg. 22. Adds: 'From sunset to early dawn.'
Mpt. 22. Astaṃitāvavādaḥ.

Sv. V.23

If a Bhikṣu speaks thus: 'The Bhikṣus exhort the Bhikṣuṇīs for the sake of gain'—that is a Pā.

Skt. 23. Āmiṣahetor bhikṣavo bhikṣuṇīr avavādanti...
Pāli 24. Āmisahetu bhikkhū bhikkhuniyo ovadanti...
Dh. 23. '... speak to the Bhikṣu thus:...' "For food."
Mhs. 24. The same.
Ksy. 24. 'For maintenance.'
Msg. 24. 'If a Bhikṣu speaks to another Bhikṣu: "O sir, for the sake of food, you are teaching the Bhikṣuṇīs"...'
Msv. 23. '...speak to the Bhikṣu thus: ...'
'For food and offerings'.
Tib. 23. 'For a morsel of rice.'
Mpt. 23. Āmiṣakiñcitkāvavādaḥ.

Sv. V.24

Whosoever Bhikṣu shall travel by appointment on a road in the company of a Bhikṣunī, even to go as far as the village, except on the right occasion—that is a Pā.

Herein this is the right occasion: If the road on which many people are travelling or is reported to be exposed to fear and danger.

Skt. 24. Bhikṣṇyā sārdhaṃ saṃvidhāya samāno mārgaṃ pratipadyeta...

Pāli 27. Bhikkhuniyā saddhiṃ saṃvidhāya ekaddhāna maggaṃ paṭipajjeyya...

For the right occasion, the Eng. translation has given: "When the road is so insecure and dangerous that travellers on it have to carry arms."

Dh. 27, *Ksy.* 27. The same.

Mhs. 28. '...from this village to another village...'

Msg. 26. '...except there is fear and danger and being accompanied by merchants.'

Msv. 26. 'If a Bhikṣu and a bhikṣuṇī make an appointment to travel with merchants...'

Tib. 26. '...when the road on which they travel is reported to be exposed to fear and danger.'

Mpt. 26. Bhikṣuṇīsārthena saha gamanaṃ.

Sv. V.25

Whatsoever Bhikṣu shall go on board the same boat, whether going up stream or down stream, by appointment, with a Bhikṣuṇī except for the purpose of crossing over to the other side—that is a Pā.

Skt. 25. Bhikṣuṇyā sārdhaṃ saṃvidhāya samānanāvaṃ adhiruhed urdhvagāminīṃ vādhogāminīṃ....

Pāli 28. Bhikkhuniyā saddhiṃ saṃvidhāya ekaṃ nāvaṃ...

Dh. 28, *Mhs.* 29, *Ksy.* 28, *Msg.* 27, *Tib.* 27. The same.

Msv. 27. '...whether going against the waves or following the stream (Yuan-po, shu-liu).'

Mpt. 27. Sabhikṣuṇī-jalayānodhiḥ.

Sv. V.26

Whatsoever Bhikṣu shall give a robe to a Bhikṣuṇī who is not related to him—that is a Pā.

Skt. 26. Ajñātyā bhikṣuṇyāś cīvaraṃ dadyāt...

Pāli 25. Aññātikāya bhikkhuniyā cīvaraṃ dadeyya...

The words: 'aññatra parivaṭṭakā—except for exchange' are not in the Skt.

Dh. 24, *Mhs.* 26, *Msg.* 28, *Msv.* 24. Adds: 'except for exchange'.

Tib. 24, *Ksy.* 52. The same.

Mpt. 24. Cīvaradānaṃ.

Sv. V.27

Whatsoever Bhikṣu shall make a robe for a Bhikṣuṇī who is not related to him—that is a Pā.

Skt. 27. Ajñātyā bhikṣuṇyāś cīvaraṃ kuryāt...

Pāli 26. Aññātikāya bhikkhuniyā cīvaraṃ sibbeyya vā sibbāpeyya vā...

'Sibbāpeyya vā...or cause it to be stitched up' is not in Skt.

Dh. 25, *Mhs.* 27, *Ksy.* 26, *Msg.* 29, *Msv.* 25. The same.

Tib. 25. Adds: 'Or cause it to be made.'

Mpt. 25. Cīvaraṃkāraṇaṃ.

Sv. V.28

Whatsoever Bhikṣu shall alone take a seat with a Bhikṣuṇī in a covered solitary place—that is a Pā.

Skt. 28. Ekāki rahasi praticchanne āsane niṣadyāṃ kalpayet...

Pāli 30. Eko ekāya raho nisajjaṃ kappeyya...

The Eng. translation has 'one man with one woman' for 'Eko ekāya'. It would be better if we use 'alone or secretly'.

Dh. 26. The same.

Mhs. 25. Adds: 'With a śaikṣamāṇā or a śrāmaṇerī.'

Ksy. Nil.

Msg. 25. '...in a solitary place.'

Msv. 29. The same.

Tib. 28. '...on a mat in a covered solitary place.'

Mpt. 29. Rahasi sthānaṃ.

Sv. V.29

Whatsoever Bhikṣu shall alone take a seat with a woman in the open[64]—that is a Pā.

Skt. 29. Ekāki mātṛgrameṇa sārdhaṃ abhyavakāśe niṣadyām kalpayet...

Pāli 45. ...mātugāmena saddhiṃ eko ekāya nisajjaṃ kappeyya...

Dh. 45, *Mhs.* 44. The same.

Ksy, Msg, Msv. Nil.

Tib. 29. '...stands together with a nun in a covered solitary place...'

Mpt. Nil.

Sv. V.30

Whatsoever Bhikṣu shall knowingly eat food procured by the intervention of a Bhikṣuṇī, unless the laity has already undertaken (to give it to him)—that is a Pā.

Skt. 30. Bhikṣuṇīparipācitaṃ piṇḍapātaṃ paribhuṃjīta...

64. 'In the open' is not in the Pāli.

Pāli 29. ...Bhikkhunīparipācitaṃ piṇḍapātaṃ bhuñjeyya...

Dh. 29, *Mhs.* 30, *Ksy.* 30, *Msv.* 30. '...except when the householder or donor has such intentions'...

Msg. 30. 'Except the old donor.'

Tib. 30. '...in a house where he was not officially invited...'

Mpt. 30. Bhikṣuṇī paripācita piṇḍapātopabhogaḥ.

Sv. V.31

Whatsoever Bhikṣu takes food many a time, except on the right occasion—that is a Pā.

Herein this is the right occasion: When there is sickness and when robes are being given. This is called the right occasion.

Skt. 31. Paraṃparabhojanaṃ...

Pāli 33. Paraṃparabhojane...

'Cīvarakārasamayo' is not in the Skt. and Sv.

Dh. 32, *Mhs.* 31. The same.

Ksy. 31. Agrees with the Pāli.

Msg. 32. '...except at the time of sickness and at the robe time.'

Msv.[65] 31, *Tib.* 31. Adds: 'at the time of working and of travelling'.

Mpt. 31. Paraṃparabhojanaṃ.

Sv. V.32

A Bhikṣu who is not sick should take one meal only at a place where he can get one meal free. If he eats more than one—that is a Pā.

Skt. 32. Ekāvasthoṣitena bhikṣuṇā aglānenaikaṃ...

Ms. is incomplete.

Pāli 31. Eko āvasathapiṇḍo bhuṃjitabbo...

Dh. 31, *Mhs.* 33, *Ksy.* 32, *Msg.* 31. The same.

Msv. 32. 'A Bhikṣu, in the residence of the Tīrthika (or heretics) may spend one night and eat one meal. If he does beyond that limit, unless there is a cause, such as illness—that is a Pā.'

Tib. 32. '...who has arrived fresh and who is not sick, may accept one meal at a boarding house....'

Mpt. 32. Ekāvasathāvāsaḥ.

65. Both the texts have a summary in verse of the following ten rules: 'To go again and again, a boarding house, flour, food, offering, right time, wrong time, storing up, passage of the mouth and delicacies.'

Sv. V.33

In case Bhikṣus arrive at the house of a householder who offers them cake or flour as much as they like, if the Bhikṣus need it, they may accept two or three full bowls. If they should accept more than that—that is a Pā.

When they have accepted two or three full bowls, they should come out and share with other good Bhikṣus. This is the right course here.

Skt. 33. Dvau trīm vā pātrapūrām...

Ms. is incomplete.

Pāli 34. Pūvehi vā manthehi vā... dvittipattapūrā patiggahetabbā...

The 'Bhikṣu' here who goes to the house of a householder is in the singular number.

Dh. 34. Adds: 'rice', 'taking to the monastery' and 'if the Bhikṣu is not sick.'

The last sentence of the Sv. is omitted here.

Mhs. 34. Adds: 'If he does not eat it at the house of the layman.' 'If he is not sick...and does not share it with other Bhikṣus.'

Ksy. 33. Adds: 'The householder who is a true believer of the Dharma.'

'Taking to the residence and eat with the Saṅgha.'

Msg. 38. '...take it outside and eat with the Bhikṣus who are not sick. If he accepts beyond the limit and does not eat with others...'

Msv. 33, *Tib.* 33. '...there are Brāhmaṇas or householders of pure faith who hospitably offer them flour, cakes and rice...return to the residence and share with other Bhikṣus if any...'

Mpt. 33. Dvitripātrapūrātiriktagrahaṇam.

Sv. V.34

If a Bhikṣu once has finished his meal and eats again without observing the ceremony[66] (practice) of leavings of food—that is a Pā.

66. Svv. ch. 13 says: 'If a Bhikṣu having once finished his meal and got up from his seat eats rice etc., without observing the ceremony of leavings of food—that is a Pā.'

About the 'ceremony,' it explains thus in the same chapter: 'The person who wishes to observe this ceremony should put all the eatables in his bowl that he may consume. Knowing the Bhikṣu next to him who is still eating he should kneel down before him with one shoulder uncovered and should take the bowl in hand saying: "Please perform the ceremony of leavings of food for me". If that Bhikṣu does not take smoething from this food of his, then it cannot be said that he has performed the ceremony of leavings of food.'

Skt. 34. Bhuktavān pravāritaḥ akṛtaniriktaṃ...
To eat or drink the 'khādanīyabhojanīyam' is not in the Sv.
Pāli 35. Bhuttāvī pavārito anitirittaṃ...
Same as the Skt.
Dh. 35. Adds: 'When he is still being invited.'
Mhs. 35. The same.
Ksy. 34. Omits: 'To observe the ceremony of leaving over the food.'
Msg. 33. Adds: 'When he has risen up from his seat.'
Msv. 34. The same.
Tib. 34. '...takes again, being invited, food or drink, except that which has been left over...'
Mpt. 34. Akṛtanirikta khādanaṃ.

Sv. V.35

Whatsoever Bhikṣu knowing that a certain Bhikṣu has finished his meal and has not performed the ceremony of leaving over the food, shall persistingly invite and offer him eatables and drinkable as much as he likes and say: 'O Bhikṣu, you eat!' with the intention of annoying him. If he acuses this Bhikṣu to be annoyed and for no other cause than this, even for a moment—that is a Pā.

Skt. 35. Jānam bhikṣuṃ bhuktavantaṃ pravāritaṃ akṛtani rikte....
'Āyuṣmaṃ' for 'Bhikṣu' in the Sv.
Pāli 36. Bhikkhuṃ bhuttāviṃ pavāritaṃ anatirittena....
'Jānaṃ āsādanāpekkho' is very brief for Skt. '...āsādanaprekṣī kacci eṣa bhikṣur muhūrtam apy āsāditaḥ syād evam eva pratyayaṃ kṛtvā...'
Dh. 36, *Mhs.* 36. '...with the intention of making him commit an offence.' It is much shorter and the language is also different.
Ksy. 35. '...knowing another Bhikṣu has finished his meal, if he offers him more to eat—that is a Pā'. It is quite simple here.
Msg. 34. Adds: 'Rose up from his seat.'
Omits: 'If he causes...for a moment.'
Msv. 35. '...on this account, if he is caused to commit an offence or to be vexed and anxious—that is a Pā.'
Tib. 35. 'with the intention of making him fall into a moral error' is not quite the same.
Omits: 'If he causes—a moment.'
Mpt. 35. Akṛtaniriktaparavāraṇaṃ.

Sv. V.36

There is a Pātayantika in going in a body to receive a meal, except on the right occasions.

Herein the right occasion is this: When there is sickness, when robes are being made, when on a journey, when on board a boat, when there is a great assembly and when invited by the Tirthika Śrāmaṇas. This is the right occassion here to have a meal.

Skt. 36. Gaṇabhojanaṃ anyatra samayāt...

Pāli 32. Gaṇabhojane aññatra samayā...

Adds: 'Cīvaradānasamayo.'

Dh. 33, *Ksy.* 36, *Msg.* 40. These texts entirely agree with the Pāli.

Mhs. 32. Adds: 'At the robe time, when the robes are being given.' 'When the Śrāmaṇas meet.'

Msv. 36, *Tib.* 86. Omits: 'When robes are being made.'

Adds: 'When there is some work.'

The last occasion in the Tib. 'When there is a general invitation to monks' is not corresponding.

Mpt. 36. Gaṇabhojanaṃ.

Sv. V.37

Whatsoever Bhikṣu shall eat food[67] at the wrong time—that is a Pā.

Skt. 37. Akālakhādaniyabhojanīyaṃ khāded vā bhuṃjita vā.

Pāli 37. Vikāle khādanīyaṃ vā bhojanīyaṃ vā khādeyya vā bhuṃjeyya vā...

Dh. 37, *Mhs.* 38, *Msv.* 37, *Msg.* 36. The same.

Ksy. 37. 'To eat eatables at the wrong time.'

Tib. 37. 'Takes food or drink at a wrong time.'

Mpt. 37. Akālabhojanaṃ.

Sv. V.38

Whatsoever Bhikṣu shall eat food[68] that has been left over or stored up—that is a Pā.

Skt. 38. Saṃnihitavarjanaṃ khādanīyabhojaniyāṃ...

Pāli 38. Saṃnidhikārakaṃ khādanīyaṃ vā bhojanīyaṃ vā.

Dh. 38, *Mhs.* 39, *Ksy.* 38. The same.

Msg. 37. 'To eat food that has been stopped.'

Msv. 38. 'To eat food that has been touched or eaten.'

---

67. Here omits the words 'hard or soft' of the Skt., so also it is the same case in the Sv. 38 below.

68. This item, we find nowhere else except in the Tib.

Tib. 38. 'Eats food, hard or soft, that has been stored up.'
Mpt. 38. Saṃnihitavarjanaṃ.

Sv. V.39

Whatsoever Bhikṣu shall place, as food, in his mouth, anything not given to him, save only water and tooth-stick (of willow tree)—that is a Pā.

Skt. 39. Adhinnam āhāram mukhadvāreṇāhāred...
Pāli 40. Adinnaṃ mukhadvāram āhāram āhāreyya...
Dh. 39. Adds: 'Such as medicine.'
Mhs. 37. 'Except tasting water and the willow stick.'
Ksy. 39. *Tib.* 39. The same.
Msg. 35. Omits: 'As food.'
Msv. 39. Adds: 'Eat or chew.'
Mpt. 39. Apratigrāhitabhuktiḥ.

Sv. V.40

Whatsoever Bhikṣu, when he is not sick, shall ask for his own use such excellent delicacies—to wit: milk, curd, butter, ghee, oil, fish, meat and dried[69] meat of householders—that is a Pā.

Skt. 40. Praṇītabhojanāni: Kṣīraṃ navanītaṃ sarpis tailaṃ matsyo māṅsavallūro...

Six articles only. Ms. is incomplete.

Pāli 39. Paṇītabhojanāni...: navanītaṃ, telaṃ, madhu, phāṇitaṃ, maccho, maṃsaṃ, khīraṃ, dadhi, sappi.

Nine articles in all.

Language differs slightly.

Dh. 40. 'Milk, curd, fish and meat' four articles only.

A bad translation here.

Mhs. 41. 'Ghee' is omitted here. Six articles only.

Ksy. 40. '...get good food such as: 'Ghee, oil, honey, molasses, milk, curd, butter, fish, or meat.'

Nine articles.

Msg. 39. 'Ghee, oil, honey, molasses, milk, curd, fish and meat.'

Eight articles.

---

69. In both the Msv. and Tib. there is a summary in verse of the following ten rules: 'With living things, to sit in a place of sleeping, standing, a naked ascetic, army, two days, to go to the battle array, beating, threatening and depravity.'

Msv. 40. 'The excellent eatables spoken by the World-honoured one such as: Milk, curd, butter, fish, and meat...'

Five articles only.

Tib. 40. 'The Blessed Buddha prescribed the following delicacies for monks: Milk, curd, butter, fish, flesh and dried flesh...'

Six articles.

Mpt. 40. Praṇītavijñāpanaṃ.

Sv. V.41

Whatsoever Bhikṣu shall knowingly drink (or use) water with living beings in it—that is a Pā.

Skt. 41. Jānan saprāṇakam udakaṃ paribhuṃjīta...

Pāli 62. Jānaṃ sappāṇakam udakaṃ paribhuñjeyya...

Dh. 62, *Ksy.* 41, *Msg.* 51, *Msv.* 41,[70] *Tib.* 41. The same.

Mhs. 20. (Repeated or combined) see the 19th of the Sv. V.

Mpt. 41. Saprāṇijalopabhogaḥ.

Sv. V.42

Whatsoever Bhikṣu shall sit in the sleeping place of a house where a meal is going on—that is a Pā.

Skt. 42. Sabhojane kule anupraskandya āsanaṃ katpayet...

Pāli 43. Sabhojane kule anupakhajja nisajjaṃ kappeyya...

'By force' (Skt. anupraskandya= Pāli: anupakkajja) is missing in Sv.

Dh. 43. '...to sit in a place by force where valuable articles are kept in the house in which a meal is going on...'

Mhs. Nil.

Ksy. 43. '...to sit in a house by force where a meal is going on...'

Msg. 54. '...to sit in a covered place where he knows people of the family are eating....'

Msv. 42. '...to arrange his seat by force where he knows people of the family are eating...'

Tib. 42. '...knowing that a man and a woman are sleeping together in a house, goes there and sits on a couch...'

Mpt. 42. Sabhojanakulaniṣadyā.

---

70. Comparing both 42 and 43 of the Sv., we find there are great differences in all other texts.

Sv. V.43

Whatsoever Bhikṣu shall sit with a woman alone in a sleeping place of a house where a meal is going on—that is a Pā.

Skt. 43. Sabhojane kule ekākī ekayā rahasi praticchanne...

Pāli 44. Mātugāmena saddhiṃ raho paṭicchanne āsane nisajjaṃ kappeyya.

Skt. 'sabhojane' is omitted here.

Dh. 44. '...to sit in a covered place where valuable articles are kept in the house in which a meal is going on....'

Mhs. 42. Omits: 'Alone in a sleeping place.'

Msg. 70. Omits: 'In the house where a meal is going on.'

Ksy, Msv, Tib, Mpt. Nil.

Sv. V.44

Whatsoever Bhikṣu shall, with his own hand, give food to an Acelaka (naked ascetic) or to a Parivrājaka or to a Parivrājikā—that is a Pā.

Skt. 44. Acelakasya vā...svahastāt khādanīyabhojanīyaṃ dadyāt...

Pāli 41. Acelakassa vā paribbājakassa vā paribbājikāya vā sahatthā khādanīyaṃ bhojanīyaṃ vā dadeyya...

Dh. 41. Omits: 'Acelaka'.

Mhs. 40. '...give food to the naked ascetics either male or female...' Two objects of the gift instead of three of the Sv.

Ksy. 44. 'Give food to the heretics and Parivarājakas.' There is no distinction of gender.

Msg. 52, *Msv.* 44, *Tib.* 44. The same; slightly different in language.

Mpt. 44. Aceladānaṃ.

Sv. V.45

Whatsoever Bhikṣu shall go to see an army drawn up in battle-array,[71] except for a cause thereto sufficient—that is a Pā.

Skt. 45. Udyuktāṃ senāṃ darśanāyo....

Pāli 48. Uyyuttaṃ senaṃ dassanāya gaccheyya....

Dh. 48, *Mhs.* 45, *Ksy.* 45, *Msg.* 55. The same.

Msv. 45. '...to see an army in full equipment....'

Tib. 45, *Msv.* 45. Omits: 'Except when there is a sufficient cause.'

Mpt. 45. Senādarśanaṃ.

71. Literally it means: 'marching army'.

Sv. V.46

If there arises any occasion for a Bhikṣu's going to the army, he may remain there up to two nights. If he remains beyond that limit—that is a Pā.

Skt. 46. Yenodyuktāṃ senāṃ... (Ms. is incomplete)...tena bhikṣuṇā tatra senāyāṃ vasitavyaṃ...

The portion regarding the number of nights is missing in the Ms.

Pāli 49. Senāṃ gamanāya, dirattatirattaṃ tena bhikkhunā senāyaṃ vasitabbaṃ....

Two or three nights.

Dh. 49, *Ksy.* 46. '...if he remains there beyond two to three nights...'

Mhs. 46. '...up to two or three nights...'

Msg. 56. '...up to three nights...'

Msv. 46. The same.

Tib. 46. '...he may remain there for two days...'

Mpt. 46. Senāvāsaḥ.

Sv. V.47

If the Bhikṣu while remaining in the army up to two nights, sees the march of the army, the hoisting of the general-in-chief's flag, the drawing up of the battle-array and the conflict of the forces—that is a Pā.

Skt. 47. Udyūthikām senāṃ darśanāya...(Ms. missing)...mad dhvajāgran vā balāgran vā anīkadarśanaṃ vā....

Pāli: 'senābyūhaṃ' is not here.

Pāli 50. Uyyodhikaṃ vā balaggaṃ vā senābyūhaṃ vā anīkadassanaṃ gaccheyya...

Skt.: 'dhvajāgran' is not here.

Dh. 50. '...occasionally sees the battle-array, the fighting or sees the drawing up of the forces of infantry, elephants and cavalry...' This differs from the Pāli.

Mhs. 47. 'Sees battle-array and fighting' only.

Ksy. 47. '...sees with delight the army marching, other forces, flags and various reviews...'

Msg. 57. '...sees the march of the army, battle-array, flags and fighting...'

Msv. 47. '...sees the army in full equipment, the first flag (of the four flags),[72] the soldiers, the battle-array and other forces...'

---

72. Svs. ch. 11, says that the four flags are: 1. lion, 2. great bull, 3. crocodile and 4. the golden-winged bird. The last one is stated to be 'Nāga' in Tib. sources.

Tib. 47. '...should go to the battle-array, or should relish in mind the sight of the excellent flag, the excellent troops or the review....'

Mpt. 47. Udyūthikāgamanaṃ.

Sv. V.48

Whatsoever Bhikṣu being angry, malicious and displeased with another Bhikṣu shall beat him with the hand—that is a Pā.

Skt. 48. Ābhiṣaktaḥ kupitaś caṇḍīkṛto...bhikṣoḥ prahāraṃ dadyāt....

Pali 74. Bhikkhussa kupito anattamano pahāraṃ dadeyya...

Dh. 78. Same as the Pāli.

Mhs. 71. '...being angry beats another Bhikṣu.'

Ksy. 48, *Tib.* 48. Omits: 'Displesed with.'

Msg. 58, *Msv.* 48. The same.

Mpt. 48. Prahāradānaṃ.

Sv. V.49

Whatsoever Bhikṣu being angry, malicious and displeased with another Bhikṣu shall threaten him with his hand—that is a Pā.

Skt. 49. Ms. is missing completely.

Pāli 75. Bhikkhussa kupito anattamano talasattikam uggireyya...

Dh. 79. The same.

Mhs. 72, *Ksy.* 49, *Msv.* 49. '...makes a threatening gesture with the hand...'

Ksg 49. Omits: 'Displeased with.'

Msg. 59. '...makes a killing gesture with the palm...'

Tib. 49. '...threatens him even with his fist.'

Mpt. 49. Udgūraṇaṃ.

Sv. V.50

Whatsoever Bhikṣu knowing another Bhikṣu's gross offence conceals it even for one night—that is a Pā.

Skt. 50. Bhikṣor jānan duṣṭhulāṃ āpattiṃ praticchādayet...

Pāli 64. Bhikkhussa jānaṃ duṭṭhullaṃ āpattiṃ paṭicchādeyya...

Dh. 64, *Pāli* 64, *Ksy.* 50, *Msv.* 50, *Msg.* 60. Omits: 'Even for one night.'

Mhs. 74. The same.

Tib. 50. '...knowingly conceals the depravity of another monk...'

Mpt. 50. Duṣṭhulapraticchādanaṃ.

Sv. V.51

If a Bhikṣu speaks to another Bhikṣu thus: 'O venerable sir, come to the families, I shall make them give you abundant excellent eatables and drinkables'; and if the Bhikṣu without causing food to be given to another Bhikṣu, says to him thus: 'Go away! Talking with you, or sitting with you, is not pleasant to me. Talking, or sitting each one by himself, is more pleasant to me,'...doing so purposely with the intention of vexing him. And if that Bhikṣu is being troubled even for a moment, with no other reason than this—that is a Pā.

Skt. 51. 'Gaccha tvam āyuṣman na me tvayā sārdhaṃ phāṣakaṃ...'

Pāli 42. 'Gacchā' vuso na me tayā saddhiṃ kathā vā nisajjā vā phāsu hoti...'

'Gāmaṃ vā nigamaṃ vā' is not found in the Sv.

'Doing so purposely...for a moment' is not here, also is not in Dh. 46, Mhs. 76, Ksy. 52, Msg. 44, Tib. 51—Pā.

Dh. 46. '...together to go to a village.'

Adds: 'Sends him away.' See Pāli 42 above.

Msv.[73] 51. 'If that Bhikṣu is being troubled even for a moment' is not found here.

Tib. 51. '...seeking a brawl should say on that account to another monk': 'O brother, come here, let us go to the village to beg food, drink and what else is agreeable...'

See Pāli 42 above.

Mpt. 51. Bhaktacchedakāraṇaṃ.

Sv. V.52

Whatsoever Bhikṣu, who is not sick, shall, desiring to warm himself, kindle a fire out of grass, or wood, or cow-dung or rubbish personally or cause it to be kindled[74] in the open—that is a Pā.

Skt. 52. Aglāno vitapanaprekṣī...dāhayed...

Ms. is not complete.

Pāli 56. Agilāno visīvanapekkho jotiṃ samādaheyya vā samādahāpeyya vā...

'In the open' is absent here, also is not in the Msg. 41.

73. In both the Msv. and Tib. there is a summary of the following ten rules in verse; 'Pleasant, fire, community, not ordained, qualities, talking, novice-monk, disfiguring, a jewel and hot weather.'

74. The Skt.: 'Vānyatra pratyayāt' is not here, also is not in Msv. 52, Tib. 52—Pā.

Omits: 'Grass, wood etc.' It is also the same case with Ksy. 53, Mhs. 68, Msv. 52—Pā.

Dh. 57. Like the Pāli.

Msg. 41. '...grass, wood, cow-dung and husks.' See Pāli 56 above.

Tib. 52. '...for his own comfort...' See Skt. 52, above.

Mpt. 52. Agni-vṛttam.

Sv. V.53

Whatsoever Bhikṣu, when he has declared his consent to a formal proceeding of the Saṅgha conducted according to the Dharma, shall thereafter grumble about it—that is a Pā.

Skt. 54. ...Dhārṃike saṅghakaraṇiye chandam datvā...

Pāli 79. ...Dhammikānaṃ kammānaṃ chandaṃ datvā...

Dh. 76. Omits Skt.: 'Saṅgha-karaṇīye.'

Mhs. 79. The same.

Ksy. 51. Omits: 'to former proceedings...to the Dharma.'

'Shall regret.'

Msg. 43. '...later on being angry or displeased says thus: "I don't give my consent. It was not given in the proper way and that Karma could not be counted."

Msv. 53. '...having given consent to others, later on says regretfully: "Give back my consent, it was not given to you."

Tib. 53. '...gives anything to a monk of a certain community and being thereupon angry or displeased charges him with an offence which involves forfeiture saying: "I gave the thing to the community and not to yourself...'

This is quite different. Probably this version has been interpreted incorrectly.

Mpt. 53. Chanda-pratyuddhāraḥ.

Sv. V.54

Whatsoever Bhikṣu shall lie down for more than two nights in the same room with a person not ordained—that is a Pā.

Skt. 53. Anupasaṃpannena pudgalena sārdham uttaraṃ dvirātraṃ sahāgārśayyāṃ kalpayet...

Pāli 5. Anupasaṃpannena uttariṃ dvirattatirattaṃ saha seyyaṃ kappeyya...

Dh. 5. Adds: 'Up to the dawn of the third night'.

Omits: 'In the same room,' it is also in Mhs. 7—Pā.

Ksy. 54. 'Up to the third night.'

Msg. 42. 'Beyond three nights.'
Msv. 54, *Tib.* 54. The same.
Mpt. 54. Anupasaṃpannasahasvapnaḥ.

Sv. V.55

If a Bhikṣu says: "Thus I understand the meaning of the doctrine of the Buddha that: 'Practice of the obstructive qualities really does not obstruct the spiritual path,' then that Bhikṣu should be admonished by the Bhikṣus thus. "Say not so, sir! 'Thus I understand the meaning of the doctrine of the Buddha that: Practice of the obstructive qualities really does not obstruct the spiritual path.' You should not bear false witness and false accusation against the Blessed one. To make a false charge against him is not good. The Buddha does not speak such words. By many a figure the Blessed One did explain that: The obstructive qualities are really obstructing the spiritual path. Sir, you give up this evil view!" If that Bhikṣu, when he has thus been spoken to by the Bhikṣus, should persist as before, then let him be admonished for the second and the third time. If he then abandons his opinion, it is well, if not—that is a Pā.

Skt. 55. "Ye antarāyikā dharmās tāṃ pratiṣevato nālam antarāyāya..."

Pāli 68. "Yeme antarāyika dhamma vuttā bhagavatā, te paṭisevato nālam antarāyā'ti....."

We do not find 'spoken by the Buddha' in the Skt.

The repetition of the Bhikṣu's wrong view in the Skt. is omitted here and uses 'mā...evamavāca' instead.

For Skt. 'dvir api trir api' we have 'yāvatatiyam'.

Dh. 68. 'To carry out lustful desires' for 'to practise the obstructive qualities.' It is also in Ksy. 55—Pā.

This agrees with the Pāli.

Mhs. 68, *Ksy.* 55, *Msg.* 45, *Tib.* 55. The repetition of the Bhikṣu's wrong view is not here. See Dh. 68 above for Ksy. 55.

Msg. 45. Adds: 'If he does not give it up, the Saṅgha should perform a Karma.'[75] See Mhs. 48, above.

Msv. 55. '...desire is an obstacle, but it is not an obstacle when one puts it into practice.'

It is somewhat longer than other texts and the language differs also.

Tib. 55. The same; but differs somewhat from the Msv.

Mpt. 55. Dṛṣṭigatānutsargaḥ.

---

75. A final proclamation of his persisting view is to be made in a Karma, See Msgv. ch. 17.

Sv. V.56

Whatsoever Bhikṣu knew such a person who had spoken thus (as in Pā. 55), shall keep in communion with him, speak to him and sleep with him in the same place when he did not confess his guilt according to the Dharma, and did not abandon his wrong views, whereupon he had been expelled[76]—that is a Pā.

Skt. 56. Jānan tathāvādinā...saṃbhuṃjīta vā saṃvased vā tena vā sārdham sahāgaraśayyāṃ katpayet...

Pāli 69. Jānaṃ tathāvādina...saddhiṃ saṃbhuñjeyya vā saṃvāseyya vā saha vā seyyaṃ kappeyya...

'Speak to' is not in the Ṣkt. and Pāli.

'To eat' is not in the Sv., Dh. 69, and Mhs. 49—Pā.

Dh. 69. '...to keep, or sleep together or be in the same Karma.' See Pāli 69, above.

Mhs. 49. '...to sit with, talk with, sleep with and work with,' not quite corresponding. See also Pāli 69, above.

Ksy. 56. Omits: 'Confessed his guilt according to the Dharma.'

'To sleep with, eat with and be in the same Karma.'

Msg. 46. Adds: 'The Saṅgha should according to the Dharma and Vinaya perform the Karma.'

'To eat with and live in the same room.'

Msv. 56. Adds: 'To live together.'

'To enjoy or use' for the Skt. 'Saṃbhuṃjīta'. We find this kind of Chinese interpretation only here.

Tib. 56. '...welcomes him, talks with him, dwells together with him, eats in company with him or even sleeps with him in one place...'

More items are added here.

Mpt. 56. Utkṣiptānuvṛttiḥ.

Sv. V.57

If a Śrāmaṇera says: "Thus I understand the doctrine of the Buddhas: 'Indulgence in all the desires really does not obstruct the spiritual path.'" Then that Śrāmaṇera should be admonished by the Bhikṣus thus: "Say not so, you Śrāmaṇera: 'Thus I understand the meaning of the doctrine of the Buddha: Indulgence in all the desires really does not obstruct the spiritual path.' You should not bear false witness and false accusation against the Blessed One. To make a false charge against him is not good. The Buddha does not speak such words. By many a figure, the Blessed One has explained that: Indulgence in all the desires really can obstruct the spiritual path. O you Śrāmaṇera, give

76. We do not find this sentence in any other text.

up your evil view!" If that Śrāmaṇera, when he has been thus spoken to by the Bhikṣus, should persist as before, then let him be admonished for the second and the third time by the Bhikṣus. If he abandons it, it is well, if not, the Bhikṣus should speak to him thus: "From today onwards, you should not say that the Buddha is your teacher and should not walk behind the Bhikṣus. The other Śrāmaṇeras may sleep in the same place with the Bhikṣus up to one or two nights, but you will be deprived of this privilege. O fool, get out, go away beyond sight and do not stay here."

Whatsoever Bhikṣu, knowing a Śrāmaṇera to have thus been expelled, shall keep him or let him sleep in the same room—that is a Pā.

Skt. 57. "Yat kāmāṃ pratiṣevato nālam antarāyāyeti"...

Pāli 70. "Ye'me antarāyikā dhammā vuttā bhagavatā te parisevato nālam antarāyāyā'ti"...

Skt. 'kāmāṃ' is not here.

'Should not walk behind the Bhikṣus' is not here. It is also the same case with Msg. Pā. 47.

For Skt. 'upasthāpayed vā upalādayed vā tena vā sārdhaṃ sahāgāraśayyāṃ kalpayet', we have 'Upalāpeyya vā upṭṭhapeyya vā saṃbhuñjeyya vā saha vā seyyaṃ kappeyya' here.

'Would eat' is not in the Skt.

For other differences, see Pāli Pā. 68. studied above.

Dh. 70, *Mhs.* 50, *Ksy.* 57, *Msg.* 47. The repetition of the Śrāmaṇera's wrong view is not in these texts.

Other portions are the same.

Mhs. 50. 'To enjoy five kinds of sensual pleasures.'

Adds: 'To speak with.'

Ksy. 57. Omits: 'To admonish him for the second and the third time.'

Adds: 'You are not following the path of pure life.'

Msg. 47. The beginning differs from the Sv.

Adds: 'When he is not dealt with according to the Dharma...shall call him to eat and stay together...' See Pāli 70, above.

Msv. 57. '...from now on you should not say that the Tathāgata Arhat·Samyaksaṃbuddha is your teacher and should not keep company with the venerable Elder and Sabrahmacārins.' This is also found in Tib. Pā. 57.

For other differences see Msv. Pā. 55, studied above.

Tib. 57. Mostly agrees with the Msv. 57 (See above.)

Adds: 'Do not occupy the position of a monk, preceptor or the like.' This is not found in any other text(!)

Adds: 'Talks with.'

Mpt. 57. Nāśitasaṃgrahaḥ.

Sv. V.58

Whatsoever Bhikṣu shall pick up, or cause another to pick up a jewel or anything deemed a jewel, except inside of a Vihāra or residence—that is a Pā.

If there is a jewel or anything deemed a jewel, either inside the Vihāra or residence of the Bhikṣus, he should think thus: He to whom it may belong may take it away. This is the right course here.

Skt. 58. ratnaṃ vā ratnasaṃmatam vā...taṃ udgṛhṇīyād udgṛhṇayed....

Pāli 84. ratanaṃ vā ratanasaṃmataṃ vā aññatra ajjhārāmā vā ajjhāvāsathā vā uggaṇhāpeyya vā....

The language and order is a bit different from the Skt.

Dh. 82. 'Jewels or ornament of jewels.'

'In the Saṅgharāma or in the dwelling place.' This is also found in Mhs. Pā. 69.

'The recogniser should take it.'

The last sentence here differs from the Pāli.

Mhs. 69. 'Jewel or precious things.'

'It should be returned, if later on the owner asks for it.' See Dh. 82, above.

Ksy. 69. Omits: 'Residence etc.' is in the second paragraph.

'While picking up the jewel or ornaments of jewels, if he so thinks: The picker is going to give it back.'

Msg. 49. '...except for keeping it inside, with the intention of giving it back when the owner comes and asks for it...'

This text is much shorter than other texts.

Msv. 59. '...except in the Vihāra or in the house of a householder.'

'He may take it after having thought thus: I shall give it to him who recognises it.'

Tib. 59. '...in a grove, or in a dwelling place with the object of restorning it to its owner...' is not quite the same.

Mpt. 59. Ratanasaṃsparśaḥ.

Sv. V.59

If a Bhikṣu obtains a new robe, he should disfigure it with any of these three colours of disfigurement viz., either blue or mud or black. If he does not disfigure his new robe with any of these three colours of disfigurement viz., either blue or mud or black—that is a Pā.

Skt. 59. Trayāṇāṃ durvarṇīkaraṇānāṃ: nīlam vā kardamo vā kāḍiśamo vā...

Pāli 59. Tiṇṇaṃ dubbaṇṇakaraṇānaṃ: nīlaṃ vā kaddamaṃ vā kāḷasāmaṃ vā...

Dh. 60, *Mhs.* 77, *Msg.* 48. Blue, black and the colour of Mu-lan or magnolia.

Mhs. 77. '...to make a mark of three colours...' This text here is rather short.

Ksy. 68. 'If a Bhikṣu gets a new robe without disfiguring it with blue, black or magnolia colours—that is a Pā.'

Msg. 48. Adds: '...if he uses it wihout disfigurement.'

Msv. 58. Blue, mud and red.

'If he uses it without the three colours of disfigurement.'

Tib. 58. Blue, red or orange-coloured.

Mpt. 58. Āraktavastropabhogaḥ.

Sv. V.60

Whatsoever Bhikṣu takes a bath within half a month, except on the right occasion—that is a Pā.

Herein this is the right occasion: One and a half month of the remaining Spring, and the first month of Summer. These two and half months are called Hot season, and when there[77] is sickness; there has been wind and rain; when there is work and when on a journey. This is the right occasion here.

Skt. 60. Ardhamāsakaṃ snāyīta:...Tatrāyam samayaḥ...śeṣo grīṣmaṇām pūrvo māso varṣāṇāṃ...paridāghasamayaḥ avaśiṣṭaṃ glānasamayaḥ karmasamayo vātasamayo vṛṣṭisamayaḥ...māragasamayaḥ....

Pāli 57. Orenaddhamāsaṃ nahāyeyya: Tatrāyaṃ samayo: diyaḍḍho māso seso gimhānaṃ'ti vassānassa paṭhamo māso iccete aḍḍhateyyamāsā uṇhasamayo pariḷāhasamayo...

The rest is like the Skt.

Dh. 56. Adds: 'A Bhikṣu who is not sick should observe (this).'

It does not mention which months are considered to be the 'Hot season'. This is also happened in Mhs. 70, Ksy. 70, Msv. 60—Pā.

The order of the right occasions here differs from the Pāli.

Mhs. 70. 'Hot time' comes at the end. See Dh. 56, above.

Msg. 50. The ending words in the Skt. 'tatra samayaḥ' is not here.

The rest is like the Sv.

Msv. 60. Adds: 'Purposely violates the rule' and 'when there is both wind and rain'. See Dh. 56, above.

---

77. The 'wind and rain' has been placed at the end of the Skt. and the Pāli.

Tib. 60. 'Summer' for 'Spring' of the Sv.

Omits: 'When on a Journey.'

Mpt. 60. Snānaprāyaścittikaṃ.

Sv. V.61

Whatsoever Bhikṣu shall deliberately deprive any animal of life—that is a Pā.

Skt. 61. Tiryagyonigataṃ prāṇinaṃ jīvitād vyaparopayet....

Pāli 61. Pāṇaṃ jīvitā voropeyya...

Dh. 61, *Mhs.* 51, *Ksy.* 61, *Msg.* 61, *Msv.* 61, *Tib.* 61[78]. The same.

Mpt. 61. Tiryagvadhaḥ.

Sv. V.62

Whatsoever Bhikṣu shall purposely rouse suspicion in another Bhikṣu and think: 'Let this Bhikṣu be vexed even for a moment.' If there is no cause other than this—that is a Pā.

Skt. 62. Sañcintya kaukṛtyaṃ upasaṃharet kaccid asya bhikṣor muhūrtam api tāvad aphāṣaṃ bhaved...

Pāli 77. Sañcicca kukkuccaṃ upadaheyya—iti'ssa muhuttam pi aphāsu bhavissatī'ti...

Dh. 63. '...purposely vexes another Bhikṣu' only.

This is very simple in form, not quite like the Pāli.

Mhs. 52. The same.

Omits: 'If there is no other cause than this.' This is also the case in Ksy. Pā 62.

Ksy. 62. '...to vex and rouse doubt in another Bhikṣu....' This is very simple in form. See Mhs. 52, above.

Msg. 62. '...rouse doubt and repentance...'

The arrangement of words is different.

'If there is no other cause than this.' This is found here but not in the Msgv. ch. 19.

Msv. 62, *Tib.* 62. '...somehow speaks deliberately of another monk that he does not feel happiness even for a moment, and produces on that account regrets in him...' is not quite the same.

Mpt. 62. Kaukṛtyopasaṃhāraḥ.

---

78. There is a summary in verse in the Msv. and Tib. of the following ten rules: 'Brute, regret, finger, sport, together with, frightening, hiding, not formally given, groundless and going on a journey without there being any man.'

Sv. V.63

Whatsoever Bhikṣu shall poke (a person) pressingly[79] with his finger—that is a Pā.

Skt. 63. Aṅgulipratodanāt...
Pāli 52. Aṅgulipatodake....
Dh. 53, *Mhs.* 54, *Ksy.* 63, *Msv.* 63, *Tib.* 63. '...to beat and search—chi-li.
Msg. 67. 'To touch with the finger.'
Mpt. 63. Aṅgulipratodanaṃ.

Sv. V.64

Whatsoever Bhikṣu shall sport in the water—that is a Pā.

Skt. 54. Udake harṣaṇāt....
Pāli 53. Udake hassadhamme....
Dh. 52, *Mhs.* 55, *Ksy.* 64, *Msg.* 66, *Msv.* 64, *Tib.* 64. The same.
Mpt. 64. Udakaharṣaṇaṃ.

Sv. V.65

Whatsoever Bhikṣu shall sleep in the same room with a woman—that is a Pā.

Skt. 65. Mātṛgrāmeṇa sārdhaṃ sahāgāraśayyāṃ kalpayet.
Pāli 6. Mātugāmena sahaseyyaṃ kappeyya...
Dh. 4, *Mhs.* 56, *Ksy.* 65, *Msg.* 69, *Msv.* 65, *Tib.* 65. The same.
Mpt. 65. Mātṛgrāmeṇa saha svapnaḥ.

Sv. V.66

Whatsoever Bhikṣu shall frighten another Bhikṣu or cause him to be frightened even for a joke—that is a Pā.

Skt. 66. Bhikṣuṃ bhīṣayed bhīṣāpayed vāntato hāsyaprekṣyam api...
Pāli 55. Bhikkhuṃ bhiṃsapeyya...
Skt. 'bhīṣapayed' and 'hāsyaprekṣyam' is not here.
Dh. 55. The same as the Pāli.
Mhs. 73, *Msg.* 65. '...purposely frightens another Bhikṣu.'
Ksy. 66. Omits: 'Or cause him to be frightened.'
Msv. 66. The same.

---

79. The word 'pressingly' is not found in other texts.

Tib. 66. '...or makes him, even in fun, be at a loss as to what to do...' This is somewhat different.

Mpt. 66. Bhīṣaṇaṃ.

Sv. V.67

Whatsoever Bhikṣu shall hide or cause others to hide a Bhikṣu's bowl, or robe, or key or shoes or needle-case and such-like necessary articles of his life, even though in fun—that is a Pā.

Skt. 67. (Ms. missing)...vā upānahaṃ vā sūcīgharaṃ vā anyatamānyatamaṃ vā jīvitapariṣkāram upanidadhyād upanidhāpayed...

Pāli 60. pattaṃ vā cīvaraṃ vā nisidanaṃ vā sūcīgharaṃ vā kāyabandhanaṃ vā apanidheyya vā apanidhāpeyya vā...

Omits: 'Key' and 'shoes'.

Adds: 'mat', 'girdle' and 'and such-like...his life.'

Dh. 58, *Msg.* 64. Omits: 'girdle' of the Pāli text, otherwise they agree closely with the Pāli.

Mhs. 78. Articles are the same as the Pāli, but 'girdle' is not here. The rest is like the Sv.

Ksy. 67. '...bowl, or robe or other necessary articles.'

This is rather short.

Msv. 67. '...hide the bowl, or robe or other necessary articles of a Bhikṣu or a Bhikṣuṇī, or a Śikṣamāṇa or a Śrāmaṇera or a Śrāmaṇerī, except when there are other causes...'.

Tib. 67. '...bowl, robe, mat, needle or girdle or any other requisites of an ascetic life belonging to a monk, nun, monk pupil, novice-monk or novice-nun, unless there is reason to do so...'.

The first half here resembles the Pāli but the latter half is closer to the Msv. From these and such additions, we may presume that both the Msv. and the Tib. were completed at a much later date.

Mpt. 67. Gopanaṃ.

Sv. V.68

Whatsoever Bhikṣu who has given a robe to a Bhikṣu or a Bhikṣuṇī or Śikṣamāṇa, or a Śrāmaṇera or a Śrāmaṇerī shall continue to make use of it (himself)—that is a Pā.

Skt. 68. ...cīvaram uddiśya tataḥ paścāt (a)pratyuddhārya[80] paribhuṃjīta.

Pāli 59. ...sāmam cīvaraṃ vikappetvā apaccuddhārakaṃ

80. The (a) is not in the Ms. but is added here by us.

paribhuñjeyya.

The Pāli is a bit shorter than the Skt.

Dh. 59. '...to put on wihout asking the owner....'

Mhs. 81. '...take back the "pure gift" robe which was given to...'

Ksy. 59. No other names, but 'Śrāmaṇera' only.

Msg. 63. '...after having properly given away a robe to the five kinds of disciples, shall use it, as if he had not made it over...' This is very close to the Pāli.

Msv. 68. 'When a Bhikṣu is entrusted with a robe for care by another Bhikṣu, shall use it wihout asking for the owner's permission....' This is quite different.

Tib. 68. '...having presented a robe to another monk continues to use it as if not formerly given....'

Mpt. 68. Apratyuddhāryaparibhogaḥ.

Sv. V.69

Whatsoever Bhikṣu shall harass a Bhikṣu with a (charge of) Saṃghāvaśeṣa without ground—that is a Pā.

Skt. 69. Amūlakena saṃghāvaśeṣeṇa dharmeṇa dharmeṇānudhvaṃśayet.

Pāli 76. Amūlakena saṅghādisesena anuddhaṃseyya.

Dh. 80, *Msg.* 90. Adds: 'Being angry and displeased.' This addition is not found in the Pāli.

Mhs. 75. The same.

Ksy. 58. Adds: 'Dharma'. See Skt. 69—Pā.

Msv. 69, *Tib.* 69. Adds: '...knowing that Bhikṣu to be pure and without violating any rule but on account of being angry or displeased with him.'

Mpt. 69. Amūlakābhyākhyānaṃ.

Sv. V.70

Whatsoever Bhikṣu shall, by appointment, journey along the same road with a woman, even up to the next village—that is a Pā.

Skt. 70. Mātṛgrāmena sārdhaṃ saṃvidhāya samānamārgaṃ pratipadyeta...

Pāli 67. Mātugāmena sadhiṃ samvidhyāya ekaddhānamaggaṃ paṭipajjeyya...

Dh. 30. The same.

Mhs. 67. '...from this village.'

Ksy. 60. Omits: 'By appointment.'

Msg. 68. 'Even down to a village.'

Msv. 70, *Tib.* 70. Omits: 'By appointment'; adds: 'Without another man'.

Mpt. 70. Apuruṣayā striyā mārgagamanaṃ.

Sv. V.71[81]

Whatsoever Bhikṣu shall, by appointment, travel along the same road with a caravan of robbers, even as far as the next village—that is a Pā.

Skt. 71. Steyasārthena sārdhaṃ saṃvidhāya samānamārgaṃ pratipadyet...

Pāli 66. Jānaṃ theyyasatthena saddhiṃ samvidhāya ekaddhānamaggaṃ paṭipajjeyya...

'Jānaṃ' is not in the Sv. and the Skt.

Dh. 67. This agrees with the Pāli.

Mhs. 66. 'From this village to another village.'

Ksy. 71. Omits: 'By appointment.'

Msg. 72. Adds: 'Knowing' and 'even down to a village'.

Msv. 71. Adds: 'With merchants'; Omits: 'By appointment'.

Tib. 71[81]. The same.

Mpt. 71. Steyasārthagamanaṃ.

Sv. V.72

Whatsoever Bhikṣu shall confer the higher ordination upon a person whose age is below twenty—that is a Pā.

The ordination of the person is invalid and the Bhikṣus are blameworthy. This is the right course in this case.

Skt. 72. Aparipūrṇaviṃśadvarṣaṃ pudgalaṃ...ikabhāvenopa-ssaṃpādayet...

Pāli 65. Jānaṃ ūnavīsativassaṃ puggalaṃ upasaṃpādeyya, so ca puggalo anupasaṃpanno...

Dh. 65. '...higher ordination may be conferred upon a person who is 20 years old, but if a Bhikṣu knowingly confers ordination on a person below twenty—that is a Pā.

The ordination of the person is invalid and the other Bhikṣus may also scold him for his ignorance.'

81. There is a summary in verse in the Msv. and the Tib. for the following ten rules: 'Robbers, under twenty years of age, digging, invitation, training, quarrelling, going away without saying anything, discourtesy, drinking and at a wrong time.'

This is quite different from the Sv. and the Pāli.

Mhs. 61, *Ksy.* 72, *Msg.* 71. Adds: 'Knowingly.'

Ksy. 72. 'The Bhikṣusaṅgha is guilty (for this).'

Msg. 71. '...this person cannot be called to have received the higher ordination...'

Msv. 72. 'Adds: 'To enter into the Bhikṣuhood.'

Language is slightly different here.

Tib. 72. '...the monks too are disgraced'.

Mpt. 72. Ūnaviṃśavarṣopasaṃpādanaṃ.

Sv. V.73

Whatsoever Bhikṣu shall dig the ground with his own hands or employ a person to dig it or give hints, saying: 'You dig this'—that is a Pā.

Skt. 73. ...Pṛthivīm khanyāt khānayed vā; or the other reading Var. XIII: Bhikṣuḥ svahastaṃ pṛthivīṃ khanyāt khānayed vā imaṃ khanaivaṃ vadet.

The latter is closer to the Chinese Sv.

Pāli 10. Pathaviṃ khaṇeyya vā khaṇāpeyya vā...

Dh. 10, *Ksy.* 74, *Msv.* 73, *Tib.* 73. Omits: 'Or give hints... dig this.'

Mhs. 59. '...or cause others to dig it by saying: "You dig this."

Msg. 73. The same.

Mpt. 73. Khananaṃ.

Sv. V.74

A Bhikṣu may accept an invitation for four[82] months. If he accepts it beyond that limit unless there is a perpetual invitation, repeated invitation or a special invitation—that is a Pā.

Skt. 74. Cāturmāsikā Bhikṣuṇā pravāraṇa svīkartavyā...

Pāli 47. Agilānena Bhikkhunā cātumāsapaccayapavāraṇā sāditabbā...

The Skt.: 'Nityapravāraṇāyā' and 'Pratyayapravāraṇāya' absent here. 'Paccaya...with reagard to the requisites' and 'if the Bhikṣu is not sick' are additions.

Dh. 47. 'A Bhikṣu who is not sick...with regard to the giving of medicine.'[83]

82. The word 'self-satisfying' is added to each invitation here.

83. See SBE, vol. XIII., p. 48, note 1.

Adds: 'A standing invitation for life.' This is also found in Ksy. 73—Pā.

Here it does not agree with the Pāli.

Mhs. 62. 'An invitation of four months for medicine' and 'an invitation sent by himself.'

Ksy. 73. Adds: 'If the Bhikṣu is not sick.' See Dh. 47, above.

Msg. 74. Adds: 'Four months of special invitation.'

The text here is rather short.

Msv. 74. Adds: 'Invitation of earnest request.'

Tib. 74. Four exceptions: Separate, repeated, on a special occasion and perpetual invitation.

Order differs from the Sv.

Mpt. 74. Pravāritārthātisevā.

Sv. V.75

Whatsoever Bhikṣu when the recitation of the Prātimokṣa is going on, shall say: 'I have not yet learnt this rule, I shall first make inquiries concerning it from those Bhikṣus who are experts in the reciting of Sūtra, Vinaya and Abhidharma.'—that is a Pā.

If a Bhikṣu who is desirous of getting benefit of the Dharma, he should learn (the rules) of the Prātimokṣa and also should ask the Bhikṣu expert in the recitation of Sūtra, Vinaya and Abhidharma by saying: 'O venerable sir, what is the meaning of this?'

This is the proper way here.

Skt. 75. The version here does not quite agree with the Chinese Sv. For the words uttered by the Bhikṣu are:

'Nāhaṃ pudgalānāṃ mūḍhānāṃ duṣprajñānāṃ vacanāni śikṣiṣyāmi nyān ahaṃ Bhikṣuṃ prakṣyāmi...'

The other reading is closer to the Ch. Sv. especially the last portion viz., 'Idaṃ bhadanta katham asya bhāṣitasya ko'rtha... Iyaṃ tatra samīci.'[84]

The word 'mātṛkādharā' translated as 'abhidharmadharā' in the Sv.

Pāli 71. This text is quite different from both the Skt. and the Sv. The utterance of the Bhikṣu is: 'Nā tāvā'ham āvuso etasmiṃ sikkhāpade sikkhissāmi yāva na aññaṃ Bhikkhuṃ byattaṃ vinayadharaṃ paripucchāmī'ti.'

Skt. 'Sūtradharā' and 'mātṛkādharā' absent here.

Dh. 71. This mostly agrees with the Pāli; the last portion is much simpler. It says: 'He who is desirous of learning, should ask.' Cf. Pāli:

84. See JA, Nov.-Dec. 1913, p. 521, note 1.

'Sikkhāmānena Bhikkhave, Bhikkhunā aññatabbaṃ paripucchitabbaṃ paripañhitabbaṃ.'

Mhs. 63. 'If a Bhikṣu is admonished by the Bhikṣus in accordance with the Dharma after he had violated the rules many a time and shall say...'

'Sūtradharā' absent here.

'If the Bhikṣu desires to be understood, he should ask the Dharmadharā and Vinayadharā.'

Ksy. 75. This agrees with the first Skt. reading: 'Nāham pudgalānāṃ...etc.' very closely, even the word 'mātṛkādharā' is here. However this text begins with: 'If a Bhikṣu says to another Bhikṣus thus: You should learn this rule.' Which differs from the Skt. See Msv. 75, below.

Msg. 75. 'If a Bhikṣu speaks to another Bhikṣu thus: "Sir, you should learn and should not commit offences classified in the five divisions." Should that Bhikṣu reply: "I do not obey your words. If I see other Elders who are pure in the organs, learned, practised according to the Dharma and had deep-understanding, I shall ask them and practise whatever they may tell me to," except on other occasions—that is a Pā.

'Herein this is the other occasion: If a Bhikṣu who is desirous of getting benefit of the Dharma he should learn as well as ask other Bhikṣus.'

This text is more extensive in proportion than the other texts, although usually it is not the case.

Msv. 75. Roughly agrees with the first Skt. reading. Cf. Ksy. 75—Pā.

The beginning is like that of Ksy. 75—Pā.

'Those who are masters of the Tripiṭaka.'

Tib. 75. 'Whatsoever monk being addressed by a company of monks thus: "Brother, you should train yourself in this course of study"; should answer thus: "By your words I shall not submit myself to the training until I have made enquiries of Laws, precepts and tables of contents: You are like children unwise un—learned and stupid"—commits....

'A monk, even if he is desirous of attaining omniscience, should submit himself to the training. The monk who are depositaries of laws, precepts and tables of contents should also be interrogated.'

This even differs in some places from the Msv. Pā 75.

Mpt. 76. Śikṣopasaṃhārapratikṣepaḥ.

Sv. V.76

Whatsoever Bhikṣu shall stand in silence in a covered place

overhearing when Bhikṣus are quarrelling, or making a disturbance or engaged in a dispute, with the following intention: I shall keep in mind whatsoever the Bhikṣus will utter—that is a Pā.

Skt. 76. Bhikṣūṇāṃ kalahajātānāṃ bhaṇḍanajātānāṃ....tūṣṇīm upaśrutikas tiṣṭhed....

Pāli 78. Bhikkhūnaṃ bhaṇḍanajātānaṃ kalahajātānaṃ vivadāpannānaṃ upassutiṃ tiṭṭheyya...

Skt. 'Gṛhītānāṃ' and 'dhārayiṣyāmīti' are absent here.

'Etadeva paccayaṃ karitvā' is not in the Skt. and the Sv.

Dh. 77, *Ksy.* 76. '...knowing that other Bhikṣus are quarrelling, shall hear one Bhikṣu's words and tell them to another...'

Mhs. 60. The beginning: 'Having quarrelled together with and listened to silently' is different from the Sv.

Msg. 78. Agrees with the Pāli.

Msv. 76. The content here is much developed and enlarged. For instance, the intention of the Bhikṣu's overhearing is to cause other Bhikṣus to fight and quarrel which we do not find in other texts.

Tib. 76. 'Sits in silence overhearing.'

This does not agree with the Msv.

Mpt. 75. Upaśravagataṃ.

Sv. V.77

Whatsoever Bhikṣu, when the Saṅgha is engaged in conducting an enquiry, shall silently rise from his seat and go away—that is a Pā.

Skt. 77. gatāyāṃ kathāyāṃ vartamānāyāṃ tūṣṇīm utthāya prakramet samtaṃ Bhikṣum anavapṛchya...

Pāli 80. Saṅghe vinicchayakathāya vattamānaya chandaṃ adatvā uṭṭhāyāsanā pakkameyya.

Skt 'tuṣṇīm' absent here.

Both the Skt. and Pāli texts are not quite the same as the Sv.

Dh. 75, *Mhs.* 53. The same but adds: 'Without giving consent.'

Ksy. 77. '...when the Saṅgha is reciting the Vinaya rules, shall not give his consent but go away silently....'

Msg. 79. Adds: 'Without giving his consent' and 'goes away without informing others'.

Msv. 77. '...knowing that the Saṅgha is making an inquiry in accordance with the Dharma...without informing the Bhikṣus who are present, except when there is a cause...' This is somewhat enlarged.

Tib. 77. '...Without saying anything to the monks who remain unless there is reason to do so...'

Mpt. 77. Tūṣṇīṃviprakramaṇaṃ.

Sv. V.78

Whatsoever Bhikṣu shall show disrespect to other Bhikṣus—that is a Pā.

Skt. 78. Anādaravṛttāt...
Pāli 54. Anādariye...
Dh. 54. '...does note accept admonition'.
Mhs. 58. '...disrespect to his teacher and the precepts'.
Ksy. 78, *Msv.* 78. 'Disrespect' only.
Msg. 77. The same.
Tib. 78. '...does not show any courtesy'.
Mpt. 78. Anādaravṛttaṃ.

Sv. V.79

Whatsoever Bhikṣu shall drink liquor—that is a Pā.

Skt. 79. Surāmaireyamadyapānāt.
Pāli 51. Surāmerayapāne.
Dh. 51, *Mhs.* 57, *Ksy.* 79, *Msv.* 79. The same.
Msg. 76. 'Drinks[85] or sips wine.'
Tib. 79. '...drinks corn-beer or distilled liquor so as to be intoxicated...'
Mpt. 79. Surāmaireyamadyapānam.

Sv. V.80

Whatsoever Bhikṣu shall, out of hours, enter a village, without having informed other good Bhikṣus, unless there is a cause—that is a Pā.

Skt. 80. Akāle grāmaṃ praviśet santaṃ anavapṛchya...
Pāli 85. Santaṃ bhikkhuṃ anāpucchā vikāle gāmaṃ paviseyya... The order of words here differs from the Skt.
Dh. 83, *Ksy.* 80. Omits 'Good.'
Mhs. 83. Adds: 'A cause means when one is in danger. This is called a cause.'
Msg. 80. Adds: 'In the residence of the forest.'

85. The Msgv. ch. 20, says: 'Whatsoever Bhikṣu drinks wine made of molasses—that is a Pā.'

'Except there is an urgent matter.'

Msv. 80, *Tib.* 80. Omits: 'Good'; the same.

Mpt. 80. Akāla-caryā.

Sv. V.81

Whatsoever Bhikṣu has been invited to a dinner, if he goes to another family (for food) either before or after that dinner—that is a Pā.

Skt. 81. pūrvanimantritaḥ pūrvabhaktaṃ paścādbhaktaṃ kuleṣu cāritram āpadyeta...

Pāli 85. nimantito sabhatto samāno santaṃ Bhikkhuṃ anapucchā purebhattaṃ vā pacchabhattaṃ vā kulesu cārittam āpajjeyya...

Adds: 'Civaradānasamayo, civarakārasamayo...ayaṃ tattha samayo.'

Dh. 42. Agrees with the Pāli adds: 'At the time of illness.'

Mhs. 82. Adds: 'Not informing other Bhikṣus, unless there is a cause—that is a Pā. A cause means at the robe-time. This is called a cause.'

Ksy. 81. Adds: '...without having informed other Bhikṣus'.

Msg. 81. '...in a place of taking meals together'.

Adds: 'Except at the robe-time.'

Msv.[86] 81. Adds: '...without giving information'.

Tib. 81. Adds: 'Without saying anything to the host.'

Mpt. 81. Kulacaryā.

Sv. V.82

Whatsoever Bhikṣu very early in the morning before the rise of the dawn, when jewels have not yet been collected is seen going away from the threshold or by the side of the threshold of an anointed Kṣatriya king unless there is a great cause—that is a Pā.

Skt. 82. aniṣkrānte rājñi anirgṛhītesu ratneṣu indrakīle vā indrakīlabhūmim vā samatikramed...

Pāli 13. anikkhantarājake aniggataratanake pubbe appaṭisaṃ-vidito indakhīlam atikkameyya...

'Pubbe appaṭisaṃvidito' is not in the Skt.

Skt.: 'Indrakīlabhūmiṃ' absent here.

---

86. There is a summary in verse in the Msv. and the Tib.:...'Receiving a meal, dawn, first time, needle-case, mat, itches, garment, and the Sugata's robe.' The items represented by nos. 85 and 86 viz. 'bedstead' and 'stuffed with cotton' are omitted in the English translation of the Tib. text.

The Eng. translation has 'When the King has not gone forth, and the Queen has not withdrawn.' We consider this to be misleading. See SBE, vol. XIII, p. 52 and note 2. See introduction sec. V, p. lix.

Dh. 81. Omits: 'Very early in the morning before the rise of the dawn.'

Adds: 'The King has not yet come out.'

'If he passes the threshold of the palace.'

Mhs. 65. This closely agrees with the Dh. Pā 81, but omits: 'an anointed Kṣatriya' to the subject 'King'.

Ksy. 82. Omits: 'When jewels have not yet been collected.'

'...enters the gate of the palace when the King has not yet come out.'.

Msg. 82. 'If a Bhikṣu enters the gate of the palaces when the Queen has not yet kept aside the jewels. Even if he passes the threshold of the gate—that is a Pā.'

This reading is rather different.

Msv. 82. Adds: 'And jewel-like articles.'

'Enters the threshold of the palace.'

Tib. 82. Adds: 'And things considered as jewels.'

'...is seen going away from the door or threshold of the house.'

Mpt. 82. Rājakularātricaryā.

Sv. V.83

Whatsoever Bhikṣu, when the Prātimokṣa is being recited shall speak thus: 'Now for the first time do I notice that this rule, is included in the Prātimokṣa-sūtra and being recited each half month.' If the other Bhikṣus knew that he had sat in the assembly of Prātimokṣa-recitation for two or three times, not to say oftener, that Bhikṣu, is not only not made free on account of his ignorance, is to be dealt with according to the Dharma for the offence into which he has fallen. He should be scolded so that he may have regret: "O venerable sir, this is a loss[87] to you, you are not good, when the Prātimokṣa is being recited, you have no respect for it. You have not harboured such a thought that there is indeed such a thing, you do not value it, you do not get it impressed on your mind, you do not meditate on it with all your heart and you do not incline your ear to listen to the Dharma and act accordingly."—that is a Pā.

Skt. 83. Bhikṣur prātimokṣasūtre uddiśyamāne evaṃ vaded idānīm

87. Cf. Skt. 'Durlabdho na sulabdho.'

ahaṃ jānāmi...

Ms. is incomplete.

Pāli 73. Bhikkhu anvaddhamāsaṃ pātimokkhe uddissamāne evaṃ vadeyya—idāne' va kho āvuso aham ājānāmi...

The Sv. 'each half month' does not appear at the beginning.

Words of scolding are much simpler in this text.

'Uttariṃ cā'ssa moho āropetabbo' is different from the Sv.: 'He should be scolded so that...etc.'

Dh. 73. The first portion is like that of the Sv. but language differs, and the last portion is more or less like the Pāli.

Mhs. 64. Adds: 'Uposatho.'

'...his ignorance should be scolded that his practice is not good when the Prātimokṣa is being recited, he does not listen to it attentively and keeps it in mind—that is a Pā.'

Ksy. 83. Besides the proper punishment, the text here has given: 'Further, a scolding for negligence (lit. nirveda?) should be added.' That is the scolding by other Bhikṣus for his carelessness.

The last portion is more extensive in proportion than the Pāli text and somewhat closer to the Sv.

Msg. 92. Adds: 'Sūtra' besides the Prātimokṣa-sūtra.

The first portion is the same but the last portion is simpler than the Sv.

Msv. 83. 'Each half-month' comes at the beginning, so also in the Tib. Pā. 83.

We have here and in the Tib. Pā 83 more direct speeches than the Sv.

'Should be confessed in accordance with the Dharma' for Sv. 'should be dealt with.....'

Adds: 'O Āyuṣman, this Dharma is wonderful and you cannot afford to miss it.'

The last portion is nearly the same.

Tib. 83. 'This rule is embodied in the scripture and is included in it.'

'O brother, this is an evil, this is a loss to you that when the So-sor-thar-pa is recited you do not listen to it with reverence, you do not consider it something superior and holy, you do not attend to it with care...'

Mpt. 83. Śikṣāpadadravyatāvyavacāraḥ.

Sv. V.84

Whatsoever Bhikṣu shall have a needle-case made of bone, or

ivory,[88] or horn—that is a Pā.

Skt. 84. ...asthimayaṃ dantamayaṃ viṣāṇamayaṃ vā sūcigharaṃ kārayet....

Pāli 86. ...aṭṭhimayaṃ vā dantamayaṃ vā visānamayaṃ sūcigharaṃ kārāpeyya...

Adds: 'Bhedanakaṃ'.

Dh. 86, *Ksy.* 84. Adds: 'If it is completed.'

Mhs. 86. The same.

Msg. 83. Adds: 'When it is broken.'

Msv. 84, *Tib.* 84. Adds: 'It should be broken, if it is ready.'

Mpt. 84. Sūcigṛhakasampādanaṃ.

Sv. V.85

Whatsoever Bhikṣu, shall have a chair or bed made, it should be made with legs eight inches[89] in height, exclusive of the portion inside the bed or chair. If he exceeds that limit—that is a Pā.

Skt. 85. Pīṭhaṃ vā Bhikṣuṇā mañcaṃ vā kārayatā sugatāṣṭāṅguliḥ pramāṇā pādā kārayitavyā...

'Sugatāṣṭāṅguliḥ...etc.' is omitted in the Sv.

Pāli 87. Mañcaṃ vā piṭhaṃ vā kārāyamānena aṭṭhaṃgulapādakaṃ kāretabbaṃ sugatāṅgulena.

Adds: 'Chedanakaṃ.'

Dh. 84. 'Making a rope-bed or wooden bed.'

'Eight fingers of the Tathāgata's finger in height, except the portion inside and above the joint hole that has been cut off.'

Mhs. 85. '...is himself making a rope-bed or wooden bed for sitting or sleeping.'

Ksy. 85. 'Rope-bed or wooden bed.'

Msg. *84*. Omits: 'Bed or chair.'

'If it is cut beyond the limit.'

Msv. 85. 'Making big or small beds.'

'If it exceeds the limit, it should be cut off.'

Tib. 85. Adds: 'Made for the monkhood, and the excessive portion of the bedstead or chair so made, must be cut off.'

Mpt. 85. Pādakasampādanaṃ.

---

88. Literally it means: 'tooth'. The Svv. ch. 18, Pā. 84 adds: 'Trunk' besides 'tooth'.
89. Literally it means: 'finger-breadths'.

Sv. V.86

Whatsoever Bhikṣu shall stuff or cause to be stuffed a mattress (bed) with cotton—that is a Pā.

Skt. 86. Tūlasaṃstṛtām śayyām avanahed avanāhāyed vā...

Pāli 88. Mañcaṃ vā piṭhaṃ vā tulonaddhaṃ kārāpeyya...

Adds: 'Uddālanakaṃ...the stuffing shall be torn out' and 'or chair'. The causative is not here.

Dh. 85. '...to stuff a rope-bed or a wooden bed or a carpet or a mattress...'

Mhs. 84. '...to stuff a rope-bed or a chair...'

Ksy. 86. '...to stuff a rope-bed or wooden bed, with cotton...if it is ready.'

Msg. 85. '...to stuff a mattress with cotton either for sitting or for sleep. That is a Pā., even if it has been taken out.'

Msv. 86. '...to stuff a bed or a chair for the Saṅgha with cotton (from the tree), the stuffing should be taken out.'

Tib. 86. Like the Msv. Pā. 86, but the causative is here.

Mpt. 86. Avanahaḥ.

Sv. V.87

Whatsoever Bhikṣu is having a garment made for the rainy season,[90] it must be of the right measure. Herein this is the right measure—in length six spans and in breadth two spans and a half, according to the Sugata's span. If he exceeds that limit—that is a Pā.

Skt. 87. Varṣāśāṭicīvaraṃ...dīrghataḥ ṣaḍ vitastayaḥ sugatavitastyā, tiryak sārdhe dve...

Pāli 91. Vassikassāṭikam...dīghaso cha vidatthiye sugatavidatthiyā, tiriyam aḍḍhateyyā...

Adds: Chedanakaṃ...should be cut down.

Dh. 89, *Ksy.* 89. The same.

Mhs. 89. 'In length 5 spans of the Sugata's span.'

Msg. 88, *Msv.* 89, *Tib.* 89. Adds: 'It should be cut off.'

Mpt. 88. Varṣāśāṭīgataṃ.

Sv. V.88

Whatsoever Bhikṣu is having an itch-cloth[91] made, it must be made of the right measure. Herein this is the right measure—In length four

90. Literally 'Yu yu yi' means: A robe for bathing in the rain.

91. Literally it means: 'cloth for covering the body.'

spans and in breadth two spans and a half according to the Sugata's span. If he exceeds that limit—that is a Pā.

Skt. 88. Kaṇḍupraticchādanaṃ...dīrghtaś catasro vitastayaḥ sugatavitastyā tiryag dve...

Pāli 90. Kaṇḍupaṭicchādaniṃ...dīghaso catasso vidatthiyo sugatavidatthiyā tiriyaṃ dve vidatthiyo...

Adds: 'Chedanakaṃ'.

Dh. 88, *Mhs.* 88, *Ksy.* 88. 'Cloth for covering boils.' Measurement is the same.

Msg. 87. Omits: 'Should be in the right measure.'

Adds: 'It should be cut off.'

Msv. 88, *Tib.* 88. Adds: 'It should be cut off.'

Mpt. 89. Kaṇḍupraticchādanagataṃ.

Sv. V.89

Whatsoever Bhikṣu is desirous of making a rug (to sit upon) it should be made of right measure. Herein this is the right measure—in length two spans and in breadth one span and a half or adds one span to the border[92] according to the Sugata's span. If he exceeds that limit—that is a Pā.

Skt. 89. Niṣīdanaṃ...dīrghato vitasti dve sugatavitastyā tiryak sārdhavitastir daśānañ ca vitastis...

Pāli 89. Nisīdanaṃ...dīghaso dve vidatthiyo sugatavidatthiyā, tiriyaṃ diyaḍḍham dasā vidatthi...

Dh. 87, *Ksy.* 87. 'Adds half a span each to the length and breadth.'

Mhs. 87. 'Or adds one span to the border (square). The same.

Msg. 86. 'Adds one span more.'

Msv. 87. 'Adds one span to the length.'

Adds: 'It should be cut off'. This is also the same case in Tib. Pā 87.

Tib. 87. 'And one span in the borders.' See Msv. 87, above.

Mpt. 87. Niṣadanagataṃ.

Sv. V.90

Whatsoever Bhikṣu is going to have a robe made of the dimensions of the Sugata's robe, if he makes it larger—that is a Pā.

Herein this is the measure of the Sugata's robe—in length nine

---

92. Daśā—means 'thread and border.' Here we take the sense of the later, though the text takes the former.

spans and in breadth six spans, according to the Sugata's span.

This is the measure of the Sugata's robe.

Venerable sirs, the ninety Pātayantika Rules have been recited. In respect of them I ask the venerable ones, 'Are you pure in this matter?'

A second and a third time I ask the venerable ones, 'Are you pure in this matter?'

The venerable ones are pure herein. Therefore, do they keep silence. Thus do I observe.

Skt. 90. Sugatacīvarapramāṇaṃ...dīrghato nava vitastayaḥ....

Ms. is incomplete.

Pāli 92. Sugatacīvarappamāṇaṃ...dīghaso nava vidatthiyo, tiriyaṃ cha vidatthiyo...

Adds: 'Chedanakaṃ'.

Dh. 90. 'Ten spans in length.'

The composition here differs from the Sv.

Mhs. 90, *Ksy.* 90. The same.

Msg. 89. The same, but the language is simpler.

Msv. 90, *Tib.* 90. 'Ten spans in length.'

Mpt. 90. Sugatacīvaragataṃ.

VI. THE FOUR PRATIDEŚANĪYA DHARMAS

Sv. VI.1

Here are, venerable sirs, the four Pratideśanīya (Pāli: Pāṭidesanīya) Dharmas as known from the Prātimokṣa recited each half month.

Whatsoever Bhikṣu, being without illness shall accept food with his own hand from a bhikṣuṇī who is in the house of the lay disciple and is not related to him, that bhikṣu should confess his sin to the bhikṣus, saying: 'I have fallen, venerable sirs, into a blameworthy and unbecoming offence, which ought to be confessed; and now I confess it.' This is the first[93] Pratideśanīya Dharma.

Skt 1. ...ajñātyā bhikṣuṇyāḥ santikāt svahastaṃ khādanīya-bhojanīyaṃ pratigṛhya khādet vā bhuñjīta vā pratideśayitavyaṃ...

This is simpler than the Sv.

93. This ending is not found in both the Skt. and the Pāli throughout the four Pd. dharmas. cf. Mhs I below.

Pāli 1. ...aññātikāya bhikkhunīya antaragharaṃ paviṭṭhāya hatthato khādaniyaṃ vā bhojəniyaṃ vā sahatthā paṭiggahetvā khādeyya vā bhuṃjeyya vā...

'Antaragharaṃ paviṭṭhāya' is not found in the Skt.

Dh. 1. 'If a bhikṣu enters a village...'

Omits: 'The first.' See Mhs. 1, below.

Mhs. 1. 'If a bhikṣu, being without illness...on the street or in the lane...'

'This is called Pratideśanīya Dharma.' This is used at the end throughout the Four Pd. Dharmas. It is also the case with Dh., Ksy., and Msg.

Ksy. 1. Same as the Dh. Pd. 1. See Mhs. 1, above.

Msg. 2. Omits: 'With his own hand.' and '...unbecoming, which ought to be confessed; and now I confess it.' throughout the four Pd. dharmas.

'If a bhikṣu, without being sick, lives in the house of a lay disciple ...'

'Whether eats or bites.' See also Mhs. 1. above.

Msv[94] 1, *Tib.* 1. '...when a nun not related to him is on the highway during her visit to a village for alms, accepts from her with his own hand food, either soft or hard, and drinks or eats it, he should go to the grove outside and make a confession...'

'These Bhikṣus after returning to their residence outside the village should go to other bhikṣu's place and say separately......' This is used throughout the 4 Pd. dharmas.

Mpt. 1. Bhikṣunīpiṇḍakagrahaṇaṃ.

Sv. VI.2

When many bhikṣus invited to a layman's house are eating, if there is a bhikṣuṇī staying and giving directions: "Give rice to this bhikṣu, give soup to this bhikṣu,' the bhikṣus should speak to her thus: "Stand aside, sister, for a little while till the bhikṣus have finished eating." If even a single bhikṣu does not dare to exhort the bhikṣuṇī, saying: "Stand aside, sister, for a little while, till the bhikṣus have finished eating", those bhikṣus should confess to other bhikṣus, saying, 'We have fallen, venerable sirs, into a blameworthy offence, unbecoming, which ought to be confessed: and now we confess it."

This is the second Pd. dharma.

---

94. (See note 93) A summary: 'Village, another house, a learner's household and solitary place......'

Skt. 2. ...sā bhikṣuṇī bhikṣubhir evaṃ syād vacanīyā...āgamaya tāva...(Ms. is incomplete).

Pāli 2. Tehi bhikkhūhi sā bhikkhunī apasādetabbā...apasajja tāva bhaginī yava bhikkhu bhuñjantī'ti...

Dh. 2. 'Give soup to so and so, give rice to so and so.'

Mhs. 2. Adds: 'Give instructions to the server to serve more.'

The words that should be spoken to the bhikṣuṇī are omitted the second time here.

Ksy. 2. Adds: 'To give it again and again.'

Other portions are like the Mhs. Pā 2.

Msg. 3. Adds: 'Or fish or meat.'

Msv. 2. 'This bhikṣu may be given much food and excellent eatables and drinkables.'

Language at the end is quite different. 'Pd. dharma' has been translated as 'The dharma of speaking face to face.'

Tib. 2. Adds: 'Here give pulses, here give again.'

'...going to an outside grove should make a confession to the monks thus...'... 'We have committed a low and unbecoming act...'

Mpt. 2. Paṅktivaiṣamyavādānivaritabhuktiḥ.

Sv. VI.3

There are families, which the Saṅgha has declared to be families under discipline[95] (Śaikṣasaṃvṛtisaṃmatāni). If a bhikṣu knowing that such families have been declared by the Saṅgha to be families under discipline shall receive food and eatables (from them) with his own hand without previous invitation, that bhikṣu should confess to other bhikṣus, saying, 'I have fallen, venerable sirs, into a blameworthy offence, unbecoming, which ought to be confessed; and now I confess it.'

This is the third Pd. dharma.

Skt. 3. ...tathārūpebhyaḥ kulebhyaḥ śaikṣasaṃvṛtisaṃmatebhyah pūrvam animantritaḥ sa khādanīya-bhojanīyaṃ pratigṛhṇīyāt...

Pāli 3. ...tathārupesu sekhasaṃmatesu kulesu pubbe animantito agilāno khādanīyaṃ vā bhojanīyaṃ vā sahatthā paṭiggahetvā...

Adds: 'Agilāno' and 'khādeyya vā bhuñjeyya vā paṭidesetabbaṃ.'

Dh. 3, *Mhs.* 3, *Ksy.* 3. Adds: 'Without being sick.'

Msg. 4. The ending portion is much simpler than the Sv.

95. The Svv. ch. 19 tells us that if a donor knows no limit of giving away his wealth for the Saṅgha and thereby he becomes poor, the Saṇgha should formally declare that the bhikṣus, bhikṣunīs etc. should not enter his house and accept food with their own hands.

'Whether eat or bite.'

Msv. 3. For differences see Msv. Pd. 1. compared.

Tib. 3. '...in a learner's household which has been declared by the monkhood to be under a learner's regulation...'

For other portions, see Tib. Pd. 2, above.

Mpt. 3. Kulaśikṣābhaṅgapravṛttiḥ.

Sv. VI.4

There are forest-dwellings of the Saṅgha which are held to be insecure and dangerous. If a bhikṣu knowing beforehand such forest dwellings being held to be insecure and dangerous, shall accept eatables and drinkables not outside the Ārāma but inside the Ārāma, without the sanction of the Saṅgha (Saṅghakarma), this bhikṣu should confess to other bhikṣus, saying, "I have fallen, venerable sirs, into a blameworthy offence, unbecoming, which ought to be confessed; and now I confess it."

This is the fourth Pd. dharma.

Venerable sirs, the Four Pratideśanīya Dharmas have been recited.

Now I ask the venerable ones, 'Are you pure in this matter?'

A second and a third time, I ask the venerable ones, 'Are you pure in this matter?'

The venerable ones are pure herein; therefore do they keep silence.

Thus do I observe.

Skt. 4. Yāni punas tāny āraṇyakāni śayyāsanāni bhavanti sāśaṃkasaṃmatāni sapratibhayāni...

'Saṅghakarama' is absent here.

The following lines: '...pūrvam apratisamvit samāno bahir ārāmasya khādanīyabhojānīyaṃ svahastaṃ pratigṛhya aglāno khādet vā bhuñjīta vā' are quite different from the Sv.

Pāli 4. Yāni kho pana tāni āraññakāni senāsanāni sāsaṃkasaṃtāni sappaṭibhayāni...

The lines below nearly agree with the Skt. but not the Sv.: '...tathārupesu senāsanesu viharanto pubbe appaṭividitaṃ khādanīyaṃ vā bhojanīyaṃ vā ajjhārāme sahatthā paṭiggahetva agilāno khādeyya vā bhuṃjeyya vā paṭidesetabbaṃ.'

Dh. 4. Adds: 'Out of the way', 'without previously informing the donors' and 'with his own hand when he is not sick.'

Mhs. 'Without previous investigation'.

Omits the part that the bhikṣu knows the place to be held dangerous. This is also the case with ksy. Pd. 4, and Msg. Pd. 1.

Adds: 'With his own hand when he is not sick'.

Msg. 1. Omits: 'Held to be insecure and dangerous.'

'Without previous notice or information.'

Adds: 'not sick'. See Mhs. 4, above.

Msv. 4. 'Whatsoever bhikṣu, while he is dwelling in a place in the forest which is considered to be insecure and dangers shall, receive various kinds of food outside his residence, without previously sending persons to see whether there are signs of danger, that bhikṣu should return to his residence and go to the place of the bhikṣus...'

Tib. 4. '...dwelling in a hermitage situated in a region which is solitary, insecure and beset with various dangers, accepts food, soft or hard, of which he was not previously informed, in the outside grove (the life of the man who offers food being thus exposed to danger), and drinks or eats it, should go to the outside of the grove and make a confession...'

This is different from the Msv.

Mpt. 4. Vanavicayagataṃ.

VII. SAṂBAHULĀḤ ŚAIKṢA DHARMAS

Sv. VII.1

Here are, venerable sirs, the many Śaikṣa (Pāli. Sekhiya) Dharmas as known from the Prātimokṣa recited each half month.

Not to wear the inner garment[96] too high—that should be observed.

Skt. 1. Nātyutkṛṣṭaṃ cīvaraṃ[97] nivāsayiṣyāma iti śaikṣa karaṇīyā.

The translation of this would be: 'We shall not wear the robe too high—that ought to be observed'.

Pāli., Dh., Msg. Nil, from Sv. Sk. 1 to 11.

Mhs. 1, *Ksy.* 1. The Same

Msv. 2. 'The undergarment (skirt) will not be too high.'

Tib. 2. 'I shall put on my undergarment so that it is not tucked up too much.'

Mpt. 2. Nātyutkṛṣṭaṃ.

Sv. VII.2

Not to wear the inner garment too low—that should be observed.

---

96. The VNS. Sk. 2. has a transliteration of Nivasanaṃ—an undergarment.

97. (See previous page) From here onwards upto the 12th Sk. the 'cīvara' may be understood to be something in the nature of an 'undergarment' after the Ch. version, otherwise we shall not be able to explain the 13—15 Sk. dharmas in the Skt.

Skt. 2. Nātyavakṛṣṭaṃ cīvaraṃ nivāsayiṣyāma...
Mhs. 2, *Ksy.* 2, *Msv.* 3. The same.
Tib. 3. 'Not let it down too much.'
Mpt. 3. Nātyavakṛṣṭaṃ.

Sv. VII.3

Not to wear the inner garment in disorder—that should be observed.

Skt. 3. Na vikīrṇaṃ cīvaraṃ nivāsayiṣyāma...
Mhs. 3. The same.
Ksy. 3. 'Wear the inner garment in good order.'
Msv. 3, *Tib.* 3, *Mpt.* 3. Nil.

Sv. VII.4

Not to wear the inner garment like the head of an axe—that should be observed.

Skt. 4. Na nāgaśīrṣakaṃ cīvaraṃ nivāsayiṣyāma...
'Like the head of a snake.'
Mhs., *Ksy.* Nil.
Msv. 5, *Tib.* 7. 'Like the head of a snake.'
Mpt. 7. Na nāga-śiṣakaṃ nivāsanaṃ nivāsayiṣyāmīti....
Here the singular number of the person is used whereas the Skt. has the plural.

Sv. VII.5

Not to wear the inner garment like the leaf of a Tala tree—that should be observed.

Skt. 5. Na tālapatraṃ cīvaraṃ nivāsayiṣyāma...
Mhs. 4, *Ksy.* 5, *Msv.* 6, *Tib.* 5. The same.
Mpt. 5. Na tālavṛndakaṃ.

Sv. VII.6

Not to wear the inner garment like the trunk of an elephant—that should be observed.

Skt. 6. Na hastiśuṇḍaṃ cīvaraṃ nivāsayiṣyāma...
Mhs. 5. *Ksy.* 4, *Msv.* 4, *Tib.* 4. The same.
Mpt. 4. Na hastituṇḍāvalambitaṃ

Sv. VII.7

Not to wear the inner garment like a flour ball—that should be observed.

Skt. 7. Na kutmāṃsa (kulmāṣa...see Mpt. 6, below) piṇḍaṃ cīvaraṃ nivāsayiṣyāma...

Mhs. Nil.

Ksy. 6. The same.

Msv. 7. 'Not in the form of a mass of pulse.'

Tib. 6. 'Like the beards of barley.'

Mpt. 7. Na kulmāsapiṇḍakaṃ.

Not found in other texts.

Sv. VII.8

Not to wear the inner garment in fine foldings—that should be observed.

Skt. 8. Na kalāpakaṃ cīvaraṃ nīvāsayiṣyāma...

Mhs. 7. The same.

The VNS. Sk. 8 reads: 'Wear the nivāsanaṃ not like a straw bundle.'

This Sk. is not found in other texts.

Sv. VII.9

Not to wear the inner garment in the form of two ears—that should be observed.

Skt. 9. Ms. is completely missing from Sk. 9 to 11.

The VNS. SK. 9 reads: 'Not to wear the nivāsanaṃ by making it glossy.'

The Svv. Sk. 9 reads: 'Not to wear a leather (jung) nivāsana—that should be observed.'

This Sk. here is not found in other texts.

Sv. VII.10

Not to wear the inner garment like the head of a Pig—that should be observed.

I have taken this interpretation from the VNS. Sk. 10, because the Sv. text translated by Kumārajīva Sk. 10 is: 'not to wear the inner garment in the form of (something) raised up (sheng-chi). Anyway, I think, the VNS. is more clear.

The Svv. Sk. 10 reads: 'Not to wear the inner garment which is folded on both sides—that should be observed.' Of course, this is different from the above noted texts.

This Sk. is not found in other texts.

Sv. VII.11

Not to wear an inner garment of fine yarn—that should be observed.

This Sk. too is from the VNS. Sk. 11 The Sv. has (hsi sheng shu) which has no meaning at all. This seems to be a wrong reading.

The Svv. Sk. 11 is the same as the VNS.

To show the differences of the Chinese characters of 'fine yarn', we have 'Hsi sheng shu' in the Sv. and 'Hsi lou' in the two commentaries.

This Sk. too is not found in other texts.

Sv. VII.12

To wear the inner garment all round and well-arranged—that should be observed.

Skt. 12. Parimaṇḍalaṃ cīvaraṃ nivāsayiṣyāma...

Pāli 1. Parimaṇḍalaṃ nivāsessāmi...

Dh. 1, *Ksy.* 3, *Msg.* 1. The same. *Mhs.* Nil.

Msv. 1. 'To wear the skirt all round and well-arranged—that should be observed.'

Tib. 1. 'I shall[98] put on my undergarment all around me,' here the singular number of the person is like the Pāli.

Mpt. 1. Parimaṇḍalanivāsanaṃ.

Sv. V.13

Not to put on the robe too high—that should be observed.

Skt. 13. Nātyutkṛṣṭaṃ cīvaraṃ prāvariṣyāma...

From here onwards 'Cīvaraṃ' means 'robe', as we find it so clearly stated in all other texts.

See also the Sv. and Skt. Sk. 1, note 1. above compared.

Pāli., Dh., Msg. Nil.

---

98. Summary... 'Seven rules regarding the under-garment, three rules regarding the upper-garment, five rules regarding the belting, etc., five rules regarding the head-cover, etc., five rules regarding jumping, etc., five rules regarding the body, etc., nine rules regarding sitting down, and eight rules regarding giving and taking.

Ksy. 7. 'Not to wear the three robes high up...'

Msv. 9. 'This reads as: 'Not to wear the three robes very high...'

Tib. 9. 'I shall put on my upper-garment so that it is not tucked up too much.'

Mpt. 8. Nātyutkṛṣṭaṃ cīvaraṃ.

Sv. VII.14

Not to put on the robe too low—that should be observed.

Skt. 14. Nātyavakṛṣṭaṃ...

Pali., Dh., Msg. Nil.

Ksy. 8. 'Not to wear low the three robes...'

Mhs. 9, *Msv.* 10, *Tib.* 10. More or less are the same.

Mpt. 9. Nātyavakṛṣṭaṃ cīvaraṃ.

Sv. VII.15

Not to put on the robe in disorder—that should be observed.

Skt. 15. Na vikīrṇaṃ...

Pāli, Dh, Msg., Ksy. Nil.

Mhs. 10. The same.

Msv. 11. 'To wear the three robes properly.'

Tib. 11. 'I shall go amidst the houses with my clothes well-tied.'

Mpt. Nil.

Sv. VII.16

To put on the robe all round and well-adjusted—that should be observed.

Skt. Ms. is missing.

Pali 2. Parimaṇḍalaṃ pārupissāmi...

Dh. 2, *Ksy.* 9, *Msv.* 8. 'To put on the three robes...'

Mhs. Nil.

Msg. 2. The same.

Tib. 8. 'I shall put on my upper-garment all around me.'

Mpt. 10. Parimaṇḍalaṃ cīvaraṃ.

Sv. VII.17

To enter the layman's house with a well-covered body—that should be observed.

Skt. 17. Supraticchaṃ(n) na...antargṛhaṃ pravekṣyāma...

Pāli 3. Supaṭicchanno antaraghare gamissāmi...
Dh. 18, *Mhs.* 11, *Ksy.* 12, *Msg.* 3. The same.
Msv. 12. 'To cover with three robes nicely...'
Tib. 12. 'I shall go amidst the houses with my clothes well put on.'
Mpt. 12. Supraticchannaḥ.

Sv. VII.18

To sit in the layman's house with a well-covered body—that should be observed.

Skt. 18. Supraticchanna...antargṛhe niṣatsyāma...
Pāli 18. Supaṭicchanno antaraghare nisīdissāmi...
Dh. 19, *Mhs.* 12, *Msg.* 14. The same.
Ksy., *Msv.*, *Tib.*, *Mpt.* Nil.

Sv. VII.19

To enter the layman's house in a well-controlled manner—that should be observed.

The Svv. Sk. 19 says: 'To control the body well.'
Skt. 19. Susamvṛtā antargṛhaṃ pravekṣyāma...
Pāli 5. Susaṃvuto antaraghare gamissāmi...
Mpt. 11. Susaṃvṛtah.
This Sk. is not found in other texts.

Sv. VII.20

To sit in the layman's house in a well-controlled manner—that should be observed.

Skt. 20. Susaṃvṛta antargṛhe niṣatsyāma...
Pāli 20. Susaṃvuto antaraghare nisīdissāmi...
This Sk. too is not found in other texts.

Sv. V.21

To enter[99] the layman's house without casting glances—that should be observed.

Skt. 21. Anutkṣiptacakṣuṣontargṛhaṃ pravekṣyāma...
Pāli 7. Okkhittacakkhu antaraghare gamissāmi...

---

99. No. 19 in the VNS, Sk.

Dh. 20, *Mhs.* 37, *Ksy.* 14. '...without looking left or right...'
Msg. 4. '...looking properly or mindfully...'
Tib. 14. '...without moving my eyes hither and thither...'
Mpt. 14. Anutkṣiptacakṣuṣaḥ.

Sv. VII.22

To sit[100] in the layman's house without casting glances—that should be observed.

Skt. 22. Anutkṣiptacakṣuṣontargṛhe niṣatṣyāma...
Pāli 8. Okkhittacakkhu antaraghare nisīdissāmi...
Dh. 21, *Mhs.* 38, *Ksy.* 15. '...without looking left or right...'
Msg. 15. '...looking properly or mindfully...'
Msv., Tib., Mpt. Nil.

Sv. VII.23

To enter the layman's house without smelling—that should be observed.

Skt. Ms. missing.
This Sk. is not found in other texts.

Sv. VII.24

To Sit in the layman's house wihout smelling—that should be observed.

Skt. Ms. missing.
Not found in other texts.

Sv. VII.25

To enter the layman's house without presumption—that should be observed.

Skt. Ms. missing.
Ksy. The same.
Not found in other texts.

Sv. VII.26

To sit in the layman's house without presumption—that should be observed.

100. No. 20 in the VNS, Sk.

Skt. Ms. missing.
Not found elsewhere.

Sv. VII.27

To enter the layman's house with a little sound—that should be observed.

Skt. 27. Alpaśabdā antargṛhaṃ pravekṣyāma...
Pāli 13. Appasaddo antaraghare gamissāmi...
Dh. 22, *Ksy.* 13. 'Silently enters the layman's house...'
Mhs. 47. '...not with a loud sound.'
Msg. 5. The same.
Msv. 13. '...with a few words...'
Tib. 13. '...speaking few words...'
Mpt. 13. Alpaśabdaḥ.

Sv. VII.28

To sit in the layman's house with a little sound—that should be observed.

Skt. 28. Alpaśabdā antargṛhe niṣatsyāma...
Pāli 14. Appasaddo antaraghare nisīdissāmi...
Dh. 23. 'Silently sits in the layman's house...'
Mhs. 25. Adds: 'With a śaikṣamāṇā or a śrāmaṇerī'.
Ksy., Msv., Tib., Mpt. Nil.
Mhs. 48. '...not with a loud sound.'
Msg. 16. The same.

Sv. VII.29

To enter the layman's house without kneeling down—that should be observed.

Skt. Ms. missing.
Pāli 25. Na ukkuṭikāya...
Dh., Msg. Nil.
Mhs. 39, *Ksy.* 22, *Msv.* 20, *Tib.* 23. '...go amidst the houses without squatting...'
Mpt. 24. Notkuṭukikayā.

Sv. VII.30

To sit in the layman's house without kneeling down—that should be observed.

Skt. Ms. missing.
Dh. 11. 'Sit in the layman's house without squatting.'
Mhs. 40. The same.
This Sk. is not found in other texts.

Sv. VII.31

To enter the layman's house without covering the head—that should be observed.

Skt. 31. Nodguṇṭhikayā antargṛhaṃ pravekṣyāma...
Pāli 23. Na oguṇṭhito antaraghare gamissāmi.
Dh. 7, *Mhs.* 43, *Ksy.* 21, *Msg.* 7, *Msv.* 15, *Tib.* 16. The same.
Mpt. 16. Nodguṇṭhikayā

Sv. VII.32

To sit in the layman's house without covering the head—that should be observed.

Skt. 32. Nodguṇṭhikayā antargṛhe niṣatṣyāma...
Pāli 24. Na oguṇṭhito antaraghare nisīdissāmi...
Dh. 8, *Mhs.* 44, *Msg.* 18. The same.
Ksy., *Msv.*, *Tib.*, *Mpt.* Nil.

Sv. VII.33

To enter the layman's house without a turban on the head—that should be observed.

Skt. 33. Na veṣṭitaśirasontargṛhaṃ pravekṣyāma...
Not found in other texts.

Sv. VII.34

To sit in the layman's house without a turban on the head—that should be observed.

Skt. 34. Na veṣtitaśirasontargṛhe niṣatṣyāma...
Not found in other texts.

Sv. VII.35

To enter the layman's house without the arms being akimbo—that should be observed.

Skt. 35. Na skambhākṛtā antargṛhaṃ pravekṣyāma...

Pāli 21. Na khambhakato antaraghare gamissāmi...
Dh. 12, *Mhs.* 29, *Ksy.* 17, *Msg* 10, *Msv.* 18. The same.
Tib. 25. '...without leaning to any side...'
Mpt. 25. Na skambhākṛtaḥ.

Sv. VII.36

To sit in the layman's house without the arms being akimbo—that should be observed.

Skt. 36. Na skambhakṛta antargṛhe niṣatṣyāma...
Pāli 22. Na khambhakato antarghare nisīdissāmi...
Dh. 13, *Mhs.* 30, *Msg.* 22. The same.
Not found in the remaining texts (cf. Mpt. 25).

Sv. VII.37

To enter the layman's house without showing the chest—that should be observed.

Not found in other texts, except the *Upp.* Sk. 14.

Sv. VII.38

To sit in the layman's house without showing the chest—that should be observed.

Not found in other texts, except the *Upp.* Sk. 15.

Sv. VII.39

To enter the layman's house without showing the ribs—that should be observed.

Ksy. 23. '...without putting the hand at the ribs...'
Not found in other texts.

Sv. VII.40

To sit in the layman's house without showing the ribs—that should be observed.

Not found in other texts.

Sv. VII.41

To enter the layman's hosue without tucking up the robe (on one side)—that should be observed.

Skt. 37. Notkṛṣṭikākṛtā antargṛhaṃ pravekṣyāma...
Pāli 9. Na ukkhittakāya antaraghare gamissāmi...

Dh. 3, *Ksy.* 19, *Msv.* 16, *Msg.* 8. The same.

Mhs. 13. 'To enter the layman's house without tucking up the robe on the right shoulder...'

Mhs. 15. 'To enter the layman's house without tucking up the robe on the left shoulder...'

Tib. Nil.

Mpt. 17. Notkṛṣtikayā.

Sv. VII.42

To sit in the layman's house wihtout tucking up the robe (on one side)—that should be observed.

Skt. 38. Notkṛṣṭikākṛtā antargṛhe niṣatṣyāma...

Pāli 10. Na ukkhittakāya antaraghare nisīdissāmi...

Dh. 4. *Msg.* 19. The same.

Mhs. 14. 'To sit in the layman's house without tucking up the robe on the right shoulder...'

Mhs. 16. 'To sit in the layman's house without tucking up the robe on the left shoulder...'

Not found in the remaining texts.

Sv. VII.43

To enter the layman's house without tucking up the robe on the left and the right side—that should be observed.

Skt. 43. Nātyastikākṛtā antargṛhaṃ pravekṣyāma...

Pāli, Dh., Msg., Ksy., Tib. Nil.

Mhs. 17. '...not tucking up the robe on both sides...'

Mpt. 18. Notsaktikayā

Sv. VII.44

To sit in the layman's house without tucking up the robe on the left and the right side—that should be observed.

Skt. 42. Nātyastikākṛtā antargṛhe niṣatṣyāma...

Mhs. 18. '...not tucking up the robe on both sides...'

Not found in other texts.

Sv. VII.45

To enter the layman's house without letting the robe fall down—that should be observed.

Skt. 45. Na vikṣiptikākṛtā antargṛhaṃ pravekṣyāma...
Not found in other texts except in *Upp.* Sk. 16.
The VNS. Sk 37 says: To enter into, and Sk. 38: To sit in the house without letting the three robes fall and cover the feet.

Sv. VII.46

To sit in the layman's house without letting the robe fall down—that should be observed.

Skt. 46. Na vikṣipitikākṛtā antargṛhe niṣatsyāma...
Not found in other texts. See note on Sv. VII.45, above.

Sv. VII.47

To enter the layman's house without swinging the arms—that should be observed.

Skt. 47. Na bāhupracālakā...a...p...
Pāli 17. Na bāhuppacālakaṃ...a...p...
Dh. 16, *Mhs.* 33, *Ksy.* 25, *Msg.* 13, *Msv.* 26. The same.
Tib. 27. '...without shaking my hands...'
Mpt. 27. Na bāhupracālanaṃ

Sv. VII.48

To sit in the layman's house without swinging the arms—that should be observed.

Skt. 48. Na bāhupracālakā...a...n...
Pali 18. Na bāhuppacālakaṃ...a...n...
Dh. 17, *Mhs.* 34. The same.
Not found in other texts.

Sv. VII.49

To enter the layman's house without swaying the shoulder—that should be observed.

Skt. 49. Na cāṃsapracālakā...a...p...
Mhs. 23. The same.
Mpt. 29. Na soḍhaukikayā.
Not found in other texts.

Sv. VII.50

To sit in the layman's house without swaying the shoulder—that should be observed.

Skt. 50. Na cāṃsapracālakā...a...n...
Mhs. 24. The same.
Not found in the remaining texts.

Sv. VII.51

To enter the layman's house without shaking the head—that should be observed.

Skt. 51. Na śirṣapracālakā...a...p...
Pāli 19. Na sīsappacālakaṃ...a...p...
Dh. Nil.
Mhs. 21, *Ksy.* 26, *Msg.* 12, *Msv.* 27, *Tib.* 28. The same.
Mpt. 28. Na Śirṣapracālakāṃ

Sv. VII.52

To sit in the layman's house without shaking the head—that should be observed.

Skt. 52. Na śīrṣapracālakā...a...n...
Pāli 20. Na sīsappacālakaṃ...a...n...
Mhs. 22. The same.
Not found in other texts.

Sv. VII.53

To enter the layman's house without swaying the body—that should be observed.

Skt. 53. Na kāyapracālakā...a...p...
Pāli 15. Na kāyappacālakaṃ...a...p...
Dh. 14, *Mhs.* 19, *Ksy.* 27, *Msg.* 11, *Msv.* 25, *Tib.* 26. The same.
Mpt. 26. Na kāyapracālakāṃ.

Sv. VII.54

To sit in the layman's house without swaying the body—that should be observed.

Skt. 54. Na kāyapracālakā...a...n...
Pāli 16. Na Kāyappacālakaṃ...a...n...
Dh. 15. *Mhs.* 20. The same
Not found in the remaining texts.

Sv. VII.55

To enter the layman's house without interlacing the hands—that should be observed.

Skt. 55. Na hastasaṃlagnikayā...a...p...
Mhs. 25, *Ksy.* 28, *Msv.* 29, *Tib.* 30. The same.
Mpt. 30. Na hastasaṃlagnikayā.
Not found in other texts.

Sv. VII.56

To sit in the layman's house without interlacing the hands—that should be observed.

Skt. 56. Na hastasaṃlagnikayā...a. n...
Mhs. 26. The same.
Missing in other texts.

Sv. VII.57

To enter the layman's house without bending the leg—that should be observed.

Mhs. 41. 'Chi-hsing'
Ksy. 29. 'I-tsu-hsing'
Msv. 23. 'Tse-tsu-hsing'
The three texts above have different Chinese characters for 'bending the leg.'

There are also slight differences in VNS. Sk. 57 and SVV. Sk. 53. Not found in other texts.

Sv. VII.58

To sit in the layman's house without bending the leg—that should be observed.

Not found in the remaining texts save the *Mhs. Sk.* 42.

Sv. VII.59

To enter the layman's house without placing one leg upon the other—that should be observed.

Skt. 59. Na pāde pādam ādāyāntargṛhaṃ pravekṣyāma...
Mpt. 34. Na pāde pādam ādhāya.
The Svv. Sk. 55. has 'lei-pi-tso'...to sit one leg upon the other...is not found elsewhere.

This Sk. too is not found in other texts.

Sv. VII.60

To sit in the layman's house without placing one leg upon the other—that should be observed.

Skt. 60. Na pāde pādam ādāyāntargṛhe n...

Ksy. 39, *Msv.* 33, *Msg.* 21, *Tib.* 34. The same; slightly different in language.

Not found in other texts.

Sv. VII.61

Not to sit in the layman's house and place the palm against the cheek, for making the laity laugh—that should be observed.

Skt. 61. Na pāṇau hanum upādāya a...n...

Missing in all other texts.

Sv. VII.62

To receive food with a concentrated mind—that should be observed...

Skt. 62. ...Satkṛtyaudanaṃ pratigrahīṣyāma...

Pāli 27. Sakkaccaṃ piṇḍapātaṃ paṭiggahessāmi...

Dh. 26, *Mhs.* 51, *Ksy.* 40, *Msg.* 24. The same.

Msv. 39 and 43. 'To take food with care' and 'With respect.'

Tib. 40. I shall take my meal in a decent manner.'

Mpt. 40. Satkṛtya piṇḍapātaṃ pratigrahīṣyāmaḥ.

Sv. VII.63

To receive soup with a concentrated mind—that should be observed.

Skt. 63. Satkṛtya sūpikaṃ pratigrahīṣyāma.

Ksy. 46. The same.

Not found in other texts.

Sv. VII.64

To receive food without letting the contents of the bowl to be overflowing—that should be observed.

Skt. 54. Ms. missing.

Pāli 30. Samatitthikaṃ[101] piṇḍapātaṃ paṭigghessāmi...
Dh. 27, *Mhs.* 52, *Ksy.* 41. The same.
Msg. Nil.
Msv. 40. 'Not to receive[102] a bowlful of food, in addition to soup and vegetables, so that the food will not flow from the brim of the bowl; should keep a space about the size of a bending-finger, and eat with a concentrated mind—that should be observed.'
Tib. 42. 'I shall not make my bowl brimful with sauce.'
Mpt. 41. Na samatīrthikaṃ.

Sv. VII.65

To eat equal rice and soup—that should be observed.

Skt. 65. Samasūpikaṃ piṇḍapātaṃ paribhokṣyāma...
Pāli 34. Samasūpakaṃ piṇḍapātaṃ bhuñjissāmi...
Dh. 29, *Mhs.* 53, *Msg.* 25. The same.
Mpt. 42. Na samasūpikaṃ.
Missing in the remaining texts.

Sv. VII.66

To eat without scooping a particular portion—that should be observed.

Dh. 31, *Mhs.* 55, *Msg.* 26. The same.
Not found in other texts.

Sv. VII.67

Not to select good food from the bowl—that should be observed.

Skt. 67(?). Na vyutkhaṇḍaśaḥ piṇḍapātaṃ paribhokṣyāma...
Mhs. 54. 'Not to take food from all the places in the bowl...'
Not found in other texts except in Upp. Sk. 31.

Sv. VII.68

Not to make big handfuls of rice—that should be observed.

---

101. Samatitthikaṃ 'Equally full, equally heaped up' says SBE, vol. XIII, p. 62, note 5. But it is positive, that a 'na' is not translated, as we find strong evidence in Mpt. Sk. 41.

102. The Chinese Msv. text edited by the Chinese Buddhist Institute, Nanking, has divided this Sk. into two and marked it with the nos. 40-41. This, in fact, is one. See Msvv. ch. 50.

Skt. 68. Nātimahādālopaṃ kariṣyāma...
Pāli 39. Na'timahantaṃ kabalam karissāmi...
Dh. 36, *Ksy.* 62, *Msg.* 29, *Msv.* 45. The same.
Mhs. 64. 'To eat without letting the hand be full...'
Tib. 50. 'The bits eaten shall not be too big.'
Mpt. 49. Nātimahantaṃ.

Sv. VII.69

To make the handfuls of rice to just suit the mouth—that should be observed.

Skt. 69. Parimaṇḍalaṃ ālopaṃ kariṣyāma...
Pāli 40. Parimaṇḍalaṃ ālopaṃ karissāmi...
Dh. Nil.
Mhs. 65. 'To eat food without letting the mouth wide open.'
Ksy. 63. 'Without making small handfuls of rice-.'
Msg. 31. 'Picking up the handfuls of rice...'
Msv. 46. This exactly agrees with the Skt.
Tib. 51. 'The bits eaten shall be of a moderate size...'
Mpt. 50. Parimaṇḍalaṃ ālopam.

Sv. V.70

Not to open the mouth and wait for the food—that should be observed.

Skt. 70. Nānāgate ālope mukhadvāraṃ vivariṣyāma...
Pāli 41. Na anāhate kabale mukhadvāraṃ vivarissāmi...
Dh. 37, *Ksy.* 65, *Msg.* 30, *Msv.* 47. The same.

Mhs. 66. Adds: 'When the food has not yet come' (cf. Skt. 70 above).

Tib. 52. 'The mouth shall not be opened wide until the bits have been eaten up.'

Mpt. 51. Nānāgate ālope mukhadvāraṃ vivariṣyāmaḥ.

Sv. VII.71

Not to talk while food is in the mouth—that should be observed.

Skt. 71. Na sālopena mukhadvāreṇa vyāhariṣyāma...
Pāli 43. Na sakabaḷena mukhena vyāharissāmi...
Dh. 38, *Mhs.* 68, *Ksy.* 64, *Msg.* 33, *Msv.* 48. The same.

Tib. 53. 'Nothing should be spoken until the bits have been eaten up.'

Mpt. 52. Na sālopena mukhena vācaṃ Pravyāhariṣyāmaḥ.

Sv. VII.72

Not to bite the food by halves—that should be observed.

Skt. 66. Na kavaḍacchedakaṃ piṇḍapātaṃ paribhokṣyāma...
Pāli 45. Na kabalāvacchedakaṃ bhuñjissāmi...
Mhs. 70, *Ksy.* 54, *Msg.* 32, *Msv.* 57. The same.
Tib. 63. 'I shall eat without cutting my mouthfuls into several pieces.'
Dh., *Mpt.* Nil.

Sv. VII.73

Not to make a sound while the food is being chewed—that should be observed.

Skt. 73. Na śukārakaṃ piṇḍapātaṃ paribhokṣyāma...
Pāli 51. Na surusurukārakaṃ bhuñjissāmi...
Dh. 42. 'Should not purposely make a sound while the food has been chewed...'
Mhs. 62, *Ksy.* 48. The same.
Msg. 37, *Msv.* 51. '...making a Hu-tsu sound'.
Tib. 54. 'I shall not make a tsu-tsu noise.'
Mpt. 54. Na śuścukārakaṃ.

Sv. VII.74

Not to swallow unchewed food—that should be observed.

Skt. Ms. is missing.
Mhs. 74, *Msg.* 39. The same.
Not found in other texts.

Sv. VII.75

Not to cause the cheek to swell with food—that should be observed.

Skt., *Ksy.*, *Mpt.* Nil.
Pāli 46. Na avagaṇḍakārakaṃ bhuñjissāmi...
Dh. 41, *Mhs.* 69, *Msg.* 27, *Msv.* 56. The same.
Tib. 61. 'I shall not plaster my cheeks (with the remaining food).'

Sv. VII.76

Not to protrude the tongue while eating—that should be observed.

Skt. 76. Na jihvāniścārakaṃ piṇḍapātaṃ paribhokṣyāma...
Pāli 49. Na jivhāniccārakaṃ bhuñjissāmi...
Dh. Nil.
Mhs. 73, *Ksy.* 53, *Msg.* 28, *Msv.* 58. The same.
Tib. 58. 'I shall not eat by lolling out my tongue...'
Mpt. 57. Na jihvāniścārakaṃ piṇḍapātaṃ bhokṣyāmaḥ.

Sv. VII.77

Not to smell the food while eating—that should be observed.

Skt. 75. Nojjighraṃtaḥ piṇḍapātaṃ paribhokṣyāma...
Mhs. 57, *Ksy.* 50. The same.
Not found in the remaining texts.

Sv. VII.78

Not to lick the hand—that should be observed.

Skt. 78. Na hastāvalehakaṃ piṇḍapātaṃ paribhokṣyāma...
Pāli 52. Na hatthanillehakaṃ bhuñjissāmi...
Dh. 44, *Mhs.* 63, *Ksy.* 56, *Msg.* 35, *Msv.* 61, *Tib.* 64. The same.
Mpt. 63. Na hastāvalehakaṃ.

Sv. VII.79

Not to clean the bowl with the finger while eating—that should be observed.

Mhs. 56. 'Not to bend the finger to clean...'
Msg. 34. The same.
Not found in other texts.

Sv. VII.80

Not to abandon food—that should be observed.

Skt. 80. Na śiṣṭavikiraṃ(?) piṇḍapātaṃ paribhokṣyāma...
Pāli 48. Na sitthāvakārakaṃ bhuñjissāmi...
Dh. 40, *Msg.* 40. 'Not to let fall...'
Mhs. 59. The same.
Msv. 55. 'Should not scatter food with the hand...'
Ksy., *Tib.* Nil.

Mpt. 58. Na sikthapṛthakkārakaṃ.

Sv. VII.81

Not to shake the hand while eating—that should be observed.

Skt. 81. Na hastāvadhūnakaṃ piṇḍapātaṃ paribhokṣyāma...
Pāli 47. Na hatthaniddhunakaṃ bhuñjissāmi...
Dh. 45, *Mhs.* 72, *Msg.* 41, *Msv.* 62, *Tib.* 66. The same.
Ksy. Nil.
Mpt. 65. Na hastasaṃdhūnakaṃ.

Sv. VII.82

Not to receive the eating vessel with a soiled hand—that should be observed.

Skt. 82. Na sāmiṣeṇa pāṇinā pānīyasthālakaṃ pratigṛhīṣyāma...
Pāli 55. Na sāmisena hatthena pāniyathālakaṃ paṭiggahessāmi...
Dh. 47, *Msg.* 46. The same.
Mhs. 60. 'Not to hold a clean utensil with a soiled hand (after taking food)...'
Ksy. 68. 'Not to hold a water-vessel with a soiled hand...'
Msv. 66. 'Not to hold a clean water-jar...'
Tib. 70. 'I shall not take into my hand a water-pot while my hand is soiled with the leavings of a meal'.
Mpt. 68. Na samiṣeṇa pāṇinodakasthālakaṃ grahīṣyāmaḥ.

Sv. VII.83

Not to cover the soup with rice with the hope of getting more—that should be observed.

Skt. 83. Naudaneṇa sūpaṃ praticchādayiṣyāmo bhūyaskāmatāṃ upādāya...
Pāli 36. Na sūpaṃ vā vyaṃjanaṃ vā odanena paṭicchādessāmi bhiyyokamyataṃ upādāya 'ti.
'Vyamjanaṃ vā' is not in the Skt.
Dh. 33, *Mhs.* 77, *Ksy.* 43, *Msg.* 45. The same.
Msv. 49. 'Not to cover the soup and vegetables with rice and *vice-versa...'*
Tib. 46. 'I shall[103] not out of greediness cover the sauce with rice'.

103. Summary: 'Six rules regarding good eating, five rules regarding tsu-tsu, etc., and five rules regarding the licking of hand, etc.'

Mpt. 46. Na odenena sūpikaṃ praticchādayiṣyāmaḥ sūpikena vā odanaṃ (cf. Msv. Sk. 49).

Sv. VII.84

Not to ask for soup and rice for himself when he is not sick—that should be observed.

Skt. 84. Ms. is missing.
Pāli 37. Na sūpaṃ vā odanaṃ vā agilāno attano atthāya viññapetvā bhuñjissāmi...
Dh. 32. The same.
Mhs. 79. Omits: 'When he is not sick.'
Msg. 44, *Ksy.* 45. '...asking for food...'
Msv., *Tib.*, *Mpt.* Nil.

Sv. VII.85

Not to look into one's neighbour's bowl with hatred—that should be observed.

Skt. 85. Nāvadhyānaprekṣiṇāntarikasya bhikṣoḥ pātraṃ vyavalokayiṣyāma...
Pāli 38. Na ujjhānasaññī paresaṃ pattaṃ olokessāmi...
Dh. 34, *Mhs.* 80, *Ksy.* 66, *Msg.* 42. The same.
Msv. 65. '...with contempt'.
Tib. 69. '...I shall[104] not look at the bowl of a monk that sits by me with an intention of upbraising him.'
Mpt. 70. Nāvadhyānaprekṣiṇo' ntarikasya bhikṣoḥ pātraṃ avalokayiṣyāmaḥ.

Sv. VII.86

To eat with a concentrated mind and look into the bowl—that should be observed.

Skt. 86. Pātrasaṃjñinaḥ piṇḍapātaṃ paribhokṣyāma...
Pāli 32. Pattasaññī piṇḍapātaṃ bhuñjissāmi...
Dh. 35. 'Should bend the mind upon the bowl while eating...'

104. Summary: 'Four relating to upbraising, etc, ten rules relating to the begging bowl, five rules on standing, etc., five rules regarding the covered head, etc., five rules regarding the wearing of braided hair, etc., five rules regarding the riding on an elephant, etc., six rules regarding the holding of a staff, etc., in the hand, and four rules for the sick.'

Mhs. 58. 'Looking into the bowl with care while eating...'
Ksy. Nil.
Msg. 43. The same.
Msv. 64. 'Should always look into the bowl while eating.'
Tib. 43. '...look into the bowl and its borders.'
Mpt. 44. Pātrasaṃjñinaḥ.

Sv. VII.87

To eat in order—that should be observed.

Skt. Ms. is missing.
Pāli 33. Sapadānaṃ piṇḍapātaṃ bhuñjissāmi...
Dh. 30. The Same.
Mpt. 43. Sāvadānaṃ.
Not found in other texts.

Sv. VII.88

Not to throw away the bowl-rinsing water in the laity's house unless the host is informed (beforehand)—that should be observed.

Skt. 88. Na sāmiṣaṃ pātrodakaṃ antagṛhe chorayiṣyāmo gṛhiṇam anavalokya...

Pāli 56. Na sasitthakaṃ pattadhovanaṃ antaraghare choddessāmi...

Dh. 48, *Pāli* 56. Omit: 'Unless the host is informed.'

Mhs. 76. 'Not to sprinkle water in the layman's house from the bowl when there is rice in it...'

Ksy. 69. '...dirty water...'

Msg. 47. 'Not to throw the remnant of food on the ground from the bowl...'

Msv. 67. The same.

Tib. 72. '...not to pour out water soiled with the leavings of a meal into (the inner court of) a house without the permission of the master of the house.'

Mpt. 71. Na sāmiṣaṃ udakaṃ antargṛhe chorayiṣyāmaḥ santaṃ gṛhiṇam anavalokya.

Sv. VII.89

Not to preach to a person who is riding on a horse, unless he is sick—that should be observed.

Skt. 89. Nāśvārūḍhasyāglanasya dharmaṃ deśayiṣyāma...
Pāli 63. Na yānagatassa agilānassa dhammaṃ desissāmi...

Not 'horse' but 'cart'.

Dh. 59, *Mhs.* 96, *Ksy.* 81, *Msg.* 62. '...to the person who is riding and sitting in a carriage...'

Msv. 84, *Tib.* 95. The same.

Mpt. 92. Nāśvārudhāya dharmaṃ deśayiṣyāmaḥ.

Sv. VII.90

Not to preach to a person who is in front of the bhikṣu and he himself is at the back, unless he is sick—that should be observed.

Skt. 91. Na purato gacchataḥ pṛṣṭhatonugacchanta[105] aglānasya dharmaṃ deśayiṣyāma...

Pāli 71. Na pacchato gacchaṃto purato gacchantassa dhammaṃ desissāmi...

Dh. 90, *Mhs.* 90,, *Ksy.* 78, *Msg.* 61. The same.

Msv. 96. '...going in front and (the bhikṣu) himself going behind...' This is also the case found in Upp. Sk. 55.

Tib. 82. 'While going behind I shall not preach religion to a person who goes before me...'

Mpt. 80. Na pṛṣṭhato gacchantaḥ purato gacchate aglānāya dh...d...

Sv. VII.91

Not to preach to a person who is on the road while the bhikṣu is outside the road, unless he is sick—that should be observed.

Skt. 90. Notpathena gacchantaḥ purato gacchato dh...d...

Pāli 72. Na uppathena gacchanto pathena gacchantassa agilānassa dh...d...

Dh. 92, *Mhs.* 91, *Ksy.* 80, *Msg.* 63, *Msv.* 77, *Tib.* 83. The same.

Mpt. 81. Notpathena gacchantaḥ pathena gacchate aglānāya dh...d...

Sv. VII.92

Not to preach to a person who is in a high position whereas the bhikṣu is in a low position, unless he is sick—that should be observed.

Skt. 92. Na nīcāsane niṣaṇṇā uccāsane niṣaṇṇasyāglānasya dh...d...

Pāli. 69. Na nīce āsane nisīditvā ucce āsane nisinnassa agīlānassa dh...d...

105. The Skt., Pāli., Msv., Tib., and Mpt.: All have the same content of 'going ahead and going behind'. They are slightly different from the Sv.

Dh. 89, *Mhs.* 88, *Msv.* 75, *Tib.* 81. The same.

Ksy. 77. 'Not to preach the doctrine to a person who is seated and he himself is not seated.'

Msg. 50. 'Not to preach the doctrine to a person who is on a high bed while he himself is underneath...'

Mpt. 79. Na nīca-tarake niṣaṇṇa ucctarake āsane niṣaṇṇāyāglānāya dh...d...

Sv. VII.93

Not to preach the doctrine to a person who sits whilst the bhikṣu stands—that should be observed.

Skt. 93. Na sthitā niṣaṇṇasya aglānasya dh...d...
Pāli 70. Na ṭhito nisinnassa agilānassa dh...d...
Dh. 86, *Mhs.* 87, *Ksy.* 74, *Msg.* 48, *Msv.* 73, *Tib.* 79. The same.
Mpt. 77. Notthito niṣaṇṇāyāglānāya dh...d...

Sv. VII.94

Not to preach the doctrine to a person who is lying down whilst the bhikṣu sits, unless he is sick—that should be observed.

Skt. 94. Na niṣaṇṇa nipannasya dh...d...
Pāli 64. Na sayanagatassa agilānassa dh...d...
Dh. 87, *Mhs.* 89, *Ksy.* 76, *Msg.* 49, *Msv.* 74, *Tib.* 80. The same.
Mpt. 78. Na niṣaṇṇā nipannāyāglānāya dh...d...

Sv. VII.95

Not to preach the doctrine to a person who covers his head—that should be observed.

Skt. 95. Nāvaguṇṭhitaśiraso dh...d...
Pāli 67. Na oguṇṭhitasīsassa agilānassa dh...d...
Dh. 54, *Mhs.* 92, *Ksy.* 92, *Msg.* 53, *Msv.* 78, *Tib.* 84. The same
Mpt. 82. Nodguṇṭhikākṛtāyaglānāya...dh...d...

Sv. VII.96

Not to preach the doctrine to a person who has a turban on his head, unless he is sick—that should be observed.

Skt. 96. Na veṣṭitaśiraso dh...d...
Pāli 66. Na veṭṭitasīsassa agilānassa dh...d...
Dh. 55, *Ksy.* 91, *Msg.* 54, *Msv.* 92. The same.

Tib. 93. '...whose head is wrapped around...'
Mpt. 90. Na veṣṭitaśirase dh...d...

Sv. VII.97

Not to preach the doctrine to a person who is akimbo, unless he is sick—that should be observed.

Skt. 97. Na skambhākṛtasya dh...d...
Dh. 56, *Msv.* 81. The same.
Not found in all other texts.

Sv. VII.98

Not to preach the doctrine to a person who is showing his chest, unless he is sick—that should be observed.

Skt. Nil.
Mhs. 86. The same.
Not found in other texts.

Sv. VII.99

Not to preach the doctrine to a person who is showing his ribs, unless he is sick—that should be observed.

The Svv. Sk. 93 comments: 'Not to preach the doctrine to a person who is hiding (or placing) his elbow on another's shoulder...'
Not found in the remaining texts.

Sv. VII.100

Not to preach the doctrine to a person who tucks up his robe (on one side)—that should be observed.

Skt. 98. Notkṛṣtikāṛtasya aglānasya dh...d...
Pāli., Ksy., Msg. Nil.
Dh. 52, *Mhs.* 93, *Msv.* 79, *Tib.* 85. The same.
Mpt. 83. Notkṛṣtikākṛtayāglānāya dh...d...

Sv. VII.101

Not to preach the doctrine to a person who tucks up the robe on the left and the right side, unless he is sick—that should be observed.

Skt. 100. Nātyastikākrtasya aglānasya dh...d...
Mhs. 94, *Msv.* 80. The same

Mpt. 84. Notsaktikākṛitāyāglānāya dh...d...
Not found in other texts.

Sv. VII.102

Not to preach the doctrine to a person who lets his robe fall down, unless he is sick—that should be observed.

Skt. 102. Na vikṣiptikākṛtasya aglānasya dh...d...
Not found in the remaining texts except in the *Upp. Sk.* 16.

Sv. VII.103

Not to preach the doctrine to a person who wears pattens, unless he is sick—that should be observed.

Skt. 103. Na pādukārūḍhasya aglānasya dh...d...
Pāli 61. Na pādukāruḷhassa agilānassa dh...d...
Dh. 58, *Mhs.* 84, *Ksy.* 83, *Msg.* 52. The same.
Msv. 87. '...wears pattens, boots and shoes...'
Tib. Nil.
Mpt. 95. Na pādukārūḍhāya dh...d...

Sv. VII.104

Not to preach the doctrine to a person who wear leather shoes, unless his is sick—that should be osberved.

Skt. 104. Na sopānahākasya aglānasya dh...d...
Pāli 62. Na upāhanārūḷhassa agilānassa dh...d...
Dh. 57, *Mhs.* 85, *Ksy.* 84, *Msg.* 51. The same.
Msv. 88. '...wears straw sandals...'
Tib. 98. '...puts on high-heeled shoes...'
Mpt. Nil.

Sv. VII.105

Not to preach the doctrine to a person who holds a staff, unless he is sick—that should be observed.

Skt. 105. Na daṇḍapāṇer aglānasya dh...d...
Pāli 58. Na daṇḍapāṇissa agilānassa dh...d...
Dh. 96, *Mhs.* 97, *Ksy.* 85, *Msg.* 59, *Tib.* 99. The same.
Msv. Nil.
Mpt. 96. Na daṇḍapāṇaye dh...d...

Sv. VII.106

Not to preach the doctrine to a person who holds an umbrella, unless he is sick—that should be observed.

Skt. 106. Na chattrapāṇer aglānasya dh..d...
Pāli 57. Na chattapāṇissa agilānassa dh...d...
Dh. 100. The same.
Mhs. 95. '...who holds an umbrella to shade his body...'
Ksy. 87, *Msg.* 60, *Msv.* 94, *Tib.* 100. The same.
Mpt. 97. Na chattrapāṇaye dh...d...

Sv. VII.107

Not to preach the doctrine to a person who holds a knife five feet in length, unless he is sick—that should be observed.

Skt. 107. Na śastrapāṇer aglānasya dh...d...
Pāli 59. Na satthapāṇissa agilānassa dh...d...
'Five feet in length' in the SV. is not found in other texts.
Dh. 99, *Mhs.* 98, *Ksy.* 86, *Msg.* 57, *Tib.* 102. 'Knife'.
Omits: 'Five feet'.
Mpt. 98. Na śastrapāṇaye dh...d...

Sv. VII.108

Not to preach the doctrine to a person who holds a small dagger, unless he is sick—that should be observed.

Skt. 108. Na khaḍgapāṇer aglānasya dh...d...
Dh. 97. '...Chien, a double edged sword...'
Mpt. 99. Na khaḍgapāṇaye dh...d...
Not found in the remaining texts.

Sv. VII.109

Not to preach the doctrine to a person who holds bows, arrows and various kinds of weapons, unless he is sick—that should be observed.

Skt. 109. Nāyudhapāṇer aglānasya dh...d...
Pāli 60. Na āyudhapāṇissa agilānassa dh...d...
Dh. 98. 'mu, a kind of weapon.'
Mhs. 99, *Msg.* 58. '...bows and arrows...' only.
Msv., *Ksy.* Nil.
Tib. 101. '...holds a weapon in his hand...'
Mpt. 100. Nāyudhapāṇaye dh...d...

Sv. VII.110

Not to cast ordure, urine, spittle or mucus on growing grass, unless one is sick—that should be observed.

Skt. 110. Nāglānāh saharitapradeśa uccāraprasrāvaṃ kheṭaṃ siṅghāṇakaṃ vāntaṃ viriktaṃ chorayiṣyāma...
Pāli 74. Na harite agilāno uccāraṃ vā passāvaṃ khelaṃ vā karissāmi...
Dh. 49, *Msg.* 64, *Msv.* 96. The same.
Mhs. 83. Omits: 'Spittle and mucus.'
'On the blade of grass.'
Ksy. 95. Adds: 'Omits blood.'
Tib. 107. 'I shall not cast ordure, urine, spittle, snot or vomitted matter into a place covered with green grass...'
Mpt. 104. Nāglānāḥ saharitapradeśe uccāraprasrāvaṃ kheṭaṃ siṅghāṇakaṃ vāntaṃ viriktaṃ chorayiṣyāmaḥ.

Sv. VII.111

Not to cast ordure, urine, spittle or mucus into the pure water, unless one is sick—that should be observed.

Skt. 111. Nāglānā udaka uccāraprasrāvaṃ kheṭaṃ siṅghāṇakaṃ vāntaṃ viriktaṃ chorayiṣyāma...
Pāli 75. Na udake agilāno uccāraṃ vā passāvaṃ vā kheḷam vā karissāmi...
Dh. 50. The same.
Mhs. 82. Omits: 'Spittle and mucus.'
Msv. 97, *Msy* 94, *Msg.* 65. Omits: 'Pure.'
Tib. 106. 'I shall not cast ordure, urine, spittle snivel, snout or vomitted matter into the water...'
Mpt. 103. Nāglānā udaka uccāraprasrāvaṃ kheṭaṃ siṅghāṇakaṃ vāntaṃ viriktaṃ chorayiṣyāmaḥ.

Sv. VII.112

Not to discharge ordure and urine in a standing posture, unless one is sick—that should be observed.

Skt. 112. Nāglānā utthitā (sthitā?) uccāraprasrāvaṃ...
Pāli 73. Na ṭhito agilāno uccāraṃ vā passāvaṃ vā karissāmi.
Dh. 51, *Mhs.* 81, *Ksy.* 93, *Msg.* 66, *Msv.* 95, *Tib.* 105. The same.
Mpt. 102. Nāglāno utthitā uccāraprasrāvaṃ kariṣyāmaḥ.

Sv. VII.113

Not to climb on a tree higher than the height of a man, unless there is a cause for it—that should be observed.

Venerable sirs, the Many Śaikṣa Dharmas have been recited.

In respect of them I ask the venerable ones, 'Are you pure in this matter?'

A second and a third time I ask the venerable ones, 'Are you pure in this matter?'

The venerable ones are pure herein—therefore, do they keep silence.

Thus do I observe.

Skt. 113. Nāsādhikaṃ puruṣaṃ vṛkṣam ārokṣyāmonyatra pratyayād.

Pāli., Msg. Nil.

Dh. 94. '...higher than the head of a man...'

Mhs. 100. '...except when there is a great cause...'

Ksy. 96. '...except when there is a cause of fear...'

Msv. 98. '...except when there is a cause of danger...'

Tib. 108. '...unless I am urged by any danger...'

Mpt. 105. Nāsādhikaṃ puruṣyaṃ vṛkṣam adhirokṣyāma anyatrāpada iti karaṇīya(?)

VIII. THE SEVEN ADHIKARAṆAŚAMATHA DHARMAS

Sv. VIII.1

Here are, venerable sirs, the Seven Adhikaraṇaśamatha Dharmas as known from the Prātimokṣa reicted each half month.

In case of a dispute fit to be settled in presence, that must be settled in presence.

Skt. 1. 1 to 7 Ms. is incomplete and missing.

Pāli 1. ...saṃmukhāvinayo dātabbo...

Dh. 1, *Mhs.* 1, *Ksy., Msv., Tib.* 1. The same.

Msg. 1. Adds: 'If for the convenience of the matter or for the convenience of the persons concerned.'

Mpt. 1. Saṃmukhavinayaḥ

Sv. VIII.2

In case of a dispute fit to be settled from recollection, that should be conducted from recollection.

Pāli 2. Sativinayo dātabbo.

Dh. 2, *Mhs.* 2, *Ksy.* 2, *Msg.* 2, *Msv.* 2, *Tib.* 2. The same.
Mpt. 2. Smṛtivinayaḥ.

Sv. VIII.3

In case of a dispute fit to be settled for a person who is no longer out of his mind, that should be conducted when that person is no longer out of his mind.

Pāli 3. ...Amuḷhavinayo dātabbo.
Dh. 3, *Mhs.* 3, *Ksy.* 3, *Msg.* 4, *Msv.* 3. *Tib.* 3. The same.
Mpt. 3. Amūḍhavinayaḥ.

Sv. VIII.4

In case of a dispute fit to be settled on confession of guilt, that should be conducted on confession of guilt.

Pāli 4. Paṭiññāya kāretabbo.
Dh. 4, *Mhs.* 5, *Ksy.* 4, *Msg.* 4, *Msv.* 6. The same.
Tib. 7. '...by an undertaking, the proceedings must be conducted by the undertaking of the accused'.
Mpt. 7. Pratijñākārakaḥ.

Sv. VIII.5

In case of a dispute fit to be settled with an inquiry into the nature of the offence, that inquiry into the nature of offence should be made.

Pāli 6. Tassapāpiyyasikā.
Dh. 5, *Mhs.* 4, *Msg.* 5. The same.
Mhs. 4, *Ksy.* 5. '...inquiring into the root-cause'.
Tib. 5. '...to be settled with an enquiry into its true nature...'
Mpt. 5. Tatsvabhāvaiṣīyaḥ.

Sv. VIII.6

In case of a dispute fit to be settled with an enquiry into the nature of the offence by a majority (of the bhikṣus), that should be conducted with an enquiry into the nature of the offence by a majority (of the bhikṣus).

Pāli 5. Yebhuyyasikā.
Dh. 6, *Msg.* 6, *Tib.* 4. The same.
Mhs. 6, *Ksy.* 6, *Msv.* 5. '...the vinaya should be conducted by many people...'

Mpt. 4. Yad-bhūyasikīyaḥ.

Sv. VIII.7

In case various disputes arise among the Saṅgha, they should be settled and annihilated as in the manner of grass covering over the field—that should be osberved.

Venerable sirs, the Seven Adhikaraṇaśamatha Dharmas have been recited.

In respect of them, I ask the venerable ones, 'Are you pure in this matter?'

The venerable ones are pure herein; therefore, do they keep silence.

Thus do I observe.

Pāli 7. Tiṇṇavatthārako

Dh. 7, *Mhs.* 7, *Ksy.* 7, *Msg.* 7, *Msv.* 7, *Tib.* 6. 'In case of a dispute fit to be settled by being covered over as with grass, that should be conducted by being covered over as with grass.'

Mpt. 6. Tṛṇastārakaḥ.

IX. CONCLUSION

Sv.

Venerable sirs!

Recited is the Introduction of the Vinaya.

Recited are the Four Pārājika Rules.

Recited are the Thirteen Saṃghāvaśeṣa Rules.

Recited are the Two Aniyata Rules.

Recited are the Thirty Niḥsargika Pātayantika Rules.

Recited are the Ninety Pātayantika Rules.

Recited are the Many Śaikṣa Rules.

Recited are the Seven Adhikaraṇaśamatha Rules.

All these have been embraced in the Vinaya-sūtra of the Buddha and are recited each half month as known in the Prātimokṣa, as well as other texts of conduct in accordance with the Dharma.

To these, O venerable sirs, you should, amongst you, rejoice in, cherish in your heart without dispute, just as a mixture of water and milk, and observe them carefully.

This should be observed.

The Vipaśyī Bhagavān Tathāgata Arhat Samyaksaṃbuddha preached this Vinaya-sūtra to an assembly of sixty-two lacs of bhikṣus who surrounded him on all sides:

> 1. Patience[106] is the best path, and Nirvāṇa
> Is most supreme, says the Buddha.
> He is not an ascetic,
> Who insults others.

The Śikhī Bhagvān Tathagata Arhat Samyaksaṃbuddha preached this Vinaya-sūtra to an assembly of eight lacs of bhikṣus who surrounded him on all sides:

> 2. Just as a person who possesses eyes and
> Insight escapes all dangers,
> So the wise men in the world
> Are able to avoid all sins.

The Sui Yeh (Viśvabhū?)[107] Bhagavān Tathāgata Arhat Samyaksaṃbuddha preached this Vinaya-sūtra to an assembly of one lac of bhikṣus who surrounded him on all sides:

> 3. Not to vex,[108] not to speak others' fault,
> Practise as to what has been taught
> In the Vinaya-sūtra, to be moderate in
> Eating, taking delight in solitude and
> Earnestness, and keeping the mind pure,
> ...This is indeed the teaching of the Buddha.

The Krakucchanda Bhagavān Tathāgata Arhat Samyakasaṃ-buddha preached this Vinaya-sūtra to an assembly of forty thousand bhikṣus who surrouned him on all sides:

> 4. Just[109] as a bee alights on a flower and
> Destroys not its colour nor its scent,
> But takes a sip and departs.
> So also a bhikṣu enters a village,
> Does not disturb others' affairs,

---

106. Dhmp. Buddhavagga, Verse 6.
107. The Chinese text has the words Sui Yeh? Cf. Skt. verse 5-6.
108. Dhmp. Buddhavagga, verse 7.
109. Cf. Dhmp. Pupphavagga, verses 6-7.

Nor does he look into what is done and
Undone, but observes his own behaviour
And meditates what is good
And what is not good.

The Kanakamuni Bhagavān Tathāgata Arhat Samykasaṃbuddha preached this Vinaya-sūtra to an assembly of thirty thousand bhikṣus who surrounded him on all sides:

5. If one wishes to attain
The highest state of mind, he should
Never allow it to get astray, but
Diligently study the Good Dharmas of
The Noble ones, thinking concentratedly of
Peace; then he may have no more sorrow.

The Kāśyapa Bhagavān Tathāgata Arhat Samykasaṃbuddha preached this Vinaya-sūtra to an assembly of twenty thousand bhikṣus who surrounded him on all sides:

6. Not[110] to commit any sin,
To practise virtue and
To Purify one's mind,
That is the teaching of the Buddhas.

Our Śākyamuni Bhagavān Tathāgata Arhat Samykasaṃbuddha preached this Vinaya-sūtra to one thousand two hundred and fifty excellent bhikṣus who surrounded him on all sides:

7. Good[111] is the restraint of the body,
The restraint in speech is good.
A bhikṣu restrained in all things
Is freed from all sins.

8. The bhikṣu guards his speech and mind,
And lets not his body practise any evil

---

110. Dhmp. Buddhavagga, verse 5.
111. Dhmp. Bhikkhuvagga, verse 2.

...After purifying his activity in these three directions...
Attains the road preached by the sages.

9. If people beat and scold you,
Never treat them with the same;
Never hate the persons who hate you,
But keep a pure mind towards the angry,
And restrain yourself while seeing
Other people practise evil things.

10. The seven Buddhas who can protect the
World are honoured by mankind.
I have explained in detail the
Vinaya-sūtra uttered by them.

11. All the Buddhas and their disciples
Pay respect to this Vinaya-sūtra.
Having paid homage to it,
They should respect one another.

12. It is through the sense of modesty and
Humility that one gets perfection
And is able to attain Nirvāṇa.

I have finished the recitation of the Vinaya-sūtra, let the Saṅgha therefore, perform the Poṣadha with concentration.

Skt.

Thre are seventeen verses here, though some of them are incomplete. The names of the seven Buddhas appeared in the following verses:

Vipaśyī in verse 1.
Śikhī in verse 3.
Viśvabhū in verse 5.
Krakucchanda in verse 7.
Kanakamuni in verse 10.
Kāśyapa in verse 12.
Śākyasiṃha in verse 14.

These verses are mostly corresponding to the Sv. though they do not mention the number of bhikṣus present when the verses were uttered.

They are roughly the same as shown in the following table:

Sv.	*Skt.*
1.	1-2
2.	3-4
3.	5-6
4.	7-9
5.	10-11
6.	13*
7.	15
8.	16
9.	17
10-12.	Nil

Pāli

We do not find any verse or names of the seven Buddhas here.

Dh.

The seven verses uttered by the seven Buddhas are quite the same, though the language differs slightly now and then.

There is an additon of 12 verses stating the benefit of observing the Śīla and disadvantages for those who violate the precepts.

Mhs., Msg.

The verses and the names of the Buddhas are the same. No number of the bhikṣus has been mentioned. Moreover, the words 'pure saṅgha' are added in the texts.

At the end of the Msg., there is an addition of six verses in praise of the wonderful rewards of observing the Vinaya rules.

Ksy.

There is no mention of the seven Buddhas nor the verses uttered by them. The arrangement resembles the Pāli text. However, there are nine verses of a quite different type though they are also in the nature of encouraging people to observe the Śīla.

---

*Ms. of the 14th verse of the Skt. is incomplete

Msv.

The first 9 verses, uttered by the seven Buddhas, including Śākyamuni, are roughly the same, though there is some difference in the attribution of the verses. Then come seven verses out of which the first mentions the names of the Buddhas, the second and third correspond with SV. 10 and 11. The remaining four verses have been drawn from a source common with the Tib. The total number of verses are thus 16.

Tib.

There are 18 verses in total in this text in the concluding stanzas. There is no indication that the verses were uttered by the seven Buddhas, nor the number of bhikṣus who attended the meetings.

The following table will show how they correspond to the Sv:

Tib.	*Sv.*
1. (23)	1
2. (24)	2
3. (25)	3
4-5. (26-27)	4
6. (28)	5
7. (29)	Nil
8. (30)	6
9. (31)	7
10. (32)	8
Nil	9
11. (33)	Nil
12. (34)	10
13. (35)	11-12
14-18 (36-40	Nil

The extra four verses: 12, 13, 14 and 15 in the Msv (as mentioned above), do correspond with Tib. 14, 15, 17 and 18 respectively.

Mpt.

We do not find anything more in this text.

III

APPENDICES

Appendix I

CLASSIFICATION OF THE PRĀTIMOKṢA RULES OF THE SARVĀSTIVĀDIN SCHOOL

	I *Pj.*	*II* *Saṃ.*	*III* *Ani.*	*IV* *Np.*	*V* *Pā*	*VI* *Pd.*	*VIII* *Adhik.*
1. Rules relating to the opposite sex.	1	1, 2, 3, 4, 5,	1, 2	(4) (5) (17)	5, 21, 22, 24, 25, (26), (27), 28, 29, (30), 43, 65, 70.	(1), (2).	
2. Rules relating to food, drink, medicine etc.				30.	(23), 30, 31, 32, 33, 34, 35, 36, 37, 38, 39, 40, 41, 42, 44, 51, 74, 79, 80.	1 2, 3, 4.	
3. Rules relating to robes, bowls, rugs, bedding etc.				1, 2, 3, 4, 5, 6, 7, 8, 9, 10, 11, 12, 13, 14, 15, 16, 17, 21, 22 23, 24, 25, 26, 27, 28.	14, 15, 18, 26, 27, 59, 67, 68, 84, 85, 86, 87, 88, 89, 90,		

	I *Pj.*	*II* *Saṃ.*	*III* *Ani.*	*IV* *Np.*	*V* *Pā*	*VI* *Pd.*	*VIII* *Adhik.*
4. Rules relating to housing, staying, association, bathing and confort etc.		6, 7, 12			16, 17, 20 52, 54, (57) 56, 60, (65).		
5. Rules relating to wrong views, ill-speech, lying, misbehaviour, quarrelling and split of the Saṅgha.	4.	8, 9, 10, 11, 13.			1, 2, 3, 7, 9, 12, 13, 23, 48, 49, 55, 57, 62, 63, 69, 76, 78.		
6. Rules relating to the Saṅgha-karma, advice, confession, preaching and reciting of the Vinaya etc.					4, (5), 6, 8, 10, 50, 53, 75, 77, 72, 83,		1, 2, 3, 4, 5, 6, 7.
7. Rules realting to trade, digging, wandering, touching money and treasures etc.		18, 19, 20, 29,			58, 73, 81, 82,		
8. Rules relating to killing, stealing, frightening, playing, association with the army and thief.	2, 3.				11, 61, 19, (41), 45, 46, 47, 71.		

Appendix II

PĀTAYANTIKA RULES NOT FOUND IN THE SV. BUT FOUND IN OTHER TEXTS

(a) *Pāli* 23. Whatsoever Bhikkhu shall go to the dwelling place of Bhikkhunīs and there exhort the Bhikkhunīs, except on the (right) occasion—that is a Pācittiya.

Herein this is the right occasion: (to wit), when a Bhikkhunī is ill. This is the right occasion in this passage:

"Bhikkhunupassayaṃ upasaṃkamitvā bhikkhuniyo ovadeyya."

This Rule is also mentioned in the Upp. Pā. 23.

Mhs. 23. Adds: 'When he is not deputed by the Saṅgha'.

Language here is simpler.

Ksy. 23. '...to give instruction and preach the doctrine to the Bhikkhunīs who are not sick...'s.d.

Msg. 23. Adds: 'Without informing other good Bhikṣus.'

This Pā. 23 of the Pāli text is not found in Dh., Sv., Skt., Msv., Tib. and Mpt.

(b) *Pāli* 82. Whatsoever Bhikku shall divert to the use of any individual property dedicated to the Saṅgha, knowing it to be so—that is a Pācittiya:

"Jānam saṅghikaṃ lābham pariṇataṃ puggalassa pariṇāmeyya."

This is also found in Upp. Pā. 10.

Mhs. 91. '...knowing the donor is desirous of giving things to the Saṅgha, shall divert them to others...' n.c.

Ksy. 9. '...knowing others who give articles to the Saṅgha shall divert them to his acquaintance...' n.c.

Msg. 91. '...knowing articles which are for the Saṅgha shall divert them to other people...' n.c.

This is to be compared with the Msg. Pā 9.

This Pā. 82 of Pāli is not found in Dh., Sv., Skt., Msv., Tib. and Mpt.

(c) *Mhs.* 43, *Msv.* 28, *Ksy.* 29. Whatsoever Bhikṣu shall sit alone with a woman in a covered place—that is a Pā.

(d) *Ksy.* 42. Whatsoever Bhikṣu knowing that the other family is taking meals shall enter their house directly—that is a Pā.

(e) *Mhs.* 20. It is a combination of the Sv. Pā. 19 and Pā. 41. therefore, we have placed the same number in both the places along with other texts in the table of the Pātayantika dharmas.

(f) *Msg.* 53. Whatsoever Bhikṣu shall knowingly sit in a place where the act of coition used to take place in the family that invited him to meals—that is a Pā.

(g) *Msv.* 43. Whatsoever Bhikṣu shall stand by force in a covered place in the family that invited him to meals—that is a Pā.

(h) *Tib.* 43. Whatsoever Bhikṣu shall stand in a solitary covered part of a house in which he knows that a man and a woman are sleeping together, commits a sin which requires expiation.

See Mpt. 43 below.

(i) *Mpt.* 43. Sthānaṃ.

Appendix III

CLASSIFICATION OF THE ŚAIKṢA DHARMAS OF THE SARVĀSTIVĀDIN SCHOOL

			Total
1. On Wearing and covering	nos.	1 to 18	32
		31 to 34	
		37 to 46	
2. On walking and proper manner	nos.	19 to 30	30
		35 to 36	
		47 to 61, 113	
3. On eating and washing bowls	nos.	62 to 88,	27
4. On preaching	nos.	89 to 109	21
5. On urination	nos.	110 to 112	3
		Total	113

Appendix IV

CLASSIFICATION OF THE PRĀTIMOKṢA RULES OF THE SARVĀSTIVĀDIN SCHOOL

Sv. I. Concordance of the Four Pārājikas

	Skt.	*Pāli.*	*Dh.*	*Mhs.*	*Ksy.*	*Msg.*	*Upp.*	*Msv.*	*Tib.*	*Mpt.*
1. Committing a carnal act	1	1	1	1	1	1	1	1	1	1
2. Taking things not given	2	2	2	2	2	2	2	2	2	2
3. Depriving of human life	3	3	3	3	3	3	3	3	3	3
4. Telling of supernatural power	4	4	4	4	4	4	4	4	4	4

Sv. II. Concordance of the Thirteen Saṃghāvaśeṣas

1. Emission of semen	1	1	1	1	1	1	1	1	1	1
2. Bodily contact with women	2	2	2	2	2	2	2	2	2	2
3. Addressing with wicked words	3	3	3	3	3	3	3	3	3	3
4. Praising of bodily service	4	4	4	4	4	4	4	4	4	4
5. Acting as a go-between	5	5	5	5	5	5	5	5	5	5
6. Building a house independently	6	6	6	6	6	6	6	6	6	6

	Skt.	*Pāli.*	*Dh.*	*Mhs.*	*Ksy.*	*Msg.*	*Upp.*	*Msv.*	*Tib.*	*Mpt.*
7. Building a house dependently	7	7	7	7	7	7	7	7	7	7
8. A false charge of pārājika	8	8	8	8	8	8	8	8	8	8
9. A charge of pārājika based on something else	9	9	9	9	9	9	9	9	9	9
10. Causing dissension in a Saṅgha	10	10	10	10	10	10	10	10	10	10
11. Siding with a Bhikṣu's wrong views	11	11	11	11	11	11	11	11	11	11
12. Ill-fame and expelling	12	13	12	13	12	13	12	12	12	12
13. Refusing other's admonition	13	12	13	12	13	12	13	13	13	13
Sv.' III. Concordance of the Two Aniyatas										
1. Sitting in a concealed place fit for lustful purposes	1	1	1	1	1	1	...	1	1	1
2. Sitting in the open, fit for lustful purposes	2	2	2	2	2	2	...	2	2	2
IV. Concordance of the Thirty Niḥsargika Pātayantikas										
1. An extra robe	1	1	1	1	1	1	1	1	1	1
2. Without the three robes	2	2	2	2	2	2	2	2	2	2
3. Not to wait for materials over one month	3	3	3	3	3	3	3	3	3	3
4. Robe from an unrelated Bhikṣuṇī	4	5	4	4	4	4	4	5	5	5

	Skt.	*Pāli.*	*Dh.*	*Mhs.*	*Ksy.*	*Msg.*	*Upp.*	*Msv.*	*Tib.*	*Mpt.*
5. Robe washed by an unrelated Bhikṣuṇī	5	4	5	5	5	5	5	4	4	4
6. Asking an unrelated house-holder for a robe	6	6	6	6	6	6	6	6	6	6
7. Accepting two robes only	7	7	7	7	7	7	7	7	7	7
8. Giving direc-tion of making a robe	8	8	8	8	8	8	8	8	8	8
9. Giving direc-tions before the robe-fund is offered	9	9	9	9	9	9	9	9	9	9
10. Messenger with robe-fund	10	10	10	10	10	10	10	10	10	10
11. A rug made of silk	11	11	11	21	11	13	11	11	11	11
12. A rug made of black wool	12	12	12	22	12	11	12	12	12	12
13. A rug to be consisted of three parts	13	13	13	23	13	12	13	13	13	13
14. A rug to be used for six years	14	14	14	24	15	14	14	14	14	14
15. A new rug to be added with old pieces	15	15	15	25	14	15	15	15	15	15
16. Carrying away the goat's wool	16	16	16	26	16	16	16	16	16	16
17. Wool washed by an unrelated Bhikṣuṇī	17	17	17	27	17	17	17	17	17	17
18. Receiving gold or silver	18	18	18	30	20	18	18	18	18	18

	Skt.	*Pāli.*	*Dh.*	*Mhs.*	*Ksy.*	*Msg.*	*Upp.*	*Msv.*	*Tib.*	*Mpt.*
19. Exchanging in money-business	19	19	19	29	19	20	19	19	19	19
20. Engaging in buying and selling	20	20	20	28	18	19	20	20	20	20
21. Keeping a spare bowl	21	21	21	20	21	21	21	21	21	21
22. New bowl in exchange of an old one	22	22	22	19	22	22	22	22	22	22
23. Yarn woven by an unrelated weaver	23	26	23	11	23	26	23	23	23	23
24. Giving instruction for weaving the robe	24	27	24	12	24	27	24	24	24	24
25. To get back a given away robe	25	25	25	13	25	24	25	25	25	25
26. Robe as a Special gift	27	28	28	18	26	28	26	26	26	26
27. Keeping one of the three robes in a hut	28	29	29	16	28	29	27	27	27	27
28. Time for making a rainy season robe	26	24	27	17	27	25	28	28	28	28
29. Diverting articles of the Saṅgha	29	30	30	14	29	30	29	29	29	29
30. Not to keep ghee, oil etc. for over 7 days	30	23	26	15	30	23	30	30	30	30

Sv. V. Concordance of the Ninety Pātayantikas

1. **Telling a lie**	1	1	1	1	1	1	1	1	1	1

	Skt.	*Pāli.*	*Dh.*	*Mhs.*	*Ksy.*	*Msg.*	*Upp.*	*Msv.*	*Tib.*	*Mpt.*
2. Using abusive language	2	2	2	2	2	2	2	2	2	2
3. Slandering	3	3	3	3	3	3	3	3	3	3
4. Stirring up a settled matter	4	63	66	5	4	4	4	4	4	4
5. Not more than five or six words to women	5	7	9	4	5	5	5	5	5	7
6. Reciting clause by clause	6	4	6	6	6	6	6	6	6	8
7. Telling super human power to the unordained	7	8	8	8	7	7	7	8	8	6
8. Telling a bhikṣu's offence to the unordained	8	9	7	9	8	8	8	7	7	5
9. Appropriating the Saṅgha's property	9	81	74	80	9	9	9	9	9	9
10. Disregarding the minor rules	10	72	72	10	10	10	10	10	10	10
11. Destroying vegetation	11	11	11	11	11	11	12	11	11	11
12. Deriding others	12	13	13	13	12	13	11	12	12	12
13. Worrying others	13	12	12	12	13	12	14	13	13	13
14. Spreading bedstead in the open	14	14	14	14	14	14	15	14	14	14
15. Spreading bedstead in the room	15	15	15	15	15	15	16	15	15	15
16. Driving a bhikṣu out	16	17	17	16	17	16	17	16	16	16
17. Encroaching upon a bhikṣu's space	17	16	16	17	16	17	18	17	17	17

	Skt.	*Pāli.*	*Dh.*	*Mhs.*	*Ksy.*	*Msg.*	*Upp.*	*Msv.*	*Tib.*	*Mpt.*
18. Sitting forcefully on a bedstead	18	18	18	18	18	18	19	18	18	18
19. Sprinkling water	19	20	19	20	19	19	20	19	19	19
20. Building a big house	20	19	20	19	20	20	21	20	20	20
21. Exhorting the bhikṣuṇīs without deputation	21	21	21	21	21	21	22	21	21	21
22. Exhorting the bhikṣuṇīs after sunset	22	22	22	22	22	22	23	22	22	22
23. Exhorting for the sake of gain	23	24	23	24	24	24	25	23	23	23
24. Travelling with a bhikṣuṇī by appointment	24	27	27	28	27	26	26	26	26	26
25. To go on board by appointment	25	28	28	29	28	27	27	27	27	27
26. Giving a robe to an unrelated bhikṣuṇī	26	25	24	26	25	28	28	24	24	24
27. Making a robe for an unrelated bhikṣuṇī	27	26	25	27	26	29	29	25	25	25
28. Sitting with a bhikṣuṇī in secret	28	30	26	25	...	25	.30	29	28	28
29. Sitting alone with a woman	29	45	45	44	...	...	31	...	29	...
30. Food procured by a bhikṣuṇī	30	29	29	30	30	30	32	30	30	30
31. Taking meals in turn	31	33	32	31	31	32	33	31	31	31
32. One meal at a public rest-house	32	31	31	33	32	31	34	32	32	32

	Skt.	*Pāli.*	*Dh.*	*Mhs.*	*Ksy.*	*Msg.*	*Upp.*	*Msv.*	*Tib.*	*Mpt.*
33. A limit for taking cakes	33	34	34	34	33	38	35	33	33	33
34. Observing the ceremony of leavings of food	34	35	35	35	34	33	36	34	34	34
35. Stirring up a bhikṣu's longing for good	35	36	36	36	35	34	37	35	35	35
36. Going in a body for meals	36	32	33	32	36	40	38	36	36	36
37. Eating at the wrong time	37	37	37	38	37	36	39	37	37	37
38. Eating what has been put by	38	38	38	39	38	37	40	38	38	38
39. Placing things in the mouth not given	39	40	39	37	39	35	41	39	39	39
40. Asking for delicacies when not sick	40	39	40	41	40	39	42	40	40	40
41. Drinking water with living beings in it	41	62	62	20	41	51	43	41	41	41
42. Sitting in the sleeping place of an eating family	42	43	43	...	43	54	44	42	42	42
43. Sitting in secret with a woman in an eating family	43	44	44	42	...	70	45	...	...	...

	Skt.	*Pāli.*	*Dh.*	*Mhs.*	*Ksy.*	*Msg.*	*Upp.*	*Msv.*	*Tib.*	*Mpt.*
44. Giving food to ascetics	44	41	41	40	44	52	46	44	44	44
45. Seeing the army-manoeuvre	45	48	48	45	45	55	47	45	45	45
46. Time for remaining in the army	46	49	49	46	46	56	48	46	46	46
47. Seeing activities of the forces	47	50	50	47	47	57	49	47	47	47
48. Beating another bhikṣu	18	74	78	71	48	58	50	48	48	48
49. Giving threatening gestures	49	75	79	72	49	59	51	49	49	49
50. Concealing other's serious offence	50	64	64	74	50	60	52	50	50	50
51. Sending away without giving food	51	42	46	76	52	44	53	51	51	51
52. Kindling a fire	52	56	57	58	53	41	54	52	52	52
53. Grumbling about settled proceedings	54	79	76	79	51	43	55	53	53	53
54. Sleeping with an unordained person	53	5	5	7	54	42	56	54	54	54
55. Persisting in wrong views	55	68	68	48	55	45	57	55	55	55
56. Siding with persons persistent in wrong views	56	69	69	49	56	46	58	56	56	56
57. Sleeping with a persistent Śramaṇera	57	70	70	50	57	57	59	57	57	57

	Skt.	*Pāli.*	*Dh.*	*Mhs.*	*Ksy.*	*Msg.*	*Upp.*	*Msv.*	*Tib.*	*Mpt.*
58. Picking up jewels	58	84	82	69	69	49	60	59	59	59
59. Disfiguring the robe with colours	59	58	60	77	68	48	61	58	58	58
60. Bathing once in a half month	60	57	56	70	70	50	62	60	60	60
61. Destroying life of living beings	61	61	61	51	61	61	63	61	61	61
62. Causing uneasiness	62	77	63	52	62	62	64	62	62	62
63. Poking with the finger	63	52	53	54	63	67	65	63	63	63
64. Sporting in the water	64	53	52	55	64	66	66	64	64	64
65. Sleeping in the same place with a woman	65	6	4	56	65	69	67	65	65	65
66. Frightening a bhikṣu	66	55	55	73	66	65	68	66	66	66
67. Hiding a bhikṣu's bowl or robe	67	60	58	78	67	64	69	67	67	67
68. Using again the robe given away	68	59	59	81	59	63	70	68	68	68
69. Charging with a false Saṃghāvaśeṣa offence	69	76	80	75	58	90	71	69	69	69
70. Travelling together with a woman by appointment	70	67	30	67	60	68	73	70	70	70
71. Travelling together with robbers	71	66	67	66	71	72	72	71	71	71

	Skt.	*Pāli.*	*Dh.*	*Mhs.*	*Ksy.*	*Msg.*	*Upp.*	*Msv.*	*Tib.*	*Mpt.*
72. Ordination to an underaged person	72	65	65	61	72	71	74	72	72	72
73. Digging the ground	73	10	10	59	74	73	75	73	73	73
74. Requisites for four months	74	47	47	62	73	74	76	74	74	74
75. Suspicious about the rules	75	71	71	63	75	75	77	75	75	76
76. Overhearing other's dispute	76	78	77	60	76	78	78	76	76	76
77. Declining to give consent	77	80	75	53	77	79	79	77	77	77
78. Disrespecting other bhikṣus	78	54	54	58	78	77	80	78	78	78
79. Drinking liquor	79	51	51	57	79	76	81	79	79	79
80. Going to a village at a wrong time	80	85	83	83	80	80	82	80	80	80
81. Begging elsewhere when invited	81	46	42	82	81	81	83	81	81	81
82. Crossing the palace threshold	82	83	81	65	82	82	84	82	82	82
83. Pretending not knowing the rules	83	73	73	64	83	92	...	83	83	83
84. Having a needle case made	84	86	86	86	84	83	86	84	84	84
85. Height of a bedstead	85	87	84	85	85	84	87	85	85	85
86. Bedstead stuffed with cotton	86	88	85	84	86	85	88	86	86	86

	Skt.	Pāli.	Dh.	Mhs.	Ksy.	Msg.	Upp.	Msv.	Tib.	Mpt.
87. Measure of making a garment for the rainy season	87	91	89	89	89	88	89	89	89	88
88. Measure of making an itch-cloth	88	90	88	88	88	87	90	88	88	89
89. Measure of making a rug	89	89	87	87	87	86	91	87	87	87
90. Measure of the Sugata's robe	90	92	90	90	90	89	92	90	90	90

Sv. VI. Concordance of the Four Pratideśanīyas

1. Bhikṣuṇī giving food in a layman's house	1	1	1	1	1	2	1	1	1	1
2. Bhikṣuṇī's direction in a layman's house	2	2	2	2	2	3	2	2	2	2
3. Householders declared to be under training	3	3	3	3	3	4	3	3	3	3
4. Receiving food inside a forest dwelling	4	4	4	4	4	1	4	4	4	4

VII. Concordance of the Śaikṣa Dharmas

1. Not to wear the inner-garment high	1	...	...	1	1	...	...	2	2	2
2. Not to wear the inner-garment low	2	...	...	2	2	...	...	3	3	3
3. Not to wear the inner-garment in disorder	3	...	...	3	3	...	1	...	...	...

	Skt.	*Pāli.*	*Dh.*	*Mhs.*	*Ksy.*	*Msg.*	*Upp.*	*Msv.*	*Tib.*	*Mpt.*
4. Not to wear the inner-garment like an axe	4	...	...	...	...	...	...	5	7	7
5. Not to wear the inner-garment like the Tala tree	5	...	...	4	5	...	...	6	5	5
6. Inner-garment like an elephant-trunk	6	...	...	5	4	...	...	4	4	4
7. Inner-garment like a flour ball	7	...	...	...	6	...	...	7	6	6
8. Inner-garment in fine foldings	8	...	...	7	...	...	...	...	...	...
9. Inner-garment in the form of two ears	* Ms.	...	...	...	...	...	...	...	...	...
10. Inner-garment like a pig-head	Ms.	...	...	...	...	...	...	...	...	...
11. Inner-garment of fine yarn	Ms.	...	...	...	...	...	...	...	...	...
12. Wearing the inner-garment all round	12	1	1	...	3	1	...	1	1	1
13. Not to put on the robe high	13	...	...	8	7	...	...	9	9	8
14. Not to put on the robe low	14	...	...	9	8	...	...	10	10	9
15. Not to put on the robe in disorder	15	...	...	10	...	...	2	11	11	...
16. Putting on the robe all round	Ms.	2	2	...	9	2	...	8	8	10
17. Entering well-covered	17	3	18	11	12	3	3	12	12	12
18. Sitting well-covered	18	4	19	12	...	14	4	...	...	...

*This indicates that the Ms. of the Skt. text is missing completely.

	Skt.	*Pāli.*	*Dh.*	*Mhs.*	*Ksy.*	*Msg.*	*Upp.*	*Msv.*	*Tib.*	*Mpt.*
19. Entering well-controlled	19	5	...	...	...	...	...	...	...	11
20. Sitting well controlled	20	6	...	...	...	...	...	...	...	...
21. To enter with-out casting glances	21	7	20	37	14	4	7	...	14	14
22. To sit with-out casting glances	22	8	21	38	15	15	8	...	...	...
23. To enter with-out smelling	Ms.	...	...	...	...	...	...	...	...	...
24. To sit with-out smelling	Ms.	...	...	...	...	...	...	...	...	...
25. Entering without presumption	Ms.	...	...	...	16	...	...	...	...	...
26. Sitting without presumption	Ms.	...	...	...	...	...	...	...	...	...
27. Entering with a little sound	27	13	22	47	13	5	9	13	13	13
28. Sitting with a little sound	28	14	23	48	...	16	10	...	...	...
29. To enter with-out kneeling down	Ms.	25	...	39	22	...	11	20	23	24
30. To sit with-out kneeling down	Ms.	...	11	40	...	...	...	...	...	...
31. To enter with-out covering the head	31	23	7	43	21	7	12	15	16	16
32. To sit with-out covering the head	32	24	8	44	...	18	13	...	...	...
33. Entering with-out a turban	33	...	...	...	...	...	...	...	...	...

	Skt.	*Pāli.*	*Dh.*	*Mhs.*	*Ksy.*	*Msg.*	*Upp.*	*Msv.*	*Tib.*	*Mpt.*
34. Sitting without a turban	34	...	...	...	...	...	...	...	...	...
35. To enter without being akimbo	35	21	12	29	17	10	...	18	25	25
36. To sit without being akimbo	36	22	13	30	...	22	...	...	...	...
37. To enter without showing the chest	...	...	...	...	...	...	14	...	...	...
38. To sit without showing the chest	...	...	...	...	...	...	15	...	...	...
39. To enter without showing the ribs	...	...	...	...	23	...	...	...	...	...
40. To sit without showing the ribs	...	...	...	...	...	...	...	...	...	...
41. To enter without tucking up the robe	37	9	3	13 15	19	8	17	16	...	17
42. To sit without tucking up the robe	38	10	4	14 16	...	19	18	...	...	...
43. To enter without tucking up both the sides	41	...	...	17	...	...	...	17	...	18
44. To sit without tucking up both the sides	42	...	...	18	...	...	...	...	...	...
45. To enter without letting the robe fall	45	...	...	...	...	...	16	...	...	...
46. To sit without letting the robe fall	46	...	...	...	...	...	...	...	...	...
47. To enter without arm-swinging	47	17	16	33	25	13	19	26	27	27

	Skt.	*Pāli.*	*Dh.*	*Mhs.*	*Ksy.*	*Msg.*	*Upp.*	*Msv.*	*Tib.*	*Mpt.*
48. To sit without arm-swinging	48	18	17	34	...	...	...	...	...	...
49. To enter without shoulders swaying	49	...	...	23	...	...	...	...	...	29
50. To sit without shoulders-swaying	50	...	...	24	...	...	...	...	...	...
51. To enter without head-moving	51	19	...	21	26	12	21	27	28	28
52. To sit without head-moving	52	20	...	22	...	...	22	...	...	...
53. To enter without body-swaying	53	15	14	19	27	11	20	25	26	26
54. To sit without body-swaying	54	16	15	20	...	...	...	...	...	...
55. To enter without interlacing the hand	55	...	...	25	28	...	...	29	30	30
56. To sit without interlacing the hand	56	...	...	26	...	...	...	...	...	...
57. To enter without bending the leg	...	...	...	41	29	...	...	23	...	...
58. To sit without bending the leg	...	...	...	42	...	...	...	...	...	...
59. To enter without placing one leg upon the other	59	...	...	...	...	...	...	...	...	34
60. To sit without placing one leg upon the other	60	...	...	...	39	21	...	33	34	...
61. Not to place the palm against the cheek	61	...	...	...	...	...	...	...	...	...

	Skt.	*Pāli.*	*Dh.*	*Mhs.*	*Ksy.*	*Msg.*	*Upp.*	*Msv.*	*Tib.*	*Mpt.*
62. Receiving food with concentration	62	27	26	51	40	24	25 30	39 43	40	40
63. Receiving soup with concentration	63	...	...	...	46	...	...	...	...	...
64. Not to let the bowl overflow	Ms.	30	27	52	41	...	...	40	42	41
65. Taking rice and soup equally	65	34	29	53	...	25	27	...	...	42
66. Without scooping	Ms.	...	31	55	...	26	29	...	...	...
67. Without selecting good food	67	...	...	54	...	...	31	...	...	...
68. Without making big handfuls	68	39	36	64	62	29	33	45	50	49
69. Handfuls to suit the mouth	69	40	...	65	63	31	34	46	51	50
70. Not to wait by opening the mouth	70	41	37	66	65	30	35	47	52	51
71. No talk when food is in the mouth	71	43	38	68	64	33	36	48	53	52
72. Without biting the food in half	66	45	...	70	54	32	54	57	63	...
73. Without sound while chewing	73	51	42	62	48	37	38	51	54	54
74. Without swallowing unchewed food	Ms.	...	...	74	...	39	...	...	...	...
75. Without swelling up the cheek	...	46	41	69	...	27	...	56	61	...

	Skt.	*Pāli.*	*Dh.*	*Mhs.*	*Ksy.*	*Msg.*	*Upp.*	*Msv.*	*Tib.*	*Mpt.*
76. Without protruding the tongue	76	49	...	73	53	28	...	58	58	57
77. Without smelling the food	75	...	...	57	50	...	41	...	...	...
78. Without licking the hand	78	52	44	63	56	35	45	61	64	63
79. Not to clean with the finger	...	...	...	56	...	34	...	...	...	...
80. Not to abandon food	80	48	40	59	...	40	...	55	...	58
81. To eat without hand-shaking	81	47	45	72	...	41	47	62	66	65
82. Soiled hand not to touch vessels	82	55	47	60	68	46	49	66	70	68
83. Not to cover with rice	83	36	33	77	43	45	51	49	46	46
84. Without asking soup and rice for himself	Ms.	37	32	79	45	44	50	...	...	...
85. Without looking into other's bowl	85	38	34	80	66	42	52	65	69	70
86. To eat looking into the bowl	86	32	35	58	...	43	...	64	43	44
87. To eat in order	Ms.	33	30	...	...	...	...	...	...	43
88. Throwing away bowl-rinsing water	88	56	48	76	69	47	53	67	72	71
89. A person riding on horse back	89	63	59	96	81	62	54	84	95	92
90. In front and at the back side	91	71	90	90	78	61	55	76	82	80

	Skt.	*Pāli.*	*Dh.*	*Mhs.*	*Ksy.*	*Msg.*	*Upp.*	*Msv.*	*Tib.*	*Mpt.*
91. On the road and outside the road	90	72	92	91	80	63	56	77	83	81
92. High and low positions	92	69	89	88	77	50	58	75	81	79
93. Sitting and standing	93	70	86	87	74	48	59	73	79	77
94. Lying and sitting	94	64	87	89	76	49	60	74	80	78
95. Covering his head	95	67	54	92	92	53	61	78	84	82
96. A turban on the head	96	66	55	...	91	54	62	92	93	90
97. A person being akimbo	97	...	56	...	...	...	...	81	...	...
98. Showing the chest	...	...	...	86	...	...	...	...	...	...
99. Showing the ribs	...	...	...	...	...	...	...	...	...	...
100. Tucking up robe on one side	98	...	52	93	...	...	...	79	85	83
101. Tucking up robe on both sides	100	...	...	94	...	...	...	80	...	84
102. Letting the robe fall	102	...	...	...	...	...	63	...	...	...
103. Wearing pattens	103	61	58	84	83	52	65	87	...	95
104. Wearing leather shoes	104	62	57	85	84	51	64	88	98	...
105. Holding a staff	105	58	96	97	85	59	66	...	99	96
106. Holding an umbrella	106	57	100	95	87	60	67	94	100	97
107. Holding a knife	107	59	99	98	86	57	68	...	102	98
108. Holding a small dagger	108	...	97	...	...	...	...	...	...	99
109. Holding a bow and other weapons	109	60	98	99	...	58	69	...	101	100

	Skt.	*Pāli.*	*Dh.*	*Mhs.*	*Ksy.*	*Msg.*	*Upp.*	*Msv.*	*Tib.*	*Mpt.*
110. Not to cast ordure etc., on green grass	110	74	49	83	95	64	70	96	107	104
111. Not to cast ordure etc., in water	111	75	50	82	94	65	71	97	106	103
112. Not to ease oneself while standing	112	73	51	81	93	66	72	95	105	102
113. Not to climb up a tree	113	...	94	100	96	...	...	98	108	105

Sv. VIII. Concordance of the Seven Adhikaraṇaśamathas

	Skt.	*Pāli.*	*Dh.*	*Mhs.*	*Ksy.*	*Msg.*	*Upp.*	*Msv.*	*Tib.*	*Mpt.*
1. Settled in presence	1	1	1	1	1	1	1	1	1	1
2. Settled from recollection	2	2	2	2	2	2	2	2	2	2
3. No longer out of his mind	3	3	3	3	3	3	3	3	3	3
4. On confession of guilt	4	4	4	5	4	4	4	6	7	7
5. Inquiring into the nature	5	6	5	4	5	5	5	4	5	5
6. To be settled by a majority	6	5	6	6	6	6	6	5	4	4
7. Like the grass covering the field	7	7	7	7	7	7	7	7	6	6

Appendix V

THE PRĀTIMOKṢA AND THE VINAYA

When Gautama Buddha (563-483 B.C.E.), founder of Buddhism, was about to pass away his disciples expressed profound sorrow regarding their impending loss. The Buddha advised them that 'the Dharma and Vinaya' should be their teacher after his demise. This probably was the earliest reference to Vinaya. As the Vinaya and his teaching (*dharma*) could replace the Buddha, one may envision their importance in Buddhism. This also indicates that early Buddhism did not recognize a patriarchal succession. The body of ordained disciples of the Buddha was known as the Saṅgha (monastic Order).

I. The Religious Background

In pre-Buddhist India, many intellectuals of the Brāhmaṇic, Āraṇyakan and Upaniṣadic periods made attempts in quest of eternal bliss through sacrifice, penance, asceticism or meditation. This could not be called a mass-movement. However, in the sixth century B.C.E. there were many religious groups led by teachers like Mahāvīra, founder of Jainism, who was known for severe self-mortification.

When the Buddha appeared on the scene he followed a middle path of religious practices. He rejected harsh asceticism and formulated a code of conduct that appeared to be rational, practical and proper. Moreover, Buddhism stresses the three aspects of cultivation, namely, *śila, samādhi* and *prajñā* (discipline, meditation and wisdom). Śila means the upholding of the moral and ethical principles which are closely associated with one's action and intention. Any unmanifested evil intention is considered an evil action. Along with meditation, the observance of morality is the foundation upon which an edifice of perfect wisdom is built, and mukti (liberation), the ultimate objective in religion will be achieved. However, discipline is a means to an end. It is a prerequisite and not the end itself.

II. The Prātimokṣa

During the lifetime of the Buddha many disciplinary rules were established. Subsequently, they were made into a code known as the *Prātimokṣa* (Code of Conduct) (Pāli: *Pātimokkha*). The Code's classification was based on the nature of offences. There are several versions of the *Prātimokṣa* for monks and nuns in Sanskrit and Pāli. The number of rules ranges from 227 to 263 for monks and 290 to 480 for nuns. We shall briefly examine the contents of this Code:

(i) **Four *pārājikas* (defeat or unpardonable).** They deal with sex offence, stealing, killing and falsehood. The punishment is expulsion from the Order.

(ii) **Thirteen *saṅghāvaśeṣas* (Pāli: *saṅghādisesa*) (requiring suspension).** They concern association with the opposite sex, housing, false accusation, schism and rejection of admonition. Violation of the first nine rules becomes an offence immediately, while the remaining four are decided after the third admonition. The offender is subjected to the following procedure: (a) probation by living separately from the rest. The duration depends on the length of days an offence was committed; (b) a penance of six additional days will be imposed; (c) An official pardon; and (d) a reinstatement ceremony by a body of twenty ordained Bhikṣus (monks).

(iii) **Two *aniyatas* (indeterminate rules).** They concern a Bhikṣu who sits with women either in an open or concealed place, Punishment may be similar to offences related to *pārājika, saṅghāveśeṣa* or *pāyattikas*.

(iv) **Thirty *niḥsārgika pāyattikas* (Pāli: *nissaggiya pācittiya*) (requiring forfeiture).** They deal with accepting robes or rugs from related or unrelated persons, trade, improper appropriation, touching gold and silver and so forth. Violation involves forfeiture.

(v) **Ninety *pāyattikas* (Pāli: *pācittiya*) (requiring repentance).** This is an assortment of offences concerning eating, dressing, appropriation, regulatory matters and so forth. The offender is required to repent.

(vi) **Four *prātideśanīyas* (Pāli: *pāṭidesanīya*) (requiring confession).** They deal with certain circumstances under which a Bhikṣu receives his food. Violation requires confession.

(vii) **Many *śaikṣas* (Pāli: *sekhiyā*) (concerning training).** These are guidelines concerning the daily life of the monastic community such as eating, dressing, walking, sitting and so forth. There is no specific punishment here; It says only that they should be observed.

(viii) **Seven *adhikaraṇa-śamathas* (Pāli: *adhikaraṇa-samatha*) (settlement of dispute).** These are concerned with the settlement of disputes. Therefore, they are procedural matters.

The *Prātimokṣa* is essentially a code of monastic discipline concentrating on the avoidance of immoral deeds, misbehaviour or impropriety. Punishment for the offences ranges from expulsion to sanctions of probation, penance, forfeiture, repentance or confession. The aim of the Code is the preservation of spiritual purity and harmony in the Saṅgha.

III. The Vinaya Literature

The *Vinaya* is one of the branches of the Buddhist *Tripiṭaka* (Three Baskets). The Pāli version consists of three books for monks and one for nuns. They are as follows:

(i) ***Sutta Vibhaṅga* (Sanskrit: *Vinaya Vibhaṅga*) (Classification of the Vinaya).** In this work the Code of *Pātimokkha* (Sanskrit: *Prātimokṣa*) is accompained by an ancient word for word commentary. For each rule a story explains the circumstances under which it was originated. It also includes amplifications, exceptions and modifications concerning a particualr rule.

(ii) ***Khandhaka* (Division).** This is similar to the *Vinaya Vastu* (Subjects Concerning Discipline) in Sanskrit versions. It is subdivided into *Mahāvagga* (Greater Chapter) and *Cullavagga* (Lesser Chapter). The former consists of ten divisions and the latter twelve. The *Mahāvagga* begins with a brief biographical sketch of the Buddha covering the period from his attainment to Buddhahood to the conversion of Sāriputta. It contains topics such as admission to the Order, the ceremony of Uposatha and Pātimokkha (recital of the Code), the rainy season retreat, the Kaṭhina ceremony (robe offering), the formal acts of the Saṅgha, schism and so forth. The first ten divisions of the *Cullavagga* are concerned with minor disciplinary proceedings, probation, duties of monks and nuns and other matters. The last two chapters concentrate on the Councils held at Rājagṛha and Vaiśāli. They appear to be later additions, but they offer a rich mine for the study of Buddhist history.

(iii) ***Parivāra* (Accessory Materials).** It is a later composition made in Ceylon. It serves as a glossary to the *Pātimokkha,* restating the rules in a simplified manner.

(iv) ***Bhikkhunī Vibhaṅga* (The Nun's Analysis).** This is included in the *Parivāra* (*Book of the Discipline*, vi, pp. 80-122). It serves as a commentary on the rules of the *Bhikkhunī Pātimokkha.* Compared with the *Sutta Vibhaṅga* it is less elaborate and very brief. In the fifth century C.E. two commentaries on the Vinaya known as *Samantapāsādika* (Perfect Vision) and *Vinaya Viniccaya* (Vinaya Deliberation) were composed by Buddhaghoṣa and Buddhadatta respectively. The former is more critical than the latter. As Buddhism developed, there emerged about twenty Buddhist sects in India in the first five centuries B.C.E. Many of them had their own version of the Vinaya. They were known as Dharmaguptā, Mahāsaṅghika, Mahīśāsakā, Mūlasarvāstivādā, Sarvāstivādā and Theravādā, and their Vinaya texts were translated into Chinese and Tibetan languages.

IV. Sources and Social Concern

The Buddhist Vinaya adopted many ancient Indian religious traditions and practices such as the observance of celibacy, spiritual purity and vow of poverty. The creation or modification of a rule was generally the reflection of public opinion or suggesitions made by members of the Saṅgha. The Buddha maintained a policy that the activities of the Saṅgha should avoid confrontation with the laws of the state and the wishes of the people. Consequently admission to the Saṅgha would be denied, if the applicant belonged to one of the following categories: a soldier, a jailbreaker, a robber, a swindler, a debtor, a eunuch, a slave, a murderer, a leper, a cripple and one who had no parental approval (*Mahāvagga, I,* 54-76). These disqualifications helped avoid public antagonism, and resulted in selecting the physically and spiritually excellent recruits.

V. Vinaya at Work

The following subheadings provide us with some insight regarding the monastic life:

(i) **The procedure of lawmaking.** As founder of Buddhism the Buddha had absolute authority to create, abolish or modify any laws whenever the needs arose. His disciples obediently carried out his instructions. After his death the Saṅgha took an active role in official acts and in promulgating regulations. It followed a prescribed legal procedure, namely, one made a motion to the full assembly and repeated it thrice in the presence of qualified members. If no one objected, the motion carried and it became law. Thus, the Saṅgha assumed both the legislative and executive powers. In fact, any matter concerning the Saṅgha should be officially proposed, discussed and disposed of according to the aforesaid procedure.

(ii) **Elections.** Whenever a meeting of the Saṅgha is convened, a chairman is elected from its membership. The authority of the chairperson is valid until the end of the meeting. The vote of the majority decides the issue. The democratic way of conducting monastic affairs antedated modern democracy by about twenty-five centuries.

(iii) **Equality and Process of Training.** Each ordained Bhikṣu is a full-fledged member of the Saṅgha and has an equal right to vote or to hold an elected office. However, seniority has been emphasized. Anyone who was ordained a day earlier is a senior. Accordingly, he would receive salutation from his juniors. Apparently there is no equality here.

According to the Vinaya, anyone seeking admission to the Order should have a qualified upādhyāya (preceptor), who will teach him the elemenatry tenets of Buddhism and proper etiquette. Their relation is similar to that of father and son. They should observe a prescribed set of duties towards each other but the burden falls on the shoulders of the pupil. He should always attend on the preceptor, performing all personal services for him, even washing his feet. In turn the preceptor will reciprocate in a suitable way.

In the event a preceptor passed away another qualified teacher (ācārya) will be appointed to guide the pupil in higher knowledge. Their duties to each other are similar to the preceptor-pupil relationship. The period of dependence is about ten years (*Mahāvagga,* I, 32-37). When the pupil reached the age of twenty and met all the requirements, he could seek permission to receieve the higher ordination from a body of ten fully qualified Bhikṣus. After the ceremony, he is instructed to avoid the four grave offences of Pārājika, and to abide by the four sources for livelihood: (1) to live by begging, (2) to wear discarded rags, (3) to live under a tree, and (4) to use cow's urine as medicine. However, many exceptions were made in later times. Thus, one attained the status of a Bhikṣu.

(iv) **Ceremonies Associated with Nature.** Nature and society have affected the way of life of the Bhikṣus. Being dependent entirely on public charity, the Saṅgha must heed public opinion. Therefore, the behaviour of the Bhikṣus must conform to the norm of morality. If the community lost confidence in them, their existence would be threatened. This consideration brought about the introduction of the Uposatha ceremony on full moon days. On this day, the *Prātimokṣa* is recited and every participant must declare his purity concerning moral conduct, and the guilty will be suitably dealt with.

The Rainy Season Retreat (Varṣās) was due to the combined forces of Nature and human needs. The Monsoon season in India lasts about three months. During this period, constant torrential showers prevent outdoor activites, including begging of alms. The Bhikṣus must remain indoors and lunches must be provided. Moreover, the Robe Offering (Kaṭhina) ceremony is associated with the rainy season residence.

(v) **Relations between Monks and Nuns.** The Buddha expressed great reluctance on accepting women to his Order. He feared that his religion would shorten its existence should they be admitted. He laid down eight weighty conditions for them. For example, a nun should salute a newly ordained monk, even if she were of a hundred years standing. Eventually the nuns were subjected to the legal authority of the Bhikṣu-Saṅgha. The monks framed the laws for them, conducted the trials, admonished the guilty and declared the verdict. Their only privilege was to hold a preliminary enquiry in the Bhikṣuṇī-Saṅgha and report the findings to the joint assembly of monks and nuns. From then on the Bhikṣu-Saṅgha conducted the legal proceedings.

It appears that the fair sex was treated unfairly. The rationale was that woman is physically weaker than man; therefore, nuns need protection and guidance from the Bhikṣu-Saṅgha, Under these circumstances nuns are in a subordinate position.

VI. Vinaya in its International Perspective

Buddhism was introduced to the countries in East and Southeast Asia from India. Owing to the cultural and social background of these nations it underwent varied transformations. From the standpoint of a particular culture certain adjustments may be deemed necessary. However, in terms of monastic discipline it is a serious vaiolation if monks abandon celibacy. This actually happened to some Japanese and Tibetan Buddhists. But the bhikṣus in Burma, Ceylon, China and Thailand have been faithfully observing the Vinaya for centuries. As the monastic Code was framed some 2,500 years ago, it may not be suitable for people in certain geographical areas. Thus Huai-hai (d. 814 C.E.), a Chinese Zen master wrote a set of regulations known as *Pai-chang ch'ing-kuei* (Pai-chang's Rules of Purity) for members of his monastery (Taishō, no 2025). It encourages manual labour, productivity, self-reliance and the conviction of "one should not eat when one does not work." This may seem strange to some. However, he did not intend to replace the *Prātimokṣa,* but rather as a supplement. This illustrates that even a sacred ancient insititution like the Code of *Prātimokṣa* may face the challenge of changing times.

Bibliography

Bhagvat, Durga N. *Early Buddhist Jurisprudence.* Poona, 1939. A survey of the religious life of the Buddhist Order in relation to the *Vinaya.*

Dutt, Nalinaksha. *Early Monastic Buddhism.* Calcutta, 1941. A well-known Indian author traces the development of early Buddhism in the doctrinal and disciplinary areas.

Hirakawa, Akira. *A Study of the Vinaya-Piṭaka.* Tokyo, 1960. It examines the Vinaya literature from the existing sources including the various translations.

Law, Bimala Churn. *A History of Pāli Literature.* London, 1933. It examines extensively the Canonical Pāli literature and the commentaries in their historical perspective.

Pachow, W. *A Comparative Study of the Prātimokṣa: On the Basis of Its Chinese, Tibetan, Sanskrit and Pāli Versions.* Santiniketan, 1955. It examines many versions of the *Prātimokṣa* belonging to the various Buddhist sects.

Vinaya-Piṭaka. Translated by I.B. Horner as *The Book of the Discipline* in six volumes. London, 1970. A complete translation of the *Vinaya* from the Pāli text. The translator shows great erudition. A valuable contribution to the study of the *Vinaya.*

Vinaya-Piṭaka. Translated by T.W. Rhys Davids and Hermann Oldenberg as *The Vinaya Texts* in three volumes in the *Sacred Books of the East* series. Oxford, 1882. A partial translation of the *Vinaya.* The section of the *Pātimokkha* is complete.

Index

Names of books are in Italics. The words beginning with Capital letters are Sanskrit or Pāli terms, and they are proper names as well.

To avoid unnecessary complexity, we have not indexed all the Sanskrit and Pāli words mentioned in the text. However, we made entries of all the important elements contained in the Prātimokṣa Sūtra.